Philosophical Meditations on Richard Wright

Philosophical Meditations on Richard Wright

Edited by James B. Haile, III

LEXINGTON BOOKS
Lanham • Boulder • New York • Toronto • Plymouth, UK

Published by Lexington Books
A wholly owned subsidiary of The Rowman & Littlefield Publishing Group, Inc.
4501 Forbes Boulevard, Suite 200, Lanham, Maryland 20706
www.rowman.com

10 Thornbury Road, Plymouth PL6 7PP, United Kingdom

British Library Cataloguing in Publication Information Available

Library of Congress Cataloging-in-Publication Data

Philosophical meditations on Richard Wright / [edited by] James B. Haile III.
p. cm.
Includes bibliographical references and index.
ISBN 978-0-7391-4494-7 (cloth : alk. paper)
1. Wright, Richard, 1908–1960—Criticism and interpretation. 2. Literature—Philosophy. I. Haile,
James B., 1979–
PS3545.R815Z796 2012
813'.52—dc23
2012016252

Printed in the United States of America

To all those ginger-colored boys and blues-colored/toned girls whose thought thinks, speech speaks, hearing hears, and touch touches their own black souls . . . yesterday, today, and tomorrow.

Contents

Acknowledgments

Train whistles blowing and hot summer nights: Memphis seems to me so long ago, so far away; at a distance, almost dreamlike, its events mostly out of sequence. If Richard Wright has passed down anything to us, it is this: reality almost always appears at a distance, in a flash, within a glimpse. And yet, it is unmistakably and undeniably ours. This is the ambiguity of existence itself—the yes and the no—of which many speak, many write, many struggle to comprehend. We practitioners of craft have to devise ways of soberly facing reality, reconciling ourselves to it, in order to "burn it out and go on to the next conflicting phase." But what is difficult, though, is figuring out how to reconcile ourselves—by what process of thought or action? By what means are we best suited to "burn it out" and move on? That is the task of craft: to provide us with this measure, to reconcile ourselves to the conflicting events of the day and not succumb to the temptation of reducing them to a corrupting sameness. We have to live with this contradiction; "burn it out" does not mean you no longer carry it within; "what it means is that you have named it and moved on to the other "indeterminate visions." Memphis for me is just that, a dark spot of indeterminate resolution that, perhaps, without proper vision, would appear anything other than a transformative quality, which it was. This project emerges from the edges of this indeterminacy. This does not mean that each cloud has a silver lining—I am not making a *judgment*; rather, like Wright's corpus, I am offering a critical perspective, which, through craft, hopes to illuminate, but not indifferently, what thought and speech can offer us: insight into and the uncovering of what is hiding beneath experience itself. Exhortation! Exodus!

There are many persons who have helped to make this project possible, and I thank all them in concert. But, I would like to particularly thank the following persons: Dr. Lucius Outlaw, Jr., for introducing me to the work of

Charles Johnson, whom I have come to regard much like myself, leaving behind certain certainties in order to find for myself, not who I was or could be, but what I wanted to do. And in this connection between what I do and who I am, I am reminded of Wright's own cause: to "live free, freely," which always has a cost, and it is a cost that we bear, sometimes with laughter, sometimes in horror, always in honesty. I would like to thank Dr. George Yancy for telling me to "just do it." To him I say what buddies say to one another signifying meaning, enjoyment, and codified intention, "Hey, shit, I reckon, man. Hey, shit, I goddamn reckon." To brother Dr. Tommy J. Curry, I suspect I haven't minded all that you have been saying, nevertheless thanks for your encouragement and for joining me on the island of black difference-making and in making our way toward the shores of tomorrow's possibilities. Tell *me* how long the train's been gone, and, where it's going. I would like to thank Dr. Jim Swindal for his continued support of my various endeavors and projects. To ZFR, what can I say that isn't in my eyes? I wish to thank you for the last few years of my life and more. Lastly, I would like to thank Lexington Books for all their support and understanding in the completion of this project.

Introduction

Richard Wright and Philosophy

James B. Haile, III, Duquesne University

As we open into this project, placing the African American author Richard Wright into a "philosophical" context and in dialogue with the discipline of "philosophy,"[1] we are reminded of the historical and continuing processes of the construction and maintenance of disciplinary boundaries and disciplinary canons in the American academy.[2] What is it that we mean to accomplish in this text by placing an African American writer in context and conversation with the discipline of "philosophy"? That is, why hasn't a thinker such as Richard Wright been included within the discipline of "philosophy" heretofore? While it may be argued that Richard Wright was both historically and culturally situated to write with "philosophical" interests and to comment and participate in larger disciplinary debates—after all, he was intimate with French "philosophers" Jean-Paul Sartre and Simone de Beauvoir, and he did know, perhaps only in passing, writers Albert Camus and Hannah Arendt[3] — this fact alone did not make Wright unique among writers generally and certainly not among African American writers to any degree.[4] The intellectual world has always been small and intellectuals have always known of one another.[5] Yet, as disciplines in the American academy became more highly specialized, defined, and separated, particularly after World War II, boundaries around disciplines became so stringent such that today, it is quite rare for "philosophers" to speak, concretely to other disciplines—and, perhaps, vice versa.[6] Nonetheless, this project, the first book in recent memory to "philosophically" engage an African American literary figure,[7] somehow seems to require justification for its undertaking. What makes Richard Wright philosophical? Can we answer this question without pointing to his relationship with Jean-Paul Sartre, Simone de Beauvoir, or any other French, German, or

American "philosopher"?[8] That is the challenge of this project: to "philoso-phize" Richard Wright without resorting to translation, or the need of a translator.[9]

In large part this introduction, as well as the collection as a whole raises and attempts to answer the question: "What makes Richard Wright a philoso-pher, or at least worthy of philosophical study?" And, this question is in good faith; it is neither rhetorical, nor is it a way of politically arm-twisting those who remain unconvinced of Wright's "philosophical" merit. It is neither my intention nor the intention of the contributors to argue that if Wright *is not* considered a "philosopher" it is because he is black, or if Wright *is* a "philos-opher" it is only because he knew some white philosophers. Rather, this collection and its contributors intend to ask, "What makes a text philosophi-cal?" In considering the question of the importance of Wright and the "philo-sophical" content of his work we hope to (re)raise larger questions of and to the discipline itself: What is philosophy? What does it mean to "do" philoso-phy? What are its disciplinary borders? What makes any of the canonized persons worthy of philosophical study?[10] And, what is more, as we answer the question of method, and seek to establish our principles for the discipline and the activity of philosophy and philosophizing, can and will we apply our standards to every case evenly? Or, will we continue the present trend within the discipline of performing boundary work in the application of our princi-ples to particular texts and to particular authors and not others? This text and the author of note provide the case for raising and addressing such questions.

This collection is a sustained attempt to open the "philosophical" canon not only in terms of who is considered for "philosophical" treatment but what *forms* of expression are legitimate for "philosophical" discourse. I am re-minded of an incident in my own graduate school experience. In a committee meeting organized to discuss my progress in the department I was asked what my area(s) of specialization and my area(s) of competency would be. When I listed twentieth-century continental philosophy and existentialism as intended areas of specialization, they were accepted. Even African American philosophy was accepted, though a great many of us in the discipline of "philosophy," especially those on my committee, do not know precisely what those terms—African American and philosophy—mean when seated one next to the other; it is almost a scandal.[11] Yet, when I mentioned my intent of making literature and philosophy, namely, African American literature and philosophy, as an area of competency, if not an area specialization, I was told that such a combination was not philosophy "proper"—"proper" meaning "fit" for an area of specialization or an area of competency—and that perhaps I was interested in aesthetics more than "philosophy." In fact, throughout my years in the program I was told that my work was "perhaps better suited for an English or literature department" given my personal interests in literature, particularly African American literature.

Yet, it has remained my position, and this collection stands in this "reflection," that the discipline of philosophy and literature necessarily relate and intersect one another. Specifically, the two converge precisely at that moment where a person attempts to convey through the act or activity of narration some perceptive or apperceptive truth concerning themselves, their shared social world, and/or their surrounding physical world. [12] If we restrict the form of "philosophical" discourse to that of traditional "philosophical" treatises of explicit form [13] and give a pass to those we have canonically added [14] then we cannot account for and will not only ignore those thinkers who placed themselves in a number of traditional philosophy debates, ranging from social metaphysics to phenomenological encounters with the physical and social worlds to social identity, but also, and more detrimentally, we will lose out on their contribution(s) to "traditional" philosophy. [15] This is especially true of African American literature, for many African American writers and their respective works engaged and continue to engage in philosophical discourses, yet *chose* and continue to *choose not* to write what are considered formal philosophical treatises. The writer Charles Johnson—formally trained in philosophy at Stony Brook University (SUNY) in the 1970s, but who *chose* instead to write what he has termed "philosophical fiction" rather than traditional "philosophy"—raises this question to a higher pitch. [16]

We, then, have to ask two fundamental questions about African American writers and literature: first, why did these authors choose *not* to write in traditional "philosophical" ways (e.g., traditional treatises) while still engaging with philosophical ideas, and what is the significance of this choice both ethically and "philosophically"; and, two, what insights do these authors have for traditional "philosophy" generally, and African American philosophy specifically [17] given that they have chosen and continue to choose not to write traditional "philosophical" treatises? The contributors to this collection raise these questions, some more explicitly than others, by situating Wright philosophically. It is in this way—that is, asking questions and interrogating the discipline of philosophy generally, and African American philosophy specifically—that this text is both distinct and necessary.

Charles Johnson reminds us of the forgotten past and the forgotten intellectual history between philosophy and literature when he notes in his 1988 text, *Being and Race: Black Writing since 1970*,

> Our lives are inherently metaphysical insofar as each moment of perception, each blink of the eye, involves the activity of interpretation; perception is an *act*, and this observation puts the lie to that ancient stupidity that says that the process of philosophy and fiction are two different enterprises—they are sister disciplines. [18]

Johnson reminds us that neither philosophy nor literature need take a specific form and have a specific range of interest or content; that our lives, in fact, collapse the distinction that is said to exist between the two disciplines—our very being *deconstructs* boundaries. The division of the two is especially pernicious for emerging undergraduate and graduate students who are taught that "philosophical" discourse must take on the structure of an expressed treatise, whether it follows Analytic or Continental form. And, yet, in those ever-popular undergraduate courses in existential philosophy, or philosophy of/and/in literature, where the intersection between philosophy and literature is overtly recognized through plays, novels, and short stories, rarely is there methodological justification for the inclusion of these thinkers into the "philosophical" canon or their being taught in a "philosophy" class, given their overt literary style.[19] That is to say, the enforcement of the traditional philosophical criteria for the canon (style of writing, direct "reference" to other traditional philosophers) seems to be arbitrary[20] for the most part—the justification for the inclusion of some writers becomes the justification for the *exclusion* of other writers.[21]

WRITING RICHARD WRIGHT: THE ETHICS OF ART

This collection highlights the fact that literature, as well as philosophy, has its ontological roots in our desire as *homo narrans*[22] to, as Wright is wont to say, "stand, to tell, to fight, to express the inexpressibly human,"[23] that is, to take a position on the world and to share this position with others. When one places pen to pad, or, in many of our contemporary cases, finger to keyboard, one necessarily takes a "philosophical" stance[24] and *inhabits*, as one inhabits a world, a philosophical position. Moreover, a writer endeavors through his/her writing to give shape and structure to his/her experiences. But, more than the primacy of the need to discourse the world and to tell stories about it, what brings philosophy and literature together is what we can glean from each: what we search for in each is a rigorous methodological approach to understanding the world and what it means to be human. Literature and philosophy both expose the basic existential truth that we are all methods for living rather than living truths;[25] we teach one another and learn from one another how to live and how to choose.

Literature, especially fiction, for writer Charles Johnson, is necessarily philosophical in that it is a metaphysical and psychological profile of the writer—where he/she is from, his/her family background, his/her experiences, etc.—as well as the writer's historical time: the politics of the era, the economic conditions, the cultural mood, and the minutest details of cultural/popular movements. Moreover, literature reflects the tensions inherent in disclosing such "invisible" realities for a human being and the choices and decisions a writer makes. These elements of one's life, sometimes avoided or ignored in traditional philosophy's quest for "objectivity," are often the most difficult to uncover (and hence, invisible, at least to us), for they *are us*, they constitute who we are as persons. The choices we make in what to disclose about ourselves and the world and how to disclose them are not just concerns for academic philosophy or literature—they open up serious ethical questions as well. The choice made by an author of what to disclose of himself/herself and the world as well as the manner of the disclosure have real world implications for the author as well as the reader. Ralph Ellison once argued that literature was not only philosophically significant but the writer also had a moral imperative not only to disclose a world to the reader but also to choose a form that would befit his craft as an artistic endeavor. In a 1970 interview, in response to a question of how a black writer interprets and writes of his experiences of being raced in America, Ellison famously noted his position on literature generally, and black literature specifically, stating that, "craft is an aspect of morality."[26] The difficulty for a writer, in particular an American writer, and especially for a black American writer, is this ethical imperative: a writer must engage the world philosophically, that is, with a perspective, yet at the same time, engage in their craft as more than just an American or a black person, but as an artist engaging the world as a human being.

The writer is given and gives him- or herself the task of putting into discourse his or her feelings, insights, and opinions, but also must engage the reader in the plot and provide them with some investment in the journey itself. Yet, and perhaps most importantly, the writer must choose a language proper to the context. That is, the most important insight of a writer is his or her ability to stand before his or her feelings, opinions, and experiences, letting them disclose themselves, capturing, into or through discourse, the living cultural world to which one finds oneself already in contribution. The fluidity of this living culture with its implicit, complex and nuanced cultural symbols and indications is difficult in itself to measure and to capture, for it is often "metaphysical"—what is present to us intuitively, but difficult to capture in language—in the most concrete and discrete of moments: everyday existence.

When one thinks he or she has captured the essence of event, or an historical moment, for example, one finds that the language is never quite enough, by itself, to express the being of the event or the moment. To this difficulty of language and expression, the American landscape adds the problem of race and race relations. The American landscape magnifies the problems inherent in the human condition—the search for meaning, the search for an expression for one's life, the problem of group dynamics, etc.—and layers among them the peculiar, unconscious psychological desires of its people as well as the invisibility of its history and historicity, all of which go into the making of a complex situation and a complex culture. The task of an American writer, then, is to deal with this complex identity while at the same time maintaining the artistic integrity of his or her work. This, too, was Richard Wright's task. Yet, Wright, like many writers who preceded and subsequently followed him, especially black authors, struggled to locate a language proper to his living condition, to describe and disclose his narrative and the narrative he thought illuminated the existence and experiences of black people in the segregated U.S. South and the hyper(o)critical, or perhaps more aptly, "liberal," North—and, in the later years of his writing, those whose suffered globally under strictures of colonization.

Wright, interestingly, sought to circumvent the problem of expression and language by reducing the role of language itself. In *American Hunger* Wright notes that he often "strove to master words, to make them disappear."[27] Words, for Wright, seemed to get in the way of self-expression and, ironically, if one could master words themselves, they would somehow make them disappear, leaving only "a rising spiral of emotional stimuli . . . ending in an emotional climax that would drench the reader with a *sense* of a new world."[28] And, yet Wright also considered words to be weapons with which to fight, thus highlighting the tension and the ambivalent relation any writer has with literature generally.

Author Toni Morrison similarly notes of the difficulty locating a language fit to explore the experiences and psychic lives of black people, particularly black girls in her novel *The Bluest Eye*. She writes,

> My choices of language (speakerly, aural, colloquial), my reliance for full comprehension on codes embedded in black culture, my effort to effect immediate co-conspiracy and intimacy (without any distancing, explanatory fabric), as well as my attempt to shape a silence while breaking it are attempts to transfigure the complexity and wealth of Black American culture into a language worthy of the culture.[29]

Morrison's choices—how to tell a story about a lead character who is a black girl, as well as what to say and how to say it—were like those Wright made in his depiction of his own youth, coming of age under Jim Crow in *Black Boy*, and in his fiction more generally. The difficulty, though, in the specific case of African American writers lies within the tension between Americanism and blackness: ought a black writer to speak positively about blackness and the actions of black people to create a socio-mythos to counter the hegemonic white mythos, or, ought an author tell the truth of his/her experiences and those of others regardless of how it might appear to a white audience?[30] Black writers thus faced and continue to face the problem of representation and self-expression at the same time dealing with the complexities of their American situation. Yet, for Wright, speaking honestly of his own history and the narratives he learned from other black folk was more important than the task of counter mythos making. "Negro writers," Wright wrote in his essay "Blueprint for Negro Writing," "must accept the nationalist implications of their lives, not in order to encourage them, but in order to change and transcend them. They must accept the concept of nationalism because, in order to transcend it, they must *possess* and *understand* it. And a nationalist spirit in Negro writing means a nationalism carrying the highest pitch of social consciousness."[31]

Richard Wright's work forces us to ask the philosophical and ethical questions "What do we 'see' when we see black people?" and "How do we depict this in narrative form?" For Wright, black people had become ontologized—in the sense of social metaphysics and social determinism[32] —as *both* problem people as well as people with problems,[33] in each case revealing black people as "those who suffer"; and, what is more, black people became marked as those whose suffering made redemption possible. It was black suffering, for Wright, that allowed and continues to allow, the sanctity of the democratic practice of experiments in living.[34] Black suffering, thus, is what lies at the heart of American history and American culture as the unconscious psychological reality for both black and white people—one may also extend this to the international situation of coloniality as well. And, though this suffering is the foundation of American life, it was, for Wright, necessarily invisible, hidden beneath "the way of things" in their everydayness.[35]

Richard Wright's searing prose was as much a philosophical commitment as it was an ethical choice. Wright *chose* to write about the "rot, pus, filth, hate, fear, guilt, and degenerate forms of life"[36] ; he chose to challenge black suffering and to refuse its invisibility through a kind of literary realism that would, he hoped, sound in many an alarm to disrupt white "innocence" and myth-making and, to, in turn, make us *all* (both blacks and whites) responsible and accountable for the covered-over foundation of American society that binds us all, one to the other. His concerns for the structure and content of his work were as pragmatic—directed toward disclosing a world many black Americans lived and were living, a world that was mostly invisible and, often misunderstood—as they were aesthetic.

Wright's contribution to African American writing and American letters and his philosophical importance was that he provided for us a rigorous methodology for *thinking* the human condition in the world through an articulation of the black experience in America. That is, through his narratives and his characters, he placed, into discourse, the human condition—the contingency of existence, the desire for meaning, order, structure and control over life, etc.—illuminated *by* and articulated *through* African American experiences in the West. The contributors in this collection examine aspects of Richard Wright's rich and diverse oeuvre.

PHILOSOPHICAL MEDITATIONS ON RICHARD WRIGHT: THE
EDITED COLLECTION

> Crucified on the vast wheel of time, I flew round and round with the Zeitgeist,
> waving my pen and lifting faint voices to explain, expound and exhort; to see,
> foresee and prophesy, to the few who could or would listen. Thus, very evi-
> dently to me and to others I did little to create my day or greatly change it; but
> I did *exemplify* it and thus for all time my life is significant for all lives of men.
> —W. E. B. DuBois, *Dusk of Dawn*[37]

This collection of essays is about a boy, a man, an author, and a reader. It is
about Richard Wright's historical moment[38] and his reflections concerning
what to do, what to believe, how to behave, and, more generally, how to be.
What is significant about a theorist, as DuBois tells us in the above epigraph,
is his ability to exemplify his historical moment. That is, for a theorist to be
significant to others, beyond himself and his historical moment, he must be
able to translate his or her moment into something specific *and* universal—
specific enough for it to articulate the moment and not to lose its significance, and universal enough to be a narrative about human beings as they
relate to and react to a changing world.

For Wright, the importance of an artist is the exemplification of his moment, while simultaneously being more than the moment itself. The goal of
the artist, and in this case the writer, is not to transcend reality but to utilize
his or her ingenuity, creativity, and imagination to bring reality out into the
openness of the open to show others who wish not to see, or cannot see, the
truth of a certain reality as it is experienced. The writer stands between brute
facts and society acting as a conduit, an expositor of experience, and has the
task of opening and unconcealing, and though he or she only speaks from his
or her perspective, it is one that inevitably speaks for all. Ultimately, the
writer must exemplify his or her historical moment—his or her experiences
as a human being living in the world—through their work, to make clear for
others, and for themselves, their own life and the possible lives of others.

For Wright, the human being is not simply conditioned, but *experiences*
the world—experience being tantamount to the facts of a life (social, eco-
nomical, and political) combined with the human imagination. Every experience, Wright learned, has an explanation, for every experience has a situation
and a human subject. The task, then, before the writer is to measure, with
delicacy, in prose and through narration the effects of an environment on a
human subject. And, as such, the writer, especially the black writer, must
measure those reactive and creative moments of the human being interacting
with his or her environment; without this measurement, all that the writer has

are pseudoscientific claims about one's environment—e.g., hot weather makes for modified behavior; small living quarters effectively stifle one's humanity.

We must, for Wright, look for the dynamism of a human being in each situation, and look for those moments where an *experience* has taken place, and an *explanation* has been given instead of a metaphysical condition wherein one's environment is all-consuming, and simply given.[39] Literature, after all, is neither just the expression of an individual coming to terms with the world that he or she finds him/herself in as an adult, nor is it an expression of one's reconstructed past, but a confluence of the two. What Wright readily points out, but which is often ignored in his work—and in African American philosophy generally—is this human fact about black people: black people were *people*, that is, they had *experiences* and offered *explanations*, before they encountered white people, and especially afterward.[40]

As an exemplar of the modern *zeitgeist*, Wright's work depicted all of the problems of his historic moment, increasing the necessity for concern and for action, locating them in a marginalized black voice; and, it was a black youth (metaphorical or literal) who always suffered the most: "Youth is the turning point in life, the most sensitive and volatile period, the state that registers most vividly the impressions and experiences of life."[41] Each experience became a possibility for a new thought, a new insight into his condition and the human condition. In his exemplification of his moment, Wright *became* his moment, but simultaneously something more. The contributors in this collection endeavor to think of Wright, to think *with* Wright, placing themselves, as much as this is possible, in the milieu of Wright with and through the characters and experiences of black life depicted in his work. In thinking with Wright and thinking Wright's milieu we transform our moment and ourselves.

We engage the phenomena of literature to locate our imagination and to entangle and disentangle ourselves from the web of sociality. Just as literature *becomes* a space of the active engagement of our imagination toward our transformation and our freedom, Richard Wright's literature, and Wright himself, *becomes* a site for the sober acceptance of our social world and our place in it and the transformative possibilities of both. *One becomes only to become again in another, freer form.* In Wright's articulation of the experiences of a black boy, he becomes (that is, inhabits) the modern Western *zeitgeist*—of anonymity, alienation—to become something more than the moment, something significant for us. And it is through our engagement with Wright's work that we come to inhabit his moment, and learn something significant about our own moment. We become, as Wright has, transcendent methods for living a human life, yet, like Wright, remain centered in the immanent and fluid facts of our own lives.

What this volume contributes to Wright scholarship is not so much a philosophical interrogation with concepts read into Wright, or a meditation on Wright and a philosophical genre—e.g., existentialism—but a method of philosophizing. Wright not only reinterpreted what an author could say— about American society, world history, race, being black in American society and the black life-world—but also how it could be said. What is important about Wright is that he endeavored to speak to a larger human community through the experiences of being black in America and black in the West. He exemplified his moment, allowing us to write about him, and his moment, in our moment. In doing so, Wright created dialogue and continuities out of what were thought to be "Manichean divides."

The central aim of this collection is to mine Richard Wright's work, to speak on the lower frequencies, if you will, illuminating his philosophical methodology and philosophical commitments as expressed in and through his novels, critical essays, short stories, travel writings, and letters. As we mine (and mind) Wright's work and his philosophical thought we also en-counter and engage in larger disciplinary debates within and surrounding "philosophy" as a professional practice within the American academy. With this central aim and its concomitant consequence in mind, the collection has been divided into three sections: Richard Wright's Literary Imagination; Richard Wright's Philosophical Imagination; and Richard Wright Today. The collection as a whole is guided by these sections, which offer the collec-tion thematic structure. The authors reflect, in broad strokes, these themes in their writings. They endeavor to measure the breaths of Wright, and to think creatively and philosophically with Wright, utilizing their various methodo-logical approaches to think about Wright's work in itself and in conversation with contemporary debates.

RICHARD WRIGHT'S LITERARY IMAGINATION

In his chapter "Bigger–Cross Damon: Wright's Existential Challenge," Lew-is R. Gordon works to theorize black existential philosophy, both its chal-lenges and its accomplishments, and situates the work of Richard Wright— most notably *Native Son* and *The Outsider*, and in specific the lead charac-ters, Bigger Thomas and Cross Damon—within this tradition. For Gordon, Wright's work exemplifies the "irony at the heart of self-reflection" for a human being facing both the strictures of the modern(izing) world and the meaning of his or her existence in black. Gordon understands Wright's work as a meta-reflection on the near impossibility of "achieving intersubjective communication" when what is being communicated, blackness, is a "delegi-timizing term of communication." Gordon uses the characters Bigger Thomas and Cross Damon to think through not only these "paradoxes posed by existence in black" but the process by which one is able to translate these experiences into philosophical self-reflection. Bigger and Cross represent, for Gordon, critical moments in Wright's work where he seeks to rethink black existence in the West, as not *just* suffering; rather, these characters offer a "point of view" on their own lives and the lives of others, thereby generating additional dimensions of existence.

In my chapter "*Black Boy*: Phenomenology and the Existential Novel," I argue that Richard Wright makes existential and phenomenological claims in *Black Boy*. Wright's claim, I argue, is that self-disclosure as a human being in the world is not achieved simply through "philosophical" (that is, theoretical) introspection or the interrogation of the everyday, but an intense and thoroughgoing relationship to suffering. For Wright, suffering takes on a significant role for articulating one's existence in the world, not only as questions concerning the absurdity of life or the eventuality of death; rather, suffering for Wright is a thoroughgoing ontological sundering at the heart of which one's existence is not simply questioned, but fundamentally denied. I ask, within the context of this sundering, how literature itself is possible. Further, I offer Wright's *Black Boy* as an accomplishment and a grand achievement given the context out of which it emerged.

In her chapter "Experiencing Existentialism through Theme and Tone: Kierkegaard and Richard Wright," Desirée H. Melton offers a reconceptualization of existentialism and existential literature. Through her analysis of Richard Wright's works *Native Son* and *The Outsider* along with Søren Kierkegaard's *Fear and Trembling* she argues that what makes for existential literature is not simply the usage of existential concepts—such as dread and despair—but an existential *tone*, one through which the reader is able to draw a connection with the situation, that is, condition, of the character. Melton argues that Wright's novel *The Outsider*, often regarded as his most existential novel, is in fact his least existential work, for it fails to relate the situation of its lead character, Cross Damon, in a tangible enough way that the reader both makes a connection with his torment and is able to draw from his torment a certain level of empathy. Rather, the reader is left, on Melton's account, only with the vocabulary of existentialism without any of the necessary empathy for the character. Conversely, Melton argues that Wright's novel *Native Son*, though not considered existential by many scholars, does in fact strike an existential tone, and does so, ironically, without the usage of existential language.

RICHARD WRIGHT'S PHILOSOPHICAL IMAGINATION

In his chapter "Fear, Trembling and Transcendence in the Everyday of Richard Wright: A *Quare* Reading," Victor Anderson situates Richard Wright's work, specifically *Black Boy* (*American Hunger*), within the paradigm of quare theory—an oppositional ontology and episteme designed to counter the dangers and desires of conforming, not only to whiteness (as oppression) but to blackness (the black community) as well. "As in Wright's counter-memory, so in the counter-memory of many black same sex–same gender loving people, their *quare* idealities and fantasies of self-assertion, self-reclamation mark off for them transcendence in the everyday over the threat of violence and death and of being and nothingness accompanied with its opposites in the actuality of their lived experiences." Quareness becomes for Anderson not only a means through which one may negotiate one's existence but also a method of articulating, in the sense of affirmation, one's sense of reality. Anderson offers a *quare* reading of Richard Wright, which provides in a subtle manner a reading of Wright, which "reads" him. In a novel way, to read Wright, for Anderson, is to "read" Wright, which is to offer a quare understanding of the man Wright, who, in *Black Boy* and *American Hunger*, presents, in counter-memory, the boy of his own black youth and the developing youth of his adolescence. Reading Wright as quare, then, also means "reading" Wright; and, what is more, it is to understand black youth (and adolescence), not only in terms of how one represents oneself and one's past, but in terms of how one situates blackness generally as a quare constitution within the sociality of space and time.

In his chapter "Specularity as a Mode of Knowledge and Agency in Richard Wright's Work," Abdul R. JanMohamed explores elements of subjectification and subjection in Richard Wright's work, in particular *Black Boy*, as expressive of certain epistemological and ontological insights born of blackness. What is significant in Wright's work, for JanMohamed, is the dialectic of oppression in which Wright finds himself, both literally and figuratively—both as a writer projecting himself into literature, as in *Native Son*, and as a black American experiencing racialization and terror—placed between castration and death. What is more, in Wright's own consciousness as a writer and as a man, he faces both of these existential realities in a manner deeply cleaved, "on the one hand, he identifies with his castrators, with those who hold the power, on the other hand, he identifies with the castrated, with those already subjugated by the prevailing power." Wright is at once purveyor of violence and oppression *and* its victim: this for JanMohamed is the impossible dialectic of oppression. Yet, it is from this dual position that Wright actualizes at once the condition for his subjugation and the requisite tools for his liberation.

RICHARD WRIGHT TODAY

Alexa Weik's chapter, "'The Uses and Hazards of Expatriation': Richard Wright's Cosmopolitanism in Process," analyzes Richard Wright's rootless cosmopolitan claim made in his series of lectures *White Man, Listen!* where he writes, "I am a rootless man." Weik analyzes Wright's statement in terms of the kind of cosmopolitanism it espouses, in terms of Wright's own failing to live up to this particular kind of cosmopolitanism. Implicit in Weik's chapter is the problem that black Americans face when engaging with and in the language and structures of a dominant paradigm: African Americans like Wright are not at home in and are alienated from much of Western discourse; and yet not being able to find a home in another language they must face their own inherent Americanness. In a nuanced reading of Wright's *Black Power* and *White Man, Listen!* Weik offers a glimpse of the conflicts that exist in Wright, and that are present within his latter works, especially *The Outsider*. Not quite an insider in the American polity or demos and not a "world" citizen—without nation, race, or religion—Weik situates Wright as a cosmopolitan-in-process, in a continual state of phenomenological unfolding and existential self-discovery.

Jerry W. Ward, Jr.'s chapter, "On Richard Wright and Our Contemporary Situation,"[42] aptly works to close the collection as it poses, for our contemporary situation and within the prevue of disaster (both man-made and natural), the continuing significance of Richard Wright's work. Ward's final chapter helps us to navigate and rethink some of the previous chapters in this collection, giving Wright's rich oeuvre "points of reference." In a general way Ward understands Wright's work to be concerned with those "disturbing questions about the designs human beings have upon other human beings." But, and more specifically, for Ward, Wright's work was a calling forth of Wright's own strange birth, at the nexus of a changing American landscape (political, economic, and social), and his own response to the "refractions of human absurdity through the prisms" of literature (both fiction and nonfiction).

NOTES

1. Throughout this introduction the nature of discipline of philosophy and what it means to "be" a philosopher and to "do" philosophy will be implicitly questioned and explicitly critiqued. Hence, when referencing the traditional philosophical discipline, its canon as well as its practitioners (historical and contemporaneous), I will be using quotations to signify an ongoing question and to recognize the ongoing problems of the discipline, especially illuminated by African American writers, in particular Richard Wright. This ongoing questioning serves, I

hope, to highlight, not the purity of the notion or the discipline itself but the fundamental nature of the kinds of questioning undergone instead of focusing on the person(s) doing the questioning and, thus, the manner in which the questioning is accomplished.

2. See Lewis Gordon's *Disciplinary Decadence: Living Thought in Trying Times* (Boulder, CO: Paradigm Publishers, 2007) for a good discussion of the structure of the present-day American academy which, in its quest to produce workers for a capitalist system, requires specification and specialization from those who matriculate and go on to work in their field. Problematically, though, in our haste to construct and shore up disciplinary boundaries we have limited our ability to study that phenomenon we initially set forth to examine: human reality.

3. For an extensive reading of Richard Wright's relationships with philosophical figures see George Cotkin's *Existential America* (Baltimore, MD: John Hopkins University Press, 2003), especially chapter 8, "Cold Rage: Richard Wright and Ralph Ellison." Also, see Nina Kressner Cobb's article "Richard Wright: Exile and Existentialism" (*Phylon* 40, no. 4, 1979: 362–74). Also, see Richard Macksey and Frank E. Moorer's edited collection *Richard Wright: A Collection of Critical Essays* (New York: Simon and Schuster, 1984), especially section 3, "The Existential Quest: Freedom and Enclosure." Also see Michel Fabre's *From Harlem to Paris: Black American Writers in France, 1849–1980* (Champaign: University of Illinois Press, 1993), especially chapter 12, "Richard Wright: An Intellectual in Exile"; and Michel Fabre's *The World of Richard Wright* (Oxford: University Press of Mississippi, 1985), chapter 10, "Wright and the French Existentialists."

4. African American writers have expressed significant intellectual curiosity with "philosophical" debates. Many African American writers traveled abroad and were familiar with many of the "philosophical" ideas. For an example of African American writers and philosophy, see Lawrence Jackson's biography of Ralph Ellison, *Emergence of Genius* (New York: John Wiley & Sons, 2002). Also, many American writers (not to mention French and German ones as well) were well versed in the debates within continental "philosophies." For American writers and philosophy, see Ann Fulton's *Apostles of Sartre: Existentialism in America 1945–1963* (Evanston, IL: Northwestern University Press, 1999). To consider a writer's (white or black) relation to and interest in "philosophical" debates a rarity is simply to be unaware of one's own intellectual roots.

5. In the 1940s, 1950s, and 1960s the intellectual world was indeed small, or better said, close. It was not rare for a figure like Richard Wright to be familiar with French "philosopher" Jean-Paul Sartre or Hannah Arendt, or for him to know Africana theorist Leopold Senghor, or W. E. B. DuBois, or, for him to know sociologist Gunnar Myrdal—the dedication to Wright's 1957 travel journal writing, *Pagan Spain* (New York: Harper Collins, 1957), reads, "For my friends Alva and Gunnar Myrdal, who suggested this book and whose compassionate hearts have long brooded upon the degradation of human life in Spain." What we need, especially in "philosophy," is a remapping of our intellectual terrain to reflect the overlap between writers, philosophers, sociologists, historians, linguists, and anthropologists. In remapping the terrain, we can and must understand reciprocal influences to get a holistic picture of the intellectual world.

6. An important question to raise, and one that I continually raise and that can be located, implicitly, within this project is "How did the disciplinary boundaries of American philosophy develop over the twentieth century, and how/why did philosophy grow increasingly isolated from other disciplines over the last quarter of the twentieth century?" And, what is more, how, if at all, can those voices on the margins of the discipline, in this case African American voices, save the discipline from its movement toward, not so much the sanctity of prayer and the stoic "inner life," but the solipsism of interiority, or inner dialogue? While this is a very important point and goes to the heart of the major argument, the most I can do here, with the given space constraints, is gesture toward the question itself.

7. Though a few edited collections, essays, and authored books do in fact take up writers, and African American ones at that, in their relation to "philosophical" concepts and within "philosophical" discourses—there is an entire subfield of "philosophy" and/of literature of which thinkers such Hugh Silverman and Charles Johnson are among the leading proponents— we need to ask, why hasn't there been extended and sustained "philosophical" interrogation of an African American writer other than a few published essays by George Yancy (chapter 6 in

Black Body, White Gazes: The Continuing Significance of Race (Lanham, MD: Rowman & Littlefield, 2008); "Desiring *Bluest Eyes*, Desiring Whiteness: The Black Body as Torn Asunder"; and "The Black Self within the Semiotic Space of Whiteness: Reflections on the Racial Deformation of Pecola Breedlove in Toni Morrison's *Bluest Eye*" (*CLA Journal* no. 3, 2000: 299–319)? Aside from these essays, in the other essays in which writers, especially African American ones, are mentioned, even at length, they are not themselves nor are their ideas the center of the philosophical debate. Rather, they are added to further bolster an already made point. Why haven't at least African American "philosophers" taken up African Americans writers as a *primary mode* of philosophical interrogation? The question at least bears asking.

8.   For a necessary article on the problem of "epistemic convergence" wherein a black thinker is only deemed worthy of study when in direct and explicit conversation with an already canonized white thinker, see Tommy J. Curry's "The Derelict and Methodological Crisis of Africana Philosophy's Study of African Descended People under an Integrationist Milieu," *Radical Philosophy Review* 14, no. 2 (2011): 139–64.

9.   In his book *Pursuit of Truth* (Cambridge, MA: Harvard University Press, 1992) W. V. Quine raises interesting and necessary epistemological points: how is knowledge generated, and do we all need to be the *same* (ontologically) to share knowledge? This challenge is quite necessary, for epistemology has not always thought that the being of the knower conditioned the kind of knowledge produced (see Lorraine Code's *What Can She Know: Feminist Theory and the Construction of Knowledge* [Ithaca, NY: Cornell University Press, 1991] for an effective discussion of this problem in analytic epistemology). For Quine, though, there is a way out of this problem. His discussion of knowledge production and consumption hinges on an assumption of commensurability: everyone is epistemically assumed to be similar enough that one can transfer (read: communicate) any knowledge claim to another, no matter how foreign. Quine writes, "Linguists can usually avoid radical translation by finding someone who can interpret the language, however haltingly, into a somewhat familiar one. But it is only radical translation that exposes the poverty of ultimate data for the identification of meanings" (46). Further, Quine writes of the problems and solution of radical translation, that, "failing evidence to the contrary," the natives minds "are presumed to be pretty much like our own" (46). Lastly, Quine writes that since "the linguist assumes that the native's attitudes and ways of thinking are like his own . . . he accordingly *imposes* his own ontology and linguistic patterns on the native wherever compatible with the native's speech and other behavior . . . We could not wish to do otherwise . . . the radical translator is *bound to impose about as much as he discovers*" (48–49; emphasis added). But, how much is lost in translation? This point raises the problem of commensurability to that of ontological reduction of difference to sameness, wherein the "center" is thought to be decider of truth. In our attempts to include African American writers (in this case, and generally, Africana thinkers) in the philosophical canon we face a serious problem: on this account it would only be reasonable to accept African American writers into the canon to the extent that they have said something relatively close to what white "philosophers" have already established *is* philosophy. And, this is exactly the problem: what is missed in the translation? And, then, what is "philosophy"?

10.   These questions are meta-philosophical questions themselves that work to problematize and therefore illuminate the fact that we have answers for questions that remain largely unasked. And, what is more, it is to serve as a reminder that "philosophers" within the American academy have, themselves, settled on an issue that, within their own canon, is far from being settled. (See Edmond Husserl's 1954 text, *The Crisis of European Sciences and Transcendental Phenomenology* [Evanston, IL: Northwestern University Press, 1970] and Maurice Merleau-Ponty's 1960 text *Signs* [Evanston, IL: Northwestern University Press, 1964] for examples of the ongoing questioning). The question thus serves in this respect, raising the question "What is philosophy?" especially as we continue to "do" philosophy. So rarely do we ask in ourselves— in our introductory courses or in our graduate seminars—about the method of our discipline and about our implicit understandings. We are often so inundated with concepts and figures that we—students and professors—become talking jukeboxes reproducing both privilege and a historically emergent epistemology of ignorance. What we are doing here in the introduction and throughout the collection in (re)raising these questions is engaging in the philosophical tradition wherein our concepts create their own problems. This, of course, is in no way new, but

what is new, relatively speaking, is raising these questions through voices that have been placed at the margins of the discipline, or perhaps completely outside of the closed system of the discipline itself. Raising these questions to philosophy through Richard Wright allows us to ask, "If we are at another crisis point—which the exclusion of voices of color signifies—can philosophy be saved as a useful and relevant enterprise through the inclusion and mining of these marginal voices?" And, this leads to the grandest of all questions implicitly raised: Why philosophy at all for a figure such as Wright? This question, though helpful to bear in mind, works to reinscribe the hegemony of thought present in the discipline contemporaneously, wherein it is assumed that white Americans have the right to construct the field and have exclusive right over the term itself. By raising the question I hope to at least direct attention to the fact that the history of the term and practice has not been exclusively "white" and, thus, by relating Wright (or any other black thinker) to philosophy is not to justify them within the construct of "whiteness" vis-à-vis the academy.

11. It is not clear whether African American philosophy is a subfield or its own branch. That is, does African American philosophy take already established (read: traditional) methods of philosophical interrogation and traditional philosophical problems and apply them to the African American experience, making them somehow African American? Or, does African American philosophy come up with its own philosophical methodologies and its own philosophical problems altogether, making it, not a subfield, but a third field alongside the general fields of analytic and continental philosophies? (For a good and detailed critique of the methodological problems in African American philosophy see Tommy J. Curry's "The Derelictical Crisis in African American Philosophy: How African American Philosophy Fails to Contribute to the Study of African Descended People," [*Journal of Black Studies*, forthcoming]; also, Ralph Dumain's "Cornel West's Evasion of Philosophy, Or Richard Wright's Revenge," www.autodidactproject.org/my/cornel1.html). Of course, there would be, in the case of African American philosophy being a third field, overlap and boundary disputes between it and the other two fields, as there is between analytic and continental philosophies. And, who or what constitutes an African American philosopher? Are we to include only those folk who earned their doctorate in philosophy? What is more, coming up with a working definition of African American philosophy is especially difficult because we first need a working definition of what African Americans are—and there is not a more disputed and contested ground in U.S. America than African American identity. The lack of philosophical rigor on African American identity—African, American, African in America, or some hybrid of the three—adds to the complication of naming African American philosophy. For example, the lack of epistemological distinction made between African American philosophy, American philosophy (namely Pragmatism), and Africana philosophy (to name a few) also adds to the ambiguity of the term "African American philosophy." The lack of rigorous methodology for how to philosophize African Americans makes it difficult to formulate a specific canon from which theorist can draw. Instead we get a hodgepodge of "black" writers from slave narratives (Frederick Douglass) to antebellum thinkers (W. E. B. DuBois and Anna Julia Cooper) to African thinkers (Steve Biko) to Caribbean thinkers (Franz Fanon) without a method for what draws them together outside of whiteness and white racism as hegemonic. There have been efforts to define African Americans and the borders of African American philosophy—with the publication of Leonard Harris's *Philosophy Born of Struggle* (Dubuque, IA: Kendall/Hunt Publishers, 1983); Cornel West's *Prophesy Deliverance: An Afro-American Revolutionary Christianity* (Philadelphia: Westminster Press, 1982), especially chapter 3, "Four Traditions of Response," and "Philosophy and the Afro-American Experience" (*Philosophical Forum* 9, nos. 2–3 [Winter–Spring 1977–1978]: 117–48); Lucius Outlaw's *On Race and Philosophy* (New York: Routledge, 1996), especially chapter 1, "Black Folk and the Struggle in 'Philosophy'"; Thomas Slaughter's "Epidermalizing the World: A Basic Mode of Being Black" (*Man and World* 10, no. 3 [September 1977]: 303–8); Paul Jefferson's "The Question of Black Philosophy," (*Journal of Social Philosophy* 20, no. 3 [Winter 1989]: 99–109); Anthony Appiah's *In My Father's House* (New York: Oxford University Press, 1993), and "African American Philosophy?" in *African American Perspectives and Philosophical Traditions*, ed. John Pittman (New York: Routledge, 1996); William Jones's "The Legitimacy of and Necessity of Black Philosophy: Some Preliminary Considerations" (*Philosophical Forum* 9, nos. 2–3: 149–60); Charles Mills's

Blackness Visible: Essays on Philosophy and Race (Ithaca, NY: Cornell University Press, 1998); John McClendon's "The Afro-American Philosopher and the Philosophy of the Black Experience: A Bibliographical Essay on a Neglected Topic in Both Philosophy and Black Studies" (*Sage Relations Abstracts* 26, no. 1 [November 1982]: 57–73); Johnny Washington's *Alain Locke and Philosophy: A Quest for Cultural Pluralism* (Westport, CT: Greenwood Press, 1986), especially chapter 1, "What Is Black Philosophy?"; Bernard Boxill's *Blacks and Social Justice* (Lantham, MD: Rowman & Littlefield, 1992); Lewis R. Gordon's *Existentia Africana* (New York: Routledge, 2000), his *Existence in Black* (New York: Routledge, 1997), and his *Introduction to Africana Philosophy* (New York: Cambridge University Press, 2008); Paget Henry's *Caliban's Reason: Introducing Afro-Caribbean Philosophy* (New York: Routledge, 2000); and Robert Gooding-Williams's *Look a Negro: Philosophical Essays on Race, Culture, and Politics* (New York: Routledge, 2005) to name a few. For a good overview of the history of African American philosophy, especially those black people who earned their doctorates in philosophy, see George Yancy's *African American Philosophers: 17 Conversations* (New York: Routledge, 1998). And while the lack of disciplinary focus is and remains a problem, the task of this collection is not to answer the question. Rather, this collection endeavors, through establishing methodological principles by which to judge Richard Wright's work as philosophy, or as philosophical, to propose some necessary principles for judging what makes a writer philosophical.

12. One may look to the usage of autobiography by many canonical philosophers (including Plato's many dialogues, Jean-Jacque Rousseau's *Confessions*, Rene Descartes' *Meditations on First Philosophy*—arguably the beginning moment of "modern philosophy"—Immanuel Kant's pre-critical writings, Simone de Beauvoir's *Memoirs of a Dutiful Daughter*, etc.) as proof of the intersection of philosophy and literature. This fact alone, though, does not cover over the problem of vagueness in "philosophy." Rather, it exacerbates the problem. Is every moment of self-reflection and disclosure and everything that follows from them as expression philosophical? How, then, do we draw the lines of what literature is philosophical, what memoir is insightful, what autobiography is useful? Interestingly, the same committee members who told me my interest in African American literature was not philosophical teach courses in which Jean-Paul Sartre's novel *Nausea* is read, have published essays on his play *The Respectful Prostitute*, and, what is more, have an edited collection on existentialism forthcoming in which there is an excerpt from Richard Wright's *White Man, Listen!* The point being made here is that there are no rules for adjudicating literature and philosophy since many traditional philosophers wrote memoirs and/or biographies—we have to ask ourselves what it was about the form that literature takes that enticed them; how we choose, and under what principles, between what we call philosophy and what we call literature; and, lastly, we must ask ourselves *why*, perhaps the most difficult question of all of the question forms, we choose certain texts and authors as expressing philosophical content in their literature while other authors and their works are simply "literature." While this is not a problem only facing African American literature, it disproportionately affects African American literature.

13. For example, Immanuel Kant's *Critique of Pure Reason*, or Jean-Paul Sartre's *Being and Nothingness*.

14. For example, Albert Camus' *The Stranger* or Fyodor Dostoevsky's *Notes from Underground* are routinely taught in most undergraduate courses on existential "philosophy." Of particular note, Albert Camus' complicated relation to "philosophers" and his inclusion into the "philosophical" canon vis-à-vis the "existential" tradition—he openly resisted the title "existentialism" being applied to his writings, and one can assume that he may have also rejected the label "philosopher" or "philosophy" as well (or at least in the "traditional" sense we have within the academy). For more on Albert Camus' relation to the discipline of philosophy and to philosophers, see *Sartre and Camus: A Historic Confrontation*, Adrian Van Den Hoven and David A. Sprintzen, eds. (Amherst, NY: Humanity Books, 2004).

15. This is an important point. For example, one can look at Simone de Beauvoir's *Second Sex* and *America Day by Day*, or Jean-Paul Sartre's *Critique of Dialectical Reason* and "Return from the United States: What I Learned about the Black Problem," to see Richard Wright's influence on their thought. How much do Beauvoir or Sartre scholars miss out on in terms of

understanding Sartre and Beauvoir by ignoring Wright's work? How much would Wright's own philosophical insights add to the study and understanding of continental and analytic philosophers alike?

16. One of the main concerns for the inclusion of African American writers in the discipline of "philosophy" (of course, beside the obvious concerns of "race") is that their method of exchange made/makes it difficult for contemporary "philosophers" to follow/understand— there were rarely footnotes or citations, only ideas. It is, thus, incumbent upon the reader to be familiar with the ideas themselves (rather than names) and be conversant within the *world* of ideas. This is a very different way of participating in and "doing" philosophy. As such, we must ask ourselves, is our inability to understand various practices and modes of "philosophy" reflective more of our own ineptitude with ideas than of the author's lack of intellectual rigor?

17. Both of these questions are loaded. Since we have argued that "traditional philosophy" is itself an ambiguous term, and African American philosophy an even more ambiguous concept, African American literature helps to further scrutinize the disciple of philosophy and the concept of African American philosophy. It is, in this way, that African American literature can add to and help define traditional philosophy and African American philosophy. Or, at least African American literature can help traditional philosophy admit that they have no rigorous method other than prejudice.

18. Charles Johnson, *Being and Race: Black Writing since 1970* (Bloomington: Indiana University Press, 1984), 32.

19. Even Walter Kaufmann, the architect of the secular turn in existential philosophy with his seminal collection *Existentialism from Dostoevsky to Sartre* (New York: Meridian Press, 1975), writes that existentialism itself cannot be defined using traditional philosophical weighs and means; existentialism is its own animal. "Existentialism is not a philosophy," Kaufmann writes, "but a label for several widely different revolts against traditional philosophy" (11). Moreover, "existentialism is not a school of thought nor reducible to any set of tenets" (11). Rather, existentialism is constituted by "the refusal to belong to any school of thought, the repudiation of the adequacy of any body of beliefs whatever, and especially of systems, and a marked dissatisfaction with traditional philosophy as superficial, academic, and remote from life—that is the heart of existentialism" (12). What existentialism is, according to Kaufmann, is simply "a timeless sensibility" (12). It must, then, be asked of those who teach such courses or endorse such courses, what makes the work of Søren Kierkegaard, Karl Jaspers, or even Emanuel Ortega "philosophical"? What makes existentialism itself "philosophical"? And, what is more damning, if we take Kaufmann seriously, how can we *exclude* writers, especially African American writers, from the canon of existential literature?

20. "Arbitrary" here is understood as contingent in the sense that there is no determined or metaphysically transparent reason or essence for the way the discipline is shaped/constructed. The difficulty of thinking disciplinary boundaries in this manner is that it evokes an image of darkly lit rooms and old white men with pernicious looks on their faces, planning around a dusty table the fate of the discipline of philosophy. Such an image, though entertaining for those of us who wish to challenge the canon, does not leave room for an honest discussion of the reproduction of sameness within the discipline where one thinks the canon to be legitimate because it is the canon, and the canon is the canon because it is legitimate. What we have left is the task to pose the questions, "Why is it that we read the authors we do?" "Why not read other authors?" And, "who decided the subjects of inquiry were the subjects to be studied?" These questions are reflections on the meta-philosophical foundation of the canons of philosophy.

21. The difficulty remains, then, because contemporaneously, there are no well-established methodological principles for adjudicating a thinker's inclusion in the traditional "philosophic" canon. What we have, then, in the construction of our traditional philosophical canon are spurious choices of dubious aesthetics, making African American writers/thinkers (as well as other non-white writers/thinkers generally) mere afterthoughts, tacked on at the end (of courses, of scholarship, etc.) to highlight already established "philosophical" principle(s). For example, Fyodor Dostoevsky's *Notes from Underground* is often treated as an intellectual precursor to Richard Wright's novella, *The Man Who Lived Underground*. Neither African American authors nor their texts are "centered" for their philosophical insights where the canonical Western thinkers sit on the bench longing to get into the "philosophical" game. The

reconstruction of our own intellectual history and the canon is especially necessary for those of us in the academy who wish to work interdisciplinarily because it allows us to see that the boundaries themselves are drawn and, that they can be redrawn.

22. I would like to thank Duquesne University professor George Yancy for pointing this out to me. On the subject of *homo narrans* in philosophy see George Yancy's *Philosophical I: Personal Reflections on Life in Philosophy* (Lanham, MD: Rowman & Littlefield, 2002), especially the introduction, "Philosophy and the Situated Narrative Self."

23. Richard Wright, *American Hunger* (Borgro Press, 1975), 135.

24. "Philosophical" here means more than traditional "philosophy," but an answer, of sorts, to the question of philosophy: What is philosophy? Along with French philosopher Maurice Merleau-Ponty I ask and tentatively answer the question "What is philosophy?" by arguing that philosophy is but a method, a way of living. In this context, philosophy is a method of interrogation, of critical analysis. Whenever one takes a position, that is, narrates, one is engaging in philosophy: "We see the things themselves, the world is what we see" (*The Visible and the Invisible* [Evanston, IL: Northwestern University Press, 1968]).

25. The existential distinction between living truths and methods for living is centered on a kind of historicism. The latter claims the theories we develop to explain the world and our human relationships therein (between ourselves and ourselves and the world) are contingent upon our own experiences and our acknowledged and unacknowledged histories. It is in this way that none of the "facts" about the world, nor any of our theories are true in the objective sense of "Truth," but are living, changing, developing as we are. We live and our theories live. The former claims that the task of philosophy is to uncover metaphysical truths that can, and must be, separated out from any particular historical time or any particular persons.

26. Ralph Ellison, *The Collected Essays of Ralph Ellison* (New York: Modern Library Classics, 2003), 359.

27. Richard Wright, *American Hunger*, 25.

28. Richard Wright, *American Hunger*, 25; emphasis added.

29. Toni Morrison, *The Bluest Eye* (Penguin, 1994), 215–16.

30. One of the problems that black writers have faced in America is that of audience. Who was the intended audience of the work, and what role did this play in what was written and how it was written? In addition to representations of blackness and audience selection was the problem of publication and sponsorship. How did white sponsorship of black authors affect the work black authors produced and their [black authors] relation to one another? For a detailed analysis of one particular case of how this tension manifested in the lives of black artists see Valeri Boyd's *Wrapped in Rainbows: The Life of Zora Neal Hurston* (New York: Scribner, 2004).

31. *Norton Anthology of African American Literature*, ed. Nelly McKay and Henry Louis Gates (New York: W.W. Norton, 1997), 1383. Author Edward Margolies similarly notes of Wright's conception of black writing in his text *Native Sons: A Critical Study of Twentieth Century Negro American Authors* (Philadelphia: Lippincott, 1969), "Aesthetics, afterall, implies a clarity of expression, a structuring of meaning out of the vast welter of human experience. Insofar as the artist is capable of forcing to the surface the underlying conditions of his life, he is capable of acting to modify these conditions." For Wright, the activity of writing itself was merely a moment that precedes the *action* of an individual. In "raising the ground to the surface," the author makes preparation to *act* in the world.

32. For example, the contemporary culture of poverty (and poverty of culture) discourse, following publication of the infamous 1965 Moynihan Report, sought and seeks to explain cyclical poverty in urban (read: black) communities utilizing logic internal to the system itself; for example, black people are poor because their culture does not promote the work ethic and savings skills to not be poor, and, on the other hand, but on the same note, black people have this particular culture because there is something intrinsic about poverty *in* and to blackness itself, poor living conditions are but the material proof. In either case, in this thinking, the culture black people have is both structurally and ontologically—both socially determined (structural) and metaphysical (socially contrived, but could not have been otherwise)—determined. Black people, on this reading, lack agency in the process. Richard Wright was well versed in this sort of literature as was he well versed in the Chicago School of social science.

For a good article on the influence of social scientific thinking on Richard Wright, see Carla Capetti, "Sociology of an Existence: Richard Wright and the Chicago School," in *The Critical Response to Richard Wright*, Robert J. Butler, ed. (Westport, CT: Greenwood, 1995), 84–87; also, see Richard Wright, *12 Million Black Voices* (New York: Thunder's Mouth Press, 1941), especially chapters 3 and 4, "Death on City Pavements" and "Men in the Making," respectively.

33.   It is important and useful to situate Richard Wright within a larger debate that continues to take place with respect to black people, especially urban, poor, and working-class black folk. Scholar Houston Baker in *Blues Ideology and African American Literature: A Vernacular Theory* (Chicago: University of Chicago Press, 1984) skillfully argues that when thinking of black people as either those persons who have problems, or who are themselves problematic, what we are in fact thinking of are not problems per se, but the reason *why* these problems themselves exist and afflict this group of persons. The implicit argument that Baker suggests is at play here is thinking of black people as lacking the necessary socialization to take advantage of Western culture. Regrettably, Richard Wright, too, makes this argument in his early semi-autobiography *Black Boy*. Yet, Baker is able to point out that what we think about when we think of blacks as problems or having problems is a "lack" which is understood solely in economic terms as an absence. But, it is useful and instructive for philosophical insight to theorize Richard Wright's work, against itself, as illuminating not a "lack" as absence, but lack as presence. The presence of an absence; Wright's work in this way takes on a richer phenomenological understanding of the relationship of black people to space and places rather than simply the relationship of black people to material things or to larger hegemonic systems—while at the same time acknowledging the importance of these modes of analysis.

34.   The claim being made here is that African American suffering seems, at times, to be for nothing other than the abstract principles of the American nation—liberty, individuality, autonomy, democracy, etc.—that are, not in themselves, actually practiced. Wright analyzes this phenomenon in his novella, *The Man Who Lived Underground* in *Eight Men* (New York: Harper Collins Publishing, 1989). In this novella the lead character, Fred Daniels, escapes a false police prosecution by literally going underground (into the sewer system) where he discovers the underground to be a subversive world with its own subversive politics, and its own subversive epistemology. It is in the underground that Daniels begins to reconsider the fundamental structures of Western democracy—freedom, equality, guilt and innocence, as well as capitalism—and develops a counter narrative (his usage of money as wall paper instead of currency is but one example of this counter discourse). Autodidact Ralph Dumain aptly points this out when he notes that Wright "suggests that the real threat to the system comes not from radicals and agitators and segments of the population who want a piece of the action, but from people who have no such investment." Here, Wright can be understood as having a possessive disinvestment rather than a possessive investment in American ideals.

35.   A significant part of the suffering of black folk in America lies in the invisibility of the suffering. This invisibility allows white Americans to ignore the plight of their fellow citizens, or, in ironic fashion, to believe that the suffering itself has come, or is close to coming to an end. In *American Hunger* Wright recounts his experiences working for a European immigrant's restaurant in Chicago and how he would watch the white waitresses carelessly going about their lives blind to the suffering of the "real world":

> They [white waitresses] lived on the surface of their days; smiles were surface smiles, and their tears were surface tears . . . The girls never talked of their feelings; none of them possessed the insight or emotional equipment to understand themselves or others. How far apart in culture we stood! (12–13)

For Wright, American society in their privileging of whiteness as norm makes it nearly impossible for whites to recognize their own privilege—its nature and how far reaching it is—and their relation to blackness and black suffering.

36.   Richard Wright, "I Bite the Hand That Feeds Me." *Atlantic Monthly*, June 1940.

37.   W. E. B. DuBois, *Dusk of Dawn*, reprinted in *Du Bois Writings* (New York: Library of America College Editions, 1996), 555; emphasis added.

38. Though this collection is not itself biographical, there are important historical notes to bear in mind in thinking and writing Richard Wright. Because Wright was born at the turn of twentieth century in the rural South and raised under Jim Crow segregation, Wright's moment was born of and articulated under emerging historical, social scientific, and philosophical trends aimed at countering the last century of metaphysical understandings of personal identities—race and gender within the institution of chattel slavery. We can witness in Wright's novels and short stories an explicit effort to counter many of these intellectual trends and to place himself in conversation with many of the contemporary discussions. Fruitful discussion and research can and has been done on Wright's many intellectual influences and interests in the academic disciplines. See Abdul JanMohamed, *The Death-Bound Subject: Richard Wright's Archaeology of Death* (Durham, NC: Duke University Press, 2005); and Henry Louis Gates, *Richard Wright: Critical Perspectives Past and Present* (New York: Amistad Press, 1993).

39. Or, perhaps worse—a condition in which the human being is all will and fortitude, and one's environmental influences are but choices within the scope of human freedom.

40. It is also on this point that Richard Wright would be informative for African American philosophers. What, for African American philosophers, is the phenomenological relationship of man to the physical world, and man to the social world? What I have in mind here extends beyond the phenomenology of racialized experiences wherein black people negotiate their being (existence) in an anti-black world. Rather, what I have in mind here is a phenomenological investigation that accounts for the worlds of black persons in America—that is, what is the relation to the spaces black folk find themselves in (urban, rural, suburban), how do they construct places out of spaces, and what effect does this have on the cultivation of personality, identity: epistemology, and ontology. In short: why aren't African American philosophers giving us a rigorous pre-cognitive, pre-reflective, pre-individualists (pre-subjective) articulation of black being *before* one's encounter with white people and anti-black racism—unless we are willing to say there is no black self prior to whiteness! Richard Wright makes the claim of black ontological independence from whiteness in a phenomenological passage in *Black Boy*:

> Though I had long known that there were people called "white" people, it had never meant anything to me emotionally. I had seen white men and women upon the streets a thousand times, but they never looked particularly "white." To me they were merely people like other people, yet somehow strangely different because I had never come in close touch with any of them. For the most part I never thought of them; they simply existed somewhere in the background of the city as a whole. (30–31)

Notice the language Wright chooses to use to talk about white people: "they simply existed somewhere in the background of the city as a whole." Alongside trees, cracked pavements, street signs, tall buildings, etc., white people existed *as* background. The kind of phenomenology I argue for has to account for the influences of place on individuals. For a good example of the usage of space/place phenomenology concerning race and the formation of identity in contemporary scholarship see *Black Los Angeles: American Dreams and Racial Realities*, Darnell Hunt and Ana-Christina Ramon, eds. (New York: New York University Press, 2010).

41. Richard Wright, "I Bite the Hand That Feeds Me." *Atlantic Monthly*, June 1940.

42. An earlier version of this essay was presented at Grinnell College on October 27, 2005, and published in *The Katrina Papers: A Journal of Trauma and Recovery* (2008). It now incorporates ideas generated during the Wright Centennial (2008) and from conversations with colleagues in the People's Republic of China regarding Richard Wright's significance for twenty-first-century readers and is part of a work-in-progress, *Richard Wright: One Reader's Responses*.

Part I

Richard Wright's Literary Imagination

Chapter One

Bigger–Cross Damon

Wright's Existential Challenge

Lewis R. Gordon, Temple University

Richard Wright is a canonical figure in black existential thought.[1] His work, consistently nothing short of a portrait of challenges posed to the quest for liberation in the face of enmeshed and complicit freedom in the modern world, brings to the fore nearly all of the themes by which this assessment is well deserved. Black existential thought involves meditations on what it means to strive for human freedom and dignity in a world of near universal disdain for black people. It is the struggle to understand and to transcend the pessimism and at times nihilism wrought by black suffering—a form of suffering that is often erased as suffering by virtue of pertaining to black subjects—to reach out, as Frantz Fanon argued, to the Other.[2] This reaching out, signaled in black narratives from Frederick Douglass's sojourn into literacy, W. E. B. DuBois's reflections on the offering of himself as an imagined suitor to a white Other in primary school games of matrimony, and the many instances in which talent and deed are presented by subjects in a world that sees only "disqualification," faces a social world in which the dialectics of recognition seem to be held hostage to symbolic erasure.[3] As Jerry Miller has shown in "The Human Stain," the challenge of achieving intersubjective communication reaches to the meaning of what is to be communicated. How is blackness communicated when it is a delegitimizing term of communication?

Richard Wright's genius emerged, among other things, through his portrait of this problem without compromising its difficulty. His biography, after all, as a child of the inequalities and injustices faced by blacks living in the South at the turn of the century and then the travails faced in northern cities, where, albeit better, were more like comparisons of fire and frying pan, is a tale of the nearly impossible. He was not from the mulatto elite from which much of black literary production was born, and his education, sporadic and minimal, was not the surest training for a writer. Yet he managed to achieve the publication of his first short story, "The Voodoo of Hell's Half Acre," at the age of sixteen in the *Southern Register*.[4] His own life's journey and artistry are exemplars of Anna Julia Cooper's conception of worth: what he offered the world far exceeded what was invested in him.[5] Wright lived through interracial settings among the greatest white intellectuals of the twentieth century, none of whom would likely have been able to produce their work under the conditions he faced. Could, in other words, their genius have been manifested if they had lived in his shoes? Ironically, for a biography similar, at least in terms of his achievements versus the challenges he faced, Jean-Jacques Rousseau would be a more likely white candidate than most of Wright's contemporaries.[6]

Among the hallmarks of existential philosophy is a concern with irony at the heart of self-reflection. An existential philosopher must not only ask about what he or she is studying, but also about the investments he or she may have in what is being studied. These investments may be such that things could get turned on their head and opposites result: In studying more, one learns less; in reaching out, one establishes distance; in seeking freedom, one, as in the case of the American Revolution, radicalizes slavery. This meta-reflective consideration permeates Wright's writings, and it is a feature that places him in the camp of existential writers, if not philosophers. Although his preferred medium is fiction and critical essays, the results are sufficiently rich for him to be a mainstay in the study of black existential philosophy.[7]

The black existential philosopher, as opposed to, e.g., the black existential critic, is concerned with more than illustrating paradoxes posed by existence in black. The black existential philosopher pushes those paradoxes into reflection on ongoing concerns in philosophy (and, what often makes many philosophers uneasy, black political life). Of course, philosophy is here understood in a very qualified way, since what may be of primary focus in a philosophy governed by black existence may be in opposition to a philosophy that abstracts away that specificity. Modern philosophy, for instance, is presumed occupied with problems of knowledge, which spill out into concerns with or against metaphysics and ethics.[8] Not questioned in this model, however, is whether abstract versions of knowing already beg anthropological questions of knowers—whether, that is, the primary basis of beginning philosophical reflection may be expanded beyond questions of knowing to those of membership, belonging, and acting. Such a consideration brings philosophical anthropology to the fore over epistemology, and it brings along with it concerns of transformative action and critical reflection. Put differently, the encomium of knowing raises the question of the presumed knower, and to answer that question already transcends the relationship through a demand for a wider context of knowing in which repressed aspects of the knower call for an audience. Wright addresses these problems through his character studies of Bigger Thomas, the anti-hero of *Native Son*, and Cross Damon, the anti-hero of *The Outsider*, both of which reveal his philosophical psychology and philosophical anthropology.[9] These characters challenge modern narcissistic fantasies of subjects free of *akrasia* (knowingly committing evil) and by extension societal reflections premised upon the same.

The challenge of self-reflection often occasions theodicean rationalization. Theodicy, as its etymology suggests, involves the articulation of G-d's justice or goodness.[10] Because G-d is intrinsically good, whatever He/She creates must also be good. And if G-d is omnipotent and omniscient, a problem arises of accounting for G-d's goodness in a world, created by G-d, fraught with injustice and evil. The classic responses to this theodicean problematic are twofold: (1) the demonstration of injustice and evil as only apparent because of human finitude, and (2) the demonstration of injustice and evil as consequences of human freedom, endowed by G-d, and permitted because of G-d's rightful decision of staying out of human affairs. In both instances, responsibility for injustice and evil fall on human shoulders. What, however, should be surmised if G-d were not placed in the equation? It would seem at first that the matter requires simply explaining injustice and malice in human terms, but in many instances, human beings do not want to bear such responsibility. Or better yet, many human beings would prefer that *some other human beings* bear that responsibility. Thus, the theodicean problem returns through either making the society or social system stand in for the place of G-d or the dominant group functioning as such, and, with psychotic individuals, themselves functioning as G-d. In such instances, the two demonstrations return through making those who live as contradictions of the system or dominant group external exemplars of injustice and evil. In the United States, this has been (and continues to be) the rationalization through which the treatment of blacks is rationalized with the self-image of the society as a beacon of freedom. Richard Wright, as with what recurs as the role of the black writer in American society, upsets this theodicy not only by offering an account of its contradictions but also by raising the point of view of the subject who lives through them. As he later reminded Jean-Paul Sartre in their discussions of the American "Negro problem," it is not a problem of Negroes but a white problem, namely, their hatred of Negroes. Convinced by Wright's contention, Sartre brought it to his discussion of anti-Semitism in *Anti-Semite and Jew*, where he focused on the anti-Semite's construction of Jewish inferiority.[11]

Wright's critique of American racial mores is akin to W. E. B. DuBois's concerns of doubled relations, manifested not only in double standards but also forms of consciousness that emerge from the lived-reality of such doubling. He first spoke of it in terms of twoness in his pamphlet *The Conservation of the Races*, of the struggle of being both American and Negro where they are treated as antitheses of each other. [12] In *The Souls of Black Folk*, this returned in the form of second sight, where the Negro sees himself only through the eyes that created him—namely, whites. [13] The Negro terminology declined over time and the term "black" began to be placed in the formulation, but I have purposely used that term here since "black" and "Negro" are not necessarily identical. Black, although sharing many of the signifiers of Negro, also points to populations that are not necessarily Negro—such as Australian Aboriginals and varieties of South Asian peoples, as well, at times, of certain populations of "Caucasians." [14] Even more, as black began to gain currency in protest literature, especially of the 1960s, the specificity of Negro began to appear as part of a specifically American imaginative corpus. In Negro is a set of tropes, often sexualized and hyperbolic, that is alien to actual black experience yet known as a lurking (and at times seductive) expectation in the social world. Black people of African descent are often pressured, in other words, to become Negroes. [15] Whether as Negro or its more directly pejorative *Nigger*, black people know of this projection, a source of simultaneous disdain and fascination, reflected back through the eyes of others. [16] We could call this phenomenon, written of also by Fanon, as the first stage of double consciousness. There is, however, a second stage. DuBois, Wright, and Fanon, after all, are raising this phenomenon as a critical object of study. By drawing out the contradictions—showing, that is, that social, political, and historical forces created the Negro—the theodicean moment is turned back onto itself in the form of a critique of the society that generated the forms of alienation constitutive of Negro. Put differently, instead of making the Negro the problem, they ask about the society that placed human beings of African descent into the situation of facing such problems. Paget Henry has dubbed this second move "potentiated double consciousness." [17] I should like to add that it involves a clearly dialectical movement, where in realizing that the Negro, and today the black, is not the problem but is a human being facing the problem of an unjust relationship, of a structural or relational problem, a process of untangling epistemically closed notions unfolds in movements of revealed contradictions. [18]

My aim here is to outline, in existential phenomenological terms, the philosophical significance of Wright's treatment of this theodicean problem of Negro and black being. We already see one insight in the form of potentiated double consciousness. *How* Wright does this is, first, through tapping into the mythic resources of American symbolic life and revealing the reflection the society did not wish to see as its Native son: Bigger Thomas. I should like to stress that by "mythic" I do not mean the false or the fictional. I mean instead the symbolic organization of normativity in a given culture. The mythic, in this sense, as symbolic, manifests another realm or *dimension* of existence. It is the peculiarly human realm, as Ernst Cassirer points out in *Essay on Man*, wherein human being generates additional dimensions of meaning.[19] It is in this sense, e.g., that the metaphor of the veil in the thought of DuBois and the many metaphors of apartheid take on an additional force: people of color live in different social, and hence symbolic, dimensions from whites, bridged by mediating symbols or forms that expand, contract, or absorb those that resist intersymbolic, interformal, or, in more ordinary phenomenological language, intersubjective relationships. As a symbolic figure, Bigger Thomas is, then, in relation to a set of other relations, namely, the society that created him. This is Wright's message in his brilliant essay, which serves as the introduction to editions of *Native Son* from 1940 onward: "How 'Bigger' Was Born."

America, as is well known, offers itself as a crusader of freedom. To live freely, however, requires legitimate appearance. It is being able to live out in the open, as the metaphor goes, without hiddenness. Freedom also involves belonging, being, in other words, in one's own home.[20] There, one could live the corollary of the first formulation of freedom, since one can, in one's home, express oneself without the limitations imposed on, say, guests. The Negro and the black have faced the contradiction of being homeless in the only place from which they are born. Licit being in that world appears without blackness. The logic here leads to the notion of black appearance as, then, fundamentally a violation of being, an illicit appearance. Bigger Thomas, as the effort to live freely in the world from which the black was born, falls into the relations of illicit appearance—the appearance of that which should not appear—in a world premised upon an economy of white legitimation. Wright offers a dialectical typography of Bigger, drawn from his experiential field ethnography, thus: Bigger 1 was the bully from his childhood who harassed others to submit to and affirm his claim to superiority; Bigger 2 challenged white authority and lived as he pleased—"he was in prison the last time I heard from him," confesses Wright.[21] Bigger 3 was the proverbial "bad nigger." He took advantage of fellow blacks, defied the law, and his fate was often death at the machinations of a white cop. Bigger 4 played a game of death in his efforts to outwit whites and refused to be exploited. His fate, if he were not killed in the process, was the insane asylum. Bigger 5 was also perceived as a "bad nigger," but it was so only in terms of his standing up to whites. Bigger often stimulated "an intense flash of pride"[22] in other Negroes and blacks, but his fate, unfortunately, was similar to Bigger 3. Wright reflected:

The Bigger Thomases were the only Negroes I know of who consistently violated the Jim Crow laws of the South and got away with it, at least for a sweet spell. Eventually, the whites who restricted their lives made them pay a terrible price. They were shot, hanged, maimed, lynched, and generally hounded until they were either dead or their spirits broken.[23]

Notice in each instance Bigger Thomas's dance with death. In Bigger Thomas, there is placed a moment of identification in which a self is placed beyond itself into feared possibilities. Bigger, after all, appears to be a Negro or a black who is not afraid of death and is thus afforded a form of radical freedom beyond the reach of other Negro or black subjects. The logic, as Abdul JanMohamed explored in *The Death-Bound Subject*, is peculiarly Hegelian: the bondsman *becomes a bondsman* through submission through fear of death.[24] Before going further, however, let us revisit the typography for some additional considerations. Recall that Bigger 1 bullied fellow Negroes and blacks to submit to him. He used force to get others to affirm his conviction that he was not like them, that he was better than they were. We see here a classic movement of narcissism under oppressive conditions. Among oppressed peoples, there are those who buy into the Manichean logic of a world of only oppressors and the oppressed. Given that logic, the only way not to be oppressed is to oppress others.[25] That Bigger 1 forced out of others a *statement* affirming his superiority, however, brings the logic against itself. Bigger 1 did this because he *needed* the submission of others in order to effect his posed and hoped-for superiority. This effort collapses, however, into a form of dependency that must have no doubt angered Bigger 1 even more, for the way of narcissism is self-deception, of the offering of a preferred image of the self, and attachment to that self-deception creates a form of servitude maintained only by force. Since the missing element in Bigger 1's focus is the true source of his sense of inferiority—namely, whites—Bigger 1 fails from the outset. The dialectics of Bigger, if we will, requires addressing the white world, and therein are the movements of Biggers 2 to 5.

Biggers 2 to 5 are repressed terms in many Negroes and blacks, as Wright analyzed them. They are manifestations of, as Frantz Fanon later formulated, a call to be "actional."[26] This leads to identification with, as with Bigger 1, *all* those who appear actional versus those whom they oppress. In Wright's words:

I've even heard Negroes say that maybe Hitler and Mussolini are all right; that maybe Stalin is all right. They did not say this out of any intellectual comprehension of the forces at work in the world, but because they felt that these men "did things," a phrase charged with more meaning than the mere words imply. There was in the back of their minds, when they said this, a wild and intense longing (wild and intense because it was suppressed!) *to belong, to be iden-*

tified, to feel that they were *alive* as other people were, to be caught up forgetfully and exultingly in the swing of events, to feel the clean, deep, organic satisfaction of doing a job in common with others.[27]

The association of freedom with *doing*, with being actional, and the added elements of *belonging* and *being identified*, point to the dual conditions, necessary and sufficient conditions, of freedom mentioned earlier. These movements, born of frustration and premised upon a paradoxical facing of death *for the sake of life*, or at least a life worth living, suggest, as Wright argues, an expansion of Bigger as a Native son of the modern world. Freedom is, after all, one of the promised jewels of modern life in the face of more sophisticated and global implements of forced servitude. That challenge, as Frederick Douglass before Wright and Fanon afterward argued, requires *struggle* with a high price[28]: "While living in America I heard from far away Russia the bitter accents of tragic calculation of how much human life and suffering it would cost a man to live as a man in a world that denied him the right to live with dignity."[29]

Frustration and a longing to be actional were motifs that, for Wright, brought to the fore the dialectical struggle of freedom in the modern world. In an act of what phenomenologists would call "free variation," he began to thematize this condition and found it extended beyond the individuals of his initial focus. This movement is a feature of African diasporic thought that is often overlooked: whereas the dominant intellectual traditions of the West regarded themselves as the universals through which particulars gain significance and that the world of blackness was too enwrapped in specificities to be of general value, double consciousness, drawing upon the contradictions of the system, expanded an understanding of repressed terms. This move entailed a subversion of expected categories resulting in the particular holding the universal through which the avowed universal becomes relativized. Wright, in this instance, saw through Bigger Thomas his existence, as archsymbol, in the lives of any form of oppressed humanity:

> I made the discovery that Bigger Thomas was not black all the time; he was white, too, and there were literally millions of him, everywhere . . . The extension of my sense of the personality of Bigger was the pivot of my life; it altered the complexion of my experience. I became conscious, at first dimly, and then later on with increasing clarity and conviction, of a vast, muddied pool of human life in America. It was as though I had put on a pair of spectacles whose power was that of an x-ray enabling me to see deeper into the lives of men.[30]

This movement is indicative of potentiated double consciousness. It is a dialectical phenomenological movement in which greater consciousness of wider conditions is achieved through realization of systemic contradictions.

The more phenomenological aspects of the analysis come to the fore here, for Wright advances not only his consciousness but also the wider understanding of consciousness *of* the conditions themselves, of the systemic impositions of limited options:

> I began to feel with my mind the inner tensions of the people I met. I don't mean to say that I think that environment *makes* consciousness (I suppose God makes that, if there is a God), but I do say that I felt and still feel that the environment supplies the instrumentalities through which the organism expresses itself, and if the environment is warped or tranquil, the mode and manner of behavior will be affected toward deadlocking tensions or orderly fulfillment and satisfaction.[31]

Sylvia Wynter, in her provocative essay "Towards the Sociogenic Principle: Fanon, Identity, the Puzzle of Conscious Experience and What It Is Like to Be 'Black,'" poses the question of the black in terms that challenge acts of intersubjective relations in western modernity.[32] Analogizing Thomas Nagel's essay "What Is It Like to Be a Bat?"[33] Wynter asks whether the antiblack racist could go through such an imaginative act with regard to blacks. The conclusion, that the black might as well be a bat, points to the collapse of vicariousness, a consideration for acts of intersubjectivity. The refusal to look into the perspective of the black is an act of treating the black as pure exteriority, a being without an inner life. In the first stage of double consciousness, the black paradoxically has to see her- or himself as a view without a point of view. Wynter points to the sociogenic principle, raised by Fanon in *Black Skin, White Masks*, wherein racism is a function not of phylogenetic or ontogenetic but socially mediated forces. It is, harkening back to our remarks on symbols, generated by the social world, the world of communication and symbolic formation. The social world, saturated by narratives that seal blacks and whites into antithetical dimensions, leads to practices of ontological fortification—e.g., through white assertions of impossible empathy; the white, *as white*, becomes by definition a being incapable of seeing a black point of view because white identity is dependent not only on the irrelevance of a black perspective but also its impossibility. I have elsewhere described this phenomenon as bad faith, a form of lying to the self, since such an effort requires asserting, in effect, that there are human beings who are not *really* human beings.[34]

A powerful feature of Wright's work is that Bigger Thomas is not only a mythopoetic trope in a fictional narrative. Wright chose the medium of the novel to explore the *inner life* of Bigger Thomas. The novel, in other words, shows how someone *becomes* Bigger Thomas, and even more unusual, Wright achieves this without compromising Bigger's agency. The choices Bigger makes are not the only ones he could have made, but they are the ones that make sense given the circumstances under which he lived. The claustrophobic world is fraught with tragic symbols of destiny (e.g., a cornered rat whose snarl is a moment of doubled reflection; a blind woman who "sees" or at least almost sees; a drunk white woman meeting her death in the arms of a black servant). The challenge of vicarious vision is established at the outset in the family's chasing a large rat around the apartment; it portends to the reader the subconscious question facing Bigger. The accidental killing of his employer's daughter raises the question to the reader of whether he or she could even imagine a verdict of Bigger's "innocence." To face Bigger, one must see his position, imagine being in his place. That effort is, however, as already established, a direction in which many are not willing to go. In Bigger are, however, the contradictions of the system, which means that a failure to face Bigger holds within it the same with regard to the system. The theodicy of placing Bigger at an external point also has the consequence of denying the system's creation, its Native son.

Wright, as is well known, was a student of the thought of Søren Kierkegaard, who was known not only as the father of modern existentialism but also the architect of "indirect" writing.[35] Writing through pseudonyms in which his position as the author was brought into question, Kierkegaard hoped to challenge his readers to think for themselves instead of taking his words for granted. The technique of indirection is useful, as well, for bringing subjects into the world of dread and anxiety. It is also useful for the world of trauma and repression. Some things are not bearable directly. Humanity needs another way. In mythic literature, this is the way of the labyrinth at the center of which is the Minotaur.[36] The image of unbridled consumption is something from which a distance is needed. In *Black Skin, White Masks*, Fanon, too, uses techniques of indirection.[37] He first tells a tale of hopes and failures—of language, love, and the imagination—over the course of five chapters at the end of which is the subject driven to tears. From the sixth chapter onward, that subject, having washed denial away, faces reality: psychopathological dimensions of what happens to the black who has the slightest contact with the white world. This effort leads to a critique of practices of recognition. Whereas Self and Other are available to the world of those whose actions matter, those already recognized in the ethical world of intersubjective communications, for those below, those in the dimensions Fanon describes as "the zone of nonbeing," there is an asymmetrical relationship to those "above." To move "up" requires a pregiven recognition that is, unfortunately, sought in the act itself. What this means is that from the perspective of "above," there are neither selves nor others "below." To move up is, then, an intrusion, a violation. The unbearable truth to which these movements lead is marked, e.g., by the difference of struggle between whites versus between whites and blacks. In the case of the former, it is about an ethical relationship demanding realignment. In the case of the latter, it is about *entering an ethical relationship*. This means, in effect, that there is a sphere of ethical suspension or, worse, absence of ethics. This means, then, that the black always faces the political before the ethical in this relationship, the call for social transformation as a condition of ethical relationships.

It might be objected that there are many instances of blacks being appealed to as the moral conscience of the nation. One could think of the encomia of black religious leaders and their demands for conditions of human dignity and social justice. Fanon's response, shared by Wright, is that the point at which those moral voices assert themselves on an equal terrain with whites is the measure of the relationship. Even Martin Luther King, Jr., was, if we remember, considered violent in his day. Compare Malcolm X, whose moral voice was never as a subordinate to whites. No one remembers Malcolm X as anything other than a *political* figure, and a violent one at that—even though all of his actions were with *words*.[38]

That Wright is asking us to do more than identify Bigger Thomas but to *understand* him, which requires, to some extent, *identifying* with him, the question is raised whether the medium of the novel is sufficient for that project. I think the jury is still out on whether Wright achieved that in *Native Son*.[39] That is perhaps the reason why he continued his project of a global analysis of Bigger through his transformation from a native son of America into an outsider of the modern world.

Wright's 1953 novel *The Outsider* is saturated with Kierkegaardian themes, signaled from its epigraph from Walter Lowrie's introduction to *The Concept of Dread*, which reads:

> Dread is an alien power which lays hold of the individual, and yet one cannot tear oneself away, nor has a will to do so; for one fears what one desires.[40]

The anti-hero of this novel is Cross Damon, whose story is told through successive movements: "Dread," "Dream," "Descent," "Despair," "Decision." Kierkegaard was a dialectical thinker, in spite of his critiques of Hegel, and, like Richard Wright, he was concerned not only with the human effort to reach for G-d but also with the constant struggle with the demonic through which moral life offered no guarantee of either secure meaning or salvation. The existential struggle in that regard is thus through paths taken alone into relationships with absolutes—in Kierkegaard's language, from *Fear and Trembling*, with the Absolute *absolutely*.[41] This realization, Kierkegaard argued through his pseudonym Johannes de Silentio, is that the individual is *higher* than the universal. A similar path is taken by Nietzsche but from the perspective of atheism. The individual who stands above the universal—which Nietzsche reads as the decadent morals of society—is an Overman.[42] From the religious perspective, this individual/overman, if not guided by G-d, is condemned to the demonic. By this, it is meant the hubris of the self, the ego that dares to be above all humanity and, for sure, even G-d.

Wright makes this movement eponymic in the novel's anti-hero's name: Cross Damon. He is, in some interpretations, a savior and demon. This is, of course, an interpretation in a Christian universe. We should add, however, that even in that universe the word *cross*, whose etymology points to the Latin *crux* and the crucifixion of Jesus, signifies a burden. Damon in Greek mythology refers to the myth of Damon and Pythias, where Damon stands in as ransom for his friend at the risk of death should his friend not return. Pythias experiences misfortunes that almost led to his not showing up, but he arrives just in time to save his friend from execution. Moved by the loyalty of the two friends, where Damon, who was innocent, was willing to die for his friend, the king pardoned Pythias and released the two friends. We could see how the combination with *Cross* leads to a reading of one burdened by innocence. This additional theme of innocence emerges in an unusual way in Wright's tragic universe. *Damon*, as many commentators point out, is also a variation of *daimon*, e.g., which, at least for the Greeks, was another way of saying "demigod." What happens to freedom when the model is godly? Wright returns in *The Outsider* to many of the themes of *Native Son*, but this time he adds layers to the claustrophobic environment and throws in moments of *deus ex machina*: Cross Damon, through a fortunate accident in which he is believed dead, is able to assume a variety of alternate identities. He moves from Chicago to New York, and, as Lionel Lane (which, if spoken out loud, sounds like "liar in a lane," but also holds within it a conjunction of king of the beasts and god/*el*)[43] and embarks on a series of encounters that leads to his killing a communist associate and his fascist landlord. The double homicide is a resolution from Wright's early meditations on Bigger:

> I felt that Bigger, an American product, a native son of this land, carried within him the potentialities of either Communism or Fascism. I don't mean to say that the Negro boy I depicted in *Native Son* is either a Communist or a Fascist. He is not either. But he is product of a dislocated society, he is a dispossessed and disinherited man; he is all of this, and he lives amid the greatest possible plenty on earth and he is looking and feeling for a way out. Whether he'll follow some gaudy, hysterical leader who'll promise rashly to fill the void in him, or whether he'll come to an understanding with the millions of kindred fellow workers under trade-union or revolutionary guidance depends upon the future drift of events in America. But, granting the emotional state, the intensity, the fear, the hate, the impatience, the sense of exclusion, the ache for violent action, the emotional and cultural hunger, Bigger Thomas, conditioned as his organism is, will not become an ardent, or even a lukewarm, supporter of the *status quo*.[44]

Cross Damon manifests Marx's greatest fear about the lumpenproletariat: after turning on the fascist, the communist is soon to follow. This warning about Bigger and by extension Cross Damon raises an additional consideration of the mythopoetics of Wright's characters best understood in monster theory. The etymology of the word *monster* is from the Latin *monstrum*, which means divine warning or omen. The related word *demonstrate*, from the Latin *monstrare* (to show, to point out, or, more properly, with the prefix *de*, to show entirely), reminds us that to warn is also to show or to reveal. In antiquity, monsters had an important social function. As divine warnings or omens, they appeared when a community lost its way. They were often articulate creatures, through whom society was forced to set things right through rituals of acknowledged communal responsibility. Monsters were thus also pedagogical in nature; their appearance signaled something to be learned, the avoidance of which is catastrophic. They therefore also stimulate crises. *Crisis*, from the Greek *krisis* (turning point in a disease), which in turn is from the word *krenein*, means to choose, to decide. The monster, symptomatic of sick society, occasions momentous decisions. That upon which decisions are to be made are exemplified by the related word *criteria*. Brought into the modern world, the argument is straightforward: human actions set standards, criteria, by which, if imbalance leads to catastrophe, human responsibility is borne. The monster here places the human community into self-reflection, as in antiquity, but what happens in a world where, no longer moved by gods, human beings have taken their place and attempt to dictate reality? On this reading, Wright offers, through Bigger Thomas and Cross Damon, a double critique. The first is the presentation of these "monsters" as a call for America to fix itself. (Recall the historical critique of the Soviet Union of its becoming the monster it was fighting.) If America ignores these warnings, the second message is evident: advancing itself as a *daimon*, it becomes them and takes its place as a monster, as a warning, to the rest of humanity.[45]

In *The Outsider*, Wright adds to his analysis another subjective position in the presence of "law" through the district attorney Ely Houston, who in spite of the theological significance of his name is also a cripple, a metaphor for a broken system if there ever was one. The god-reference, in fact supreme god, suggests a relationship to law in which he need not appeal beyond himself. Houston is, however, as with the mythopoetics of all characters with disabilities, stronger in other senses and is not only the one who *sees* Cross Damon for who and what he is, or at least might be, but also engages him in what both of them cannot resist: argumentation, or, more to the point—*dialectics*. The exchanges between the two drive the novel to the point of both being reflections of each other: Cross Damon was hiding his identity and Houston was hiding his lack of faith in and, even worse, his rejection of the values of the legal system he swore to uphold: What is his relation to such a system but as, given the degree of discretionary powers afforded him, a god or, at least, demigod, which places him in a mirror image with Damon?

The novel's ending, with Damon's dying words of suffering innocence, raises an existential paradox. That Damon committed murder is indisputable. But to do so, he must have a *mens rea*, an evil mind. To have that, however, he needed also to be responsible for his actions. That would require him to be a man, not a child. In one reading, the Kierkegaardian theme of dread is manifested in the loss of secure ground. Damon represents what it means *really to go outside*, to go beyond values. In the Nietzschean reading, nihilism is symptomatic of greater social decay.[46] Expectations of values being brought to one's actions are failures to understand one's proper relation to values, that one must bring value to one's values. Damon, then, attempted this in the reconstruction of the self and to assert himself beyond Communism, Fascism, and the American legal system. His sense of innocence, which is an appeal to a moral system in which he could be judged justly, is then an enigma: beyond good and evil are neither innocence nor guilt. There is, however, a third consideration, and this one requires taking seriously that Cross Damon is, after all, *black*. As black, there is something he wanted and of which he was also afraid:

> "Damon, can you hear me?"
>
> "Yes," he managed to whisper.
>
> Houston's voice seemed to be closer now and the tone had changed; it was the voice of a brother asking an urgent, confidential question.
>
> "Damon, listen to me, just listen and think about what I'm asking and then try to answer . . . This is Houston still talking to you . . . Damon, you were an outsider . . . You know what I mean, don't you? You lived apart . . . Damon, tell me, why did you choose to live that way?"
>
> The damned old curious outlaw! He never forgot anything. He was still on his trail . . . Still hunting him down . . . Sure; he'd tell 'im . . .
>
> "I wanted to be free . . . To feel what I was worth . . . What living meant to me . . . I loved life too . . . much."[47]

It is clear that Cross Damon, like Bigger Thomas, was also patronized by the "doers" of his world and faced the consequences that imposed minefields along the paths available to live as a free human being. They wanted to become people who were, in the end, men. How do Bigger Thomas and Cross Damon become *men*?

This problem is one raised by Fanon in his discussion of psychopathology and the Negro (*le Nègre*).[48] How is psychotherapy possible for black subjects if there is no coherent notion of a black *adult*? With adulthood comes moral responsibility. But as we saw with Bigger Thomas, what he actually does is irrelevant from the point of view of a legal system and civil society that treat him as guilty at birth.[49] If he is always guilty, he could never be really guilty, which collapses into a form of childlike a priori innocence. To become a man, then, he must be *capable* of becoming guilty. From this reading, Cross

Damon *needed* to be guilty. Dying with a sense of innocence, then, is, for him, an existential tragedy. In his dying words: "Because in my heart . . . I'm . . . I felt . . . I'm *innocent* . . . that's what made the horror."[50]

A point of difference between the white world and the black in the United States (and, I would add, globally) is the criminal justice system. It is difficult for many black people to see black convicts as *criminals*. It is not only that there are many black people serving time for crimes they did not commit. It is also an understanding of what happens to people in a world in which guilt is presumed in a way that makes de facto guilt impossible. The black race is, in other words, a presumed criminal race. This problem derails the legitimacy of legal and ethical categories in a constant call for mobilization against structural forces and institutions. Bigger Thomas and Cross Damon, then, could be extended beyond subjects of flesh and blood. For instance, Sylvia Wynter has argued against the shift in Black Studies to recent nomenclatures of "African American" and "Africana."[51] These terms, she argues, are moments of domestication that elide the important political-epistemological assertion of *Black*. From the reading of Wright that I have offered, this is another way of saying that Black Studies is also an echo of Bigger Thomas in the white academy. If this is correct, Wynter is suggesting that there is a revolutionary potential to Bigger Thomas/Black Studies, which would mean that the consequences of Biggers 2 to 5 could be more than Wright had concluded, although Wright seems to have been aware of this when he reflected, "I've already mentioned that Bigger had in him impulses which I had felt were present in the vast upheavals of Russia and Germany. Well, somehow, I had to make these political impulses felt by the reader in terms of Bigger's daily actions, keeping in mind as I did so the probable danger of my being branded as a propagandist by those who would not like the subject matter."[52] In the thought of Fanon, the point would be reformulated thus: Black communities cannot afford to underestimate the revolutionary potential of its lumpenproletariat.[53] It is identification with the dimensions of those individuals who are in direct conflict with the contradictions of the system— black lumpenproletariats, e.g., emerge primarily from the catastrophically high unemployment rates in black communities, which leave little option but to survive through participating in the illicit economy with its promise of the ongoing possibility of violent death—that could bring forth a more critical consciousness of that system. As Wynter sees it, Black Studies offers such at the epistemological level. That level is, however, a necessary but insufficient condition for the task at hand, since, as epistemological, it faces that other challenge from Bigger and Cross Damon, memorialized earlier in the words of Karl Marx, of not just understanding the world but changing it. This is no less than a call for the epistemological to be in a *relationship* with forces of change and more, for the suggestion of Black Studies as a manifestation of Bigger raises by extension the question of whether Black existentialism is the same. But Black existentialism already holds within it a critique of episte-mology as a transcendental category or as a *philosophia prima*—namely, to do so would be to issue metaphysics of knowledge/concept/essence before existence. Put differently, existence in black is a destabilizing notion since it cannot maintain an overdetermining category. The relationality of blackness is, then, posed in such a way that even as Bigger, Black existentialism priori-tizes the agency of change over knowing—in fact, the permeability of the known as an affected notion.

We come, then, to perhaps the central critical concern of Wright's exis-tential treatment of freedom. Bigger Thomas and Cross Damon attempt their struggle for freedom, ultimately, *alone*. The only recourse for any being who is not actually a *daimon*, a demigod, is a confrontation with death. Looked at with regard to institutions, the only course for Black Studies, where there is not a "Black Studies University," is confrontation with its own destruction. But again, these may not be the only alternatives. There are *other* models of freedom, as the question of black existentialism's relation to, say, philosophy suggests. As Floyd Hayes observes:

> Wright seems to be saying that the path of the complex, powerful, knowledge-able, yet cynical outsider ends in destruction. In what appears to be Wright's rejection of existential nihilism, Damon cannot walk outside of history and society and survive. The human cannot be concerned only with the self, its fears, and desires. Wright seems really to be suggesting that people must be responsible for others as well as for themselves. [54]

If the aim is to be above humanity, then becoming a god is the only course, but if the goal is to cultivate one's humanity, that realm is between the gods and beasts. It requires defending one's humanity with fellow human beings, and that may require resisting the construction of human subjectivity as epistemically closed. The Black Studies example is a case in point. In spite of the many attacks on Afrocentrics/Africologists such as Molefi Asante and Maulana Karenga, what their critics miss is that they have taken the motif of Bigger Thomas and rallied it consistently in the form of a fight against white supremacy/Eurocentrism, and they have added an existential element of ar-guing for the agency of African people in history. This makes them admir-able in black communities. But more, they have built institutions and a com-munity through which their struggle could be understood as a black one, although they prefer the designation of "African" over "black." What solid-ifies the black identification is the white response to Afrocentricity and Afri-cology, which, in the end, is awfully shrill given the amount of power whites have in the academy. Yet critics of Afrocentricity could add that there is an extent to which it could also put the antiblack racist at ease since their absence of control over *white* institutions render them harmless. Asante's response to this, I suspect, is akin to an important aspect of Bigger's metaphysical demand to be actional: He would remind the critic that Afrocentricity aims, also, to be historical.[55] By this, in spite of Asante's rejection of Marxism, there is affinity with the revolutionary call to change the world.

Wright would no doubt have loved to be involved in these debates. He was active, albeit in a critical way, with the Pan-African movement and black political efforts to forge an international intelligentsia.[56] He seemed to have been aware of the challenges to come when he read Bigger's behavior in working-class struggles in Europe and anti-colonial ones in the global south. The message he seems to have been arguing from these dialectical forays into the depths of individual struggles for freedom is that life beyond a sickness unto death could only be meaningful, and perhaps even won, through being organized and no longer fighting alone.

NOTES

1. See, e.g., discussions of him in *Existence in Black: An Anthology of Black Existential Philosophy*, ed. Lewis R. Gordon (New York: Routledge, 1997), and *An Introduction to Africana Philosophy* (Cambridge: Cambridge University Press, 2008). Cf. also discussions of him in *Simone de Beauvoir's Force of Circumstance: The Autobiography of Simone de Beauvoir*, trans. R. Howard (New York: Paragon House, 1992); and, of course, Margaret Walker's biography of him, *Richard Wright: Demonic Genius* (New York: Warner Books, 1988).

2. See Fanon, *Black Skin, White Masks*, trans. Charles Lamm Markman (New York: Grove Press, 1967), especially "By Way of Conclusion."

3. See W. E. B. DuBois, *The Autobiography of W. E. B. Du Bois: A Soliloquy on Viewing My Life from the Last Decade of Its First Century* (New York: International Publishers, 1968).

4. Richard Wright, "The Voodoo of Hell's Half Acre," *Southern Register* (1924).

5. Anna Julia Cooper, "What Are We Worth?" from *A Voice from the South*, reprinted in *The Voice of Anna Julia Cooper, including "A Voice from the South" and Other Important Essays, Papers and Letters*, ed. Charles Lemert and Esme Bhan (Lanham, MD: Rowman & Littlefield, 1998).

6. See, e.g., Ernst Cassirer, *The Question of Jean-Jacques Rousseau*, trans. Peter Gay (Bloomington: Indiana University Press, 1963); and, also, Martin Cohen, *Philosophical Tales: Being an Alternative History Revealing the Characters, the Plots, and the Hidden Scenes That Make Up the True Story of Philosophy* (Malden, MA: Wiley-Blackwell, 2008); and Jane Anna Gordon, *Creolizing Political Theory: Reading Rousseau through Fanon* (New York: Fordham University Press, forthcoming).

7. See, e.g., my discussion of him in Lewis R. Gordon, *An Introduction to Africana Philosophy* (Cambridge: Cambridge University Press, 2008), 133–40.

8. I encourage the reader to pick up any of the endless titles on Western philosophy to see my point. Outside of texts specifically in Africana philosophy or related areas of thought, I've come across two exceptions (though there may be more): A Passion for Wisdom: Readings in Western Philosophy on Love and Desire, ed. Ellen K. Feder, Karmen MacKendrick, and Sybol Cook (Saddle River, NJ: Prentice Hall, 2004); and *American Philosophies: An Anthology*, ed. Leonard Harris, Scott L. Pratt, and Anne S. Waters (Malden, MA: Blackwell, 2002).

9. Richard Wright, *Native Son* (New York: Milestone Editions, 1940); and *The Outsider*, with an introduction by Maryemma Graham (New York: Harper Perennial, 1993). References to "How 'Bigger' Was Born" are to the introduction Wright wrote to this 1940 edition of *Native Son*.

10. Since I also write as an Afro-Jew, I use the convention of "G-d" except where maintaining faithfully the quotations of others.

11. See Ronald Hayman's *Sartre: A Biography* (New York: Carroll & Graf, 1987), 220.

12. W. E. B. DuBois, *The Conservation of the Races* (Washington, DC: Negro Academy, 1898).

13. W. E. B. DuBois, *The Souls of Black Folk: Essays and Sketches* (Chicago: A.C. McClurg & Co., 1903).

14. The people of the Caucuses come to mind. See the work of Madina Tlostanova, e.g., "The Janus-Faced Empire Distorting Orientalist Discourses: Gender, Race and Religion in the Russian/(Post)Soviet Constructions of the 'Orient,'" Worlds and Knowledges Otherwise: A Web Dossier 2, dossier 2 (2008): www.jhfc.duke.edu/wko/dossiers/1.3/.../TlostanovaW-KO2.2_000.pdf; and " How 'Caucasians' became 'Black': Circassians, Modernity and the Emancipation Discourses,'" in *Trajectories for Emancipation and Black European Thinkers*, ed. Artwell Cain and Kwame Nimako (forthcoming).

15. Frantz Fanon referred to this processes as a demand for the "secretion" of blackness. See *Black Skin, White Masks*, 122. See also my essay on the subject, "When I Was There, It Was Not: On Secretions Once Lost in the Night," *Performance Research* 2, no. 3 (September 2007): 8–15.

16. I recently walked through a gallery display of posters from Hollywood blaxploitation films. As I looked at the images—the glistened skin, the oversexualized, hypermasculine males lost in lust, the muscular, impassioned females ready both to seduce and to kill, it became clear to me that there is a distinction between what my colleague Paul Taylor amusingly calls "Negro Studies" and Black Studies. I'll return to this, but suffice it to say that the dominant culture *loves* Negro Studies and hates Black Studies.

17. Paget Henry, "Africana Phenomenology: Its Philosophical Implications," *C.L.R. James Journal* 11, no. 1 (Summer 2005): 79–112. See also Nahum Chandler, "The Souls of an Ex-White Man: W. E. B. DuBois and the Biography of John Brown," *CR: The New Centennial Review* 3, no. 1 (Spring): 179–95.

18. See, e.g., "What Does It Mean to be a Problem?" in Lewis R. Gordon, *Existentia Africana: Understanding Africana Existential Thought* (New York: Routledge, 2000), 62–95.

19. Ernst Cassirer, *Essay on Man* (New Haven, CT: Yale University Press, 1972), 24.

20. For more on this view of freedom, see Lewis R. Gordon, *No Longer Enslaved, Yet Not Quite Free* (New York: Fordham University Press, forthcoming).

21. Richard Wright, *Native Son*, 12.

22. Richard Wright, *Native Son*, 13.

23. Richard Wright, *Native Son*, 13.

24. Abdul R. JanMohamed, *The Death-Bound-Subject: Richard Wright's Archaeology of Death* (Durham, NC: Duke University Press, 2005). JanMohamed and I are here referring to the formation of self-consciousness through the dialectics of Lord and Bondsman in Hegel's *Phenomenology of Spirit*, trans. A. V. Miller (Oxford: Oxford University Press, 1979); and *The Philosophy of History* (New York: Dover Publications, 1956).

25. For more discussion, cf. Lewis R. Gordon, *Bad Faith and Antiblack Racism* (Atlantic Highlands, NJ: Humanities International Press, 1995), part 3, especially the chapter "Black Antiblackness in an Antiblack World," 104–16.

26. See Fanon, *Black Skin, White Masks*, 222.

27. Richard Wright, *Native Son*, 17; emphasis added.

28. Cf. Frederick Douglass, *Narrative of the Life of Frederick Douglass, an American Slave, Written by Himself* (New York: New American Library, 1968); and for discussion, see *Frederick Douglass: A Critical Reader*, ed. Bill E. Lawson and Frank M. Kirkland (Malden, MA: Blackwell, 1999); discussions of Douglass's fight with the slave-breaker Edward Covey in my *Existentia Africana*, 55–61, and JanMohamed's *The Death-Bound Subject*, 292–99.

29. Richard Wright, *Native Son*, 20.

30. Richard Wright, *Native Son*, 17.

31. Richard Wright, *Native Son*, 19.

32. Sylvia Wynter, "Towards the Sociogenic Principle: Fanon, Identity, the Puzzle of Conscious Experience and What It Is Like to Be 'Black,'" in *Natural Identities and Sociopolitical Changes in Latin America*, ed. Mercedes F. Durán-Cogan and Antonio Gómez-Monaria (New York: Routledge, 2001), 30–66.

33. See Thomas Nagel, "What Is It Like to Be a Bat?" in his *Mortal Questions* (Cambridge: Cambridge University Press, 1991), 165–80. For an expanded discussion of Wynter's argument and its relation to Nagel's, see Lewis R. Gordon, "Is the Human a Teleological Suspension of Man? A Phenomenological Exploration of Sylvia Wynter's Fanonian and Biodicean Reflections," in *After Man, Towards the Human: Critical Essays on the Thought of Sylvia Wynter*, ed. Anthony Bogues (Kingston, Jamaica: Ian Randle, 2006), 237–57.

34. See *Bad Faith and Antiblack Racism*, part 3.

35. For discussion, see Andrew Cross, *Kierkegaard* (New York: Routledge, 2004); and *Kierkegaard in Post/Modernity*, ed. Martin J. Beck Matuštík and Merold Westphal (Bloomington: Indiana University Press, 1995).

36. Cf. Richard K. Fenn, The Secularization of Sin: An Investigation of the Daedalus Complex (Louisville, KY: Westminster/John Knox, 1991). See also Jane Anna Gordon and Lewis R. Gordon, *Of Divine Warning: Reading Disaster in the Modern Age* (Boulder, CO: Paradigm Publishers, 2009), chap. 5, "Ruin."

37. For discussion, see Lewis R. Gordon, "Through the Zone of Nonbeing: A Reading of *Black Skin, White Masks* in Celebration of Fanon's Eightieth Birthday," *C.L.R. James Journal* 11, no. 1 (Summer): 1–43.

38. For discussion, see J. A. Gordon and L. R. Gordon, *Of Divine Warning*, chap. 4. See also William R. Jones, "Liberation Strategies in Black Theology: Mao, Martin, or Malcolm?" in *Philosophy Born of Struggle: Anthology of Afro-American Philosophy from 1917* (Dubuque, IA: Kendall/Hunt, 1983), 229–41.

39. Wright was ambivalent about his own identification with Bigger, as he remarked on his feelings about black youth in the Boys Club: "For a moment I'd allow myself, vicariously, to feel as Bigger felt—not much, just a little, just a *little*—but, still, there it was" (Wright 1940, 31).

40. Walter Lowrie, "Introduction," in Søren Kierkegaard, *The Concept of Dread*, trans. Walter Lowrie, 2nd ed. (Princeton, NJ: Princeton University Press, 1968), xii.

41. Søren Kierkegaard, *"Fear and Trembling" and "Repetition,"* ed. and trans. Howard V. Hong and Edna H. Hong (Princeton, NJ: Princeton University Press, 1983), 70.

42. See Friedrich Nietzsche, *Beyond Good and Evil: Prelude to a Philosophy of the Future*, trans. Walter Kaufmann (New York: Vintage, 1966).

43. *El*, in Hebrew, means G-d, and in Canaanite *Eli* and *Il* (supreme god). See Frank Moore Cross, *Canaanite Myth and Hebrew Epic* (Cambridge, MA: Harvard University Press, 1973).

44. Richard Wright, *Native Son*, 23–24.

45. For a developed discussion of this thesis, see J. A. Gordon and L. R. Gordon, *Of Divine Warning*, especially chaps. 2–4.

46. See Friedrich Nietzsche, "The Genealogy of Morals" and "Ecce Homo," trans. Walter Kaufmann (New York: Vintage, 1967); and Friedrich Nietzsche, *The Will to Power*, trans. Walter Kaufmann and R. J. Hollingdale (New York: Vintage, 1967).

47. Richard Wright, *The Outsider*, 584–85.

48. For discussion, cf. Ronald Judy, "Fanon's Body of Black Experience," in *Fanon: A Critical Reader*, ed. Lewis R. Gordon, T. Denean Sharpley-Whiting, and Renée T. White (Malden, MA: Blackwell, 1996), 53–73.

49. This is a phenomenon with a philosophical anthropology that is also metaphysical. See Art Massara (Jerry Miller), "Stain Removal: On Race and Ethics," *Philosophy and Social Criticism* 33, no. 4 (2007): 498–528.

50. Richard Wright, *The Outsider*, 586.

51. See Sylvia Wynter, "On How We Mistook the Map for the Territory, and Re-Imprisoned Ourselves in Our Unbearable Wrongness of Being, of *Désêtre*: Black Studies toward the Human Project," in *Not Only the Master's Tools*, ed. Lewis R. Gordon and Jane Anna Gordon (Boulder, CO: Paradigm Publishers, 2006), 85–106.

52. Richard Wright, *Native Son*, 29.

53. Frantz Fanon, *The Wretched of the Earth*, trans. Constance Farrington (New York: Grove Press, 1963).

54. Floyd Hayes, "The Concept of Double Vision in Richard Wright's *The Outsider*," in *Existence in Black: An Anthology of Black Existential Philosophy*, ed. Lewis R. Gordon (New York: Routledge, 1997), 181.

55. This portrait of Afrocentricity/Africology can be found in Molefi Asante's *An Afrocentric Manifesto* (Cambridge: Polity, 2007). See also his *Maulana Karenga: An Intellectual Portrait* (Cambridge: Polity, 2009).

56. Cf. Richard Wright, *Black Power: Three Books from Exile: Black Power; The Color Curtain; and White Man, Listen! (P.S.)*, introduction by Cornel West (New York: Harper Perennial Modern Classics, 2008).

Chapter Two

Black Boy

Phenomenology and the Existential Novel

James B. Haile, III, Duquesne University

A searing blues angst narrative set to an upbeat, almost perpetual rhythm—of surprise, interrogation, and innovation—Nina Simone's 1963 song, "Mississippi Goddamn,"[1] engages existential issues of loss, of failure and success, of affirmation and negation echoing Richard Wright's Mississippi plantation life, wholly, utterly, magisterially forging, illuminating a metaphysical connection to the boy who would become the man to write *Black Boy*.[2] Distinctly black and American in its mode of representing and communicating reality, Simone's song emerges like a phoenix, whose presence, forced upward and out, beckoning forth, like Wright's *Black Boy*, the listener to black social reality through its usage of call and response.[3] "Too slow," we are told time and again by Simone that the movement toward social freedom and equality is too slow; we are invited to participate in the mocking "too slow" response to the injustices experienced by black folk: "washing the windows / *too slow* / desegregation / *too slow* / mass participation / *too slow* / do things gradually / *too slow* / but bring more tragedy / *too slow*."[4] Simone's experience with southern, white, anti-black racism, what author Charles Chestnutt calls "tradition,"[5] "pickin' the cotton . . . you just plain rotten," forces to the surface the cry "Why don't they [white folks] see it [the injustice], I don't know, I don't know"[6] —like a water hose plunged into the black earth and turned up high, thick, viscous blackness spurts out. Simone's voice resonates, like Wright's prose, with protest—"Don't tell me, I'll tell you, me and my people are just about through"[7]—righteous indignation as well as an articulated self-affirmation—"You don't have to live next to me, just give me my equality."[8]

Yet, underneath the vitriol (read: black honesty) are subtle elements of humor, of the absurd irony of whiteness in America, especially profound in the South, specifically Mississippi, for whom *Goddamn* is the most apt of things to say—indeed, if one could burn the whole Goddamn thing down they would, or would they? The suffering, after all, makes for a special kind of clarity—what W. E. B. DuBois referred to as second sight, the makings of a special kind of ontological being born with a caul over his/her eyes, a natural seer with metaphysical insight and potency—necessary for writing/ singing "Mississippi Goddamn," and, as Simone says, *meaning every word of it.* Simone located her epistemological clarity in her being as a southerner generally, not hailing from Mississippi (rather, Tyron, North Carolina) but having "experienced" Mississippi and its Jim Crow racism.[9] Wright, too, located his prescient vision of a young "twice born soul" in his own southern roots (his being a nameless plantation near Natchez, Mississippi) and in his own anonymous, yet ubiquitous black suffering. Yet, as one tears down one's history, one is ever building it back; Wright, like Simone, reconstructed what was once thought unavailable to black folk, stripped of them in southern "tradition": the ability to think and depict the world and their own life *for* themselves.[10]

In this chapter, I will argue that Richard Wright makes existential and phenomenological claims in *Black Boy*. Wright's principle claim, I will argue, is that self-disclosure as being in the world is not achieved simply through "philosophical" (that is, theoretical) introspection[11] or the interrogation of the everyday, but an intense and thoroughgoing relationship to suffering—the loss of self and the continual reconstruction of the self[12]—through which meaning and self-expression are "accomplished." Suffering in the context of Wright's *Black Boy* is not simply the despair of finding and losing meaning in the world and dealing with the eventuality of non-being in death but a "quality of the mind," a coming to an understanding, resolutely, of the ephemeral nature of one's own life as well as the transient nature of life itself through personal ontological fissuring. That is, when one's life loses all structure what is illuminated in/about that life, generally, is that it is but the convergence of various vectors or forces[13] rather than a secure moment of one's autonomous choices (and choosing). The "quality of hurt" of Wright's life in *Black Boy*, then, is more than traditional existential analysis, but a moment of loss and of recovery brought about by *peculiar* historical forces that helped shape the experience of being black and southern within the historical shifts from slavery to antebellum Reconstruction through Jim Crow.[14] Wright's life emerged in a psychological and historical manner similar to a Freudian slip—the nation hiccuped and burped up Richard Wright. Wright's *Black Boy* is a record of the hiccup and the burp as well as the social and personal costs of such a specious emergence and a "strange birth."[15] This essay traces the suffering accounted in *Black Boy* and its significance for existential-phenomenological discovery (read: uncovering).

EXISTENTIAL PHENOMENOLOGY, LITERATURE, AND BLACKNESS

How does one gain access to one's own life, to think about or even write about one's own experiences? How does one find the language to articulate the being of his/her experiences? Can language capture the being or content of our experiences? Or, does it, in some way, only hope to capture merely our own perspective? Literature poses to us a specific phenomenological problem. Just because we have experiences, perceptions, and/or feelings does not mean that we can explain them, exhort them, transfer them to the symbolic world for others to understand. At the end of *Black Boy*, Richard Wright tells us about his initial encounter with literature in his youth, and his struggles with coming to terms with and understanding himself and others in language. He writes,

> Steeped in new moods and ideas, I bought a ream of paper and tried to write; but nothing would come, or what did come was flat beyond telling. I discovered that more than desire and feeling were necessary to write and I dropped the idea. Yet I still wondered how it was possible to know people sufficiently to write about them? Could I ever learn about life and people? [16]

Similarly, at the end of *American Hunger* Wright laments about the angst brought about by the rush of emotions and his inability to express them in language.

> I picked up a pencil and held it over a sheet of white paper, but my feelings stood in the way of my words. Well, I would wait, day and night, until I knew what to say. Humbly now, with no vaulting dream of achieving a vast unity, I wanted to try to build a bridge of words between me and the world outside, that world which was so distant and elusive that it seemed unreal. [17]

Wright experienced the phenomenological paradox and the irony of language: While we are brought out of ourselves (that is, our interiority) through our engagement with the world, we are trapped within our own selves when it comes to explaining in language our perceptual relation to the world. Existence is tragically ironic; we can experience, feel something to our very core, but when we try to explain it to others, we are lost for the words to properly signify the experience. Maurice Merleau-Ponty points out this problem in the beginning of *The Visible and the Invisible* where he writes,

We see the things themselves, the world is what we see: formula of this kind express a faith common to the natural man and the philosopher—the moment he opens his eyes; they refer to a deep-seated set of mute "opinions" implicated in our lives. But what is strange about this faith is that if we seek to articulate it into theses or statements, if we ask ourselves what is this *we*, what *seeing* is, and what *thing* or *world* is, we enter into a labyrinth of difficulties and contradictions.

What Saint Augustine said of time—that it is perfectly familiar to each, but that none of us can explain it to others—must be said of the world . . . Ceaselessly the philosopher finds himself obliged to reinspect and redefine the most well-grounded notions, to create new ones, with new words to designate them, to undertake a new reform . . . before which the natural man now no longer recognizes where he stood. [18]

Wright, too, found himself in a world, a southern world, in the face of which he found he had no language to properly articulate his feelings, his experiences, his suffering and his pain. Rather, what Wright discovered was his *urge* to flee, his urge to find a new way of life; in finding his new ways of life and living, he hoped that he would develop a new vocabulary to reflect on his southern world and his southern experiences and put them into discourse. The last pages of *Black Boy* read,

I was leaving the South to fling myself into the unknown, to meet other situations that would perhaps elicit from me other responses. And if I could meet enough of a different life, then, perhaps, gradually and slowly I might learn who I was, what I might be. I was not leaving the South to forget the South, but so that some day I might understand it, might come to know what its rigors had done to me, to its children. I fled so that the numbness of my defensive living might thaw out and let me feel the pain—years later and far away—of what living in the South had meant. [19]

The North, the place of flight, [20] offered Wright the possibility of developing a new language to understand his past, to understand what it meant to his personality given that he "could never really leave the South, for my feelings had already been formed by the South, for there had been slowly instilled into it my personality and consciousness, black though I was, the culture of the South." [21] Wright's transplantation of his southern experiences into the new soil—quite literally a new earth—of the North might allow for a new discourse, a new way of thinking, of being, of doing. In short it (the transplantation) might release him *from* the world and give the world back to him. [22] He writes,

So, in leaving, I was taking a part of the South to transplant in alien soil, to see if it could grow differently, if it could drink of new and cool rains, bend in strange winds, respond to the warmth of other suns, and, perhaps, to bloom . . .

And if that miracle ever happened, then I would know that there was yet hope in that southern swamp of despair and violence, that light could emerge even out of the blackest of the southern night.[23]

Wright hoped that by leaving the South (physically) he might find himself (again) in the North (spiritually), as well as a new way of theorizing. What Wright discovered, though, is that one never actually loses oneself, one simply alters his or her perspective. This revelation, that wherever one goes one finds oneself reflected in different ways, has its costs: throughout *Black Boy* and *American Hunger* we understand that self-discovery always does, and must entail, fundamental *risk*. An individual must be willing to lose him- or herself to find who and what they in fact are; the risk is discovering a truth that he or she did not intend or desire to find. Had Wright never left the South—like many other black and white folk—he would not have developed a new language and would have been lost in the labyrinth of socially conditioned rituals—white domination and black subservience. And, the truth that Wright learned, one that haunted him throughout his life, is that there was no place for him to be at home in the world.

The activity of translating our experience into language entails a similar risk. In this activity one may discover that they are simply incapable of translating and are forever trapped within their inner life (world) where there are, in fact, no windows. What is more, one may discover that what it means to succeed in translating experience to language is a kind of formalism in which we lose our experiences and ourselves *to* language itself.

On the other hand, one is never assured of discovering anything. Language challenges us to call forth *all* the events of our experience, even the painful experiences and demands the discipline "to keep the painful details and episodes of a brutal experience alive in one's aching *consciousness*, to finger its jagged grains, and to transcend it, not by the consolation of philosophy but by *squeezing* from it a near-tragic, near-comic lyricism"[24] without guarantee of any result.

Wright articulated with phenomenological insight the paradox of existence and the irony of language of which Merleau-Ponty spoke: while our experiences may be immediate, our articulation of them is anything but immediate. Language, spoken or written, exists within this gap of experience and expression, stands, as it were, between thing or world and us, reminding us of its (language's) failures and of its unexpected successes. And though we are always finding ourselves late, always arriving late, for there is ever a gap between our experiences and our articulations of them, our world and ourselves, we are nevertheless transformed in language. Our language is ever returning to itself—and in turn returning us to ourselves yet different—and attempting to return *to* us our/some vanished time and place of experience. Language is, thus, a reminder of who we have already become, even if we do not "know" it yet.[25] We must accept the fundamental *risks* of language if we are to ever catch a glimpse of who and what we are. For Wright, as for Merleau-Ponty, the paradox and the irony did not mean to deny either of these, but to analyze the world and ourselves with renewed notions of existence and renewed forms of language.

Wright, like Merleau-Ponty, poses the relationship between expression and the risk of expression, and yet, we have *Black Boy* as we have *The Visible and the Invisible*, bodies of literature on the impossibility of literature. Both present the paradox of existence and the irony of writing: to write is to already be late, to be late is to long for, to long for is to be absent, and to be absent is to be (most) present.

The primary task of phenomenology—as it is being used here—is to make explicit that which is implicit in our experiences, to reveal the "object" of our tacit knowledge—ourselves, as we exist in the world. The traditional problem with the phenomenological understanding/articulation of black folk is quite well known: the "object" of experience is so distorted by surrounding white racism—that is, racism's internal logic that deems blacks non-persons, sub-persons, and/or pathological persons—that what is discovered through analysis, namely one's self in the world, seems foreign to itself.[26] The difficulty, then, is articulating the "object" of black phenomenological introspection. That is, if what we always already possess is an implicit knowledge of our being in the world, and phenomenological interrogation of the everyday makes explicit our implicit knowledge, then for the "black" subject there is a fundamental problem of self-disclosure and self-knowledge. Frantz Fanon articulates this problem in his well-known words "not only must the black man be black, but he must be black in *relation* to the white man."[27] What Fanon is articulating here is the fact that the "object" of phenomenological interrogation that is *found* is "black"—a referential concept understood by white racism's internal logic—not a self adjudicated for-itself, but an externalized in-itself creating an incongruity of being and existence, an indistinguishable quality and quantity of life between the in-itself and the for-itself. What the "black" subject is supposed to recognize through its phenomenological introspection is that it is a non-person, a *relational* entity whose existence is derivative and predicated upon whiteness. But, a larger question still looms, unasked: How is it that one can implicitly know oneself as the "black" object of another's gaze, as distorted, as the polar opposite of how one sees and thinks oneself, and make explicit this knowledge?[28] That is, how do we have texts on or about the alienation of black folk, written *by* black folk? It is a difficult task to say the least. What a black person discovers, then, is the need for principles by which to adjudicate, understand, explicitly state one's being as one's own, one's experiences as one's own. This, for black folk, is done through the articulation and affirmation of one's own humanity. That is, the affirmation of all of the absurd and contrary realities of human life made explicit in black living. Black suffering, then, becomes a marker, not for the non- or sub-personhood of "blackness," but of the condition for introspection and for the possibility of self-understanding, and, for humanity. The phenomenological situation of black folk, thus, is reversed.[29] As Thomas F. Slaughter writes in his essay "Epidermalizing the World," "Being in the open, outside the system, I begin to question . . . I act in judgment . . . I gaze on the society's axiological periphery and condemn the arbitrary valorizations . . . Whereas before, my being to the world through my body was my condemnation, now, my body is my vindication . . . I rehabilitate myself."[30]

For Wright, too, human suffering is what calls the black subject forth, hails them into the clearing by reminding oneself that one is *alive* and to be alive means taking up an "organic" position in the world. Suffering allows the black subject to recognize himself/herself no matter how distorted the image in the mirror held up by society. But, it is not suffering alone that allows for self-conscious expression, or what we will later call "freedom"; suffering itself not sufficient for the kind of insight that Wright offers. Self-consciousness is a process—but the seeds of its overturning are latent within the suffering itself. For many in Wright's community, in *his own family*, this process never took. Rather, for Wright, the desperation and hunger, "lacking genuine passion . . . void of hope . . . the essential bleakness,"[31] had been settled on lives to subtend the inevitable—death. That is to say, for Wright, many in the black community and his own family had resigned themselves to the hunger and the desperation, "lacking . . . in those intangible sentiments that bind man to man,"[32] because the alternative, fighting and dying, seemed worse than the worst of suffering-life. This life, though, for Wright, was vacuous and empty.

The problem of immediate apperception of a black self within a white society is that the self has been emptied of content, laid barren, and, thus is a caricature, filled with affect—"yessah, boss"; the yes exaggerated with a protean black gate (in a shuffle)—a survival mechanism which becomes an ontology. This slow drawl means, for Wright, that the black person has refused to take from their suffering a principle, a perspective on the world. And, this is the key: to simply suffer and not glean from it the absurdity of life, a principle for living means that all one has is the suffering without meaning. When a black person of this sort thinks of himself or herself, reveals himself or herself in the world, all that they discover is, "yessah boss" in one way or another, one form or another.

The problem of whiteness or that of an anti-black society, we are told, is that it creates of a black person a zombie of sorts, a mechanical man—"he has eyes and ears and a good distended African nose, but he fails to understand the simple facts of life. *Understand*. Understand? It's worse than that.

He registers with his senses but short-circuits his brain. Nothing has meaning. He takes it in but he doesn't digest it. Already he is—well, bless my soul! Behold! A walking zombie! Already he's learned to repress not only his emotions but his humanity. He's invisible, a walking personification of the Negative, the most perfect achievement of your [white] dreams, sir! The mechanical man!"[33] —or, perhaps, a non-person, a being in the "form" of human, but not quite human—"that is not a new man who has come in, but a new kind of man, a new genus. Why, it's a Negro!"[34] To become free a black person must first recognize this world, how this world sees him/her, and yet dislocate himself/herself from "yessah boss" as an identity. In this way, black folk must always double-deal, exist on two different levels—on one level, in-itself for a white society; and, on another level, for-itself qua human being. And, while blackness exists within and for a white society, it is important to note that it cannot be reduced to it. And, yet, phenomenologically we are treading this line (it must be remembered that lines, too, have depth) quite dangerously. And, yet in this danger, as in the risk of existence and in language, is necessary and constitutive of what it means to *be*, especially acute in the ambiguities of the black American experience.

What, then, is being made explicit in a phenomenology of black living? Can one call oneself forward as a non-being, a collection of affects articulated from without? As barren, as bleak? Can one be called forth by their own negation? What is called forth by that slow southern drawl "yessah boss" followed by the "tradition" of signifying and a slow purposeful bop? Does soberly accepting this southern pain and humiliation, accepting this southern suffering destroy the "self" articulated in "yessah boss"? Does destroying the "white man" destroy the "yessah boss"? Can a physical death precede a social one? Can that be it? But, as Wright discovered, even this was somehow untrue. Could the murder of Dives, really, resurrect Lazarus? Can destruction do what faith can? One cannot, as Wright discovered, call oneself forward as a *not*,[35] nor can one call oneself forth through the simple negation of *ressentiment*.

> I can't take the pressure much longer, somebody say prayer!
> Alabama's got me so upset
> Tennessee made me lose my rest
> And everybody knows about Mississippi Goddamn!

While Wright seemed to have, on one level, accepted the terms of the racial logic—blackness as ontologically relational and derivative of whiteness—in dramatic effect and affect, he also complicated this logic with his own *Black Boy* narrative in which his own pain and suffering along with his own desire for freedom frame the narrative and work contrary to racism's internal logic of "the "blackness" of things black."[36] Wright's addition of desire and freedom to the racial logic was significant for his theorizing of the development and emergence of the human personality, and the emergence of the "self" in the world. Wright's black boy narrative intertwined factual life experience and environmental influences with individual choice to give a collage of the human subject. For Wright, though, many African Americans—his class-mates, his family and the surrounding community, for example—did not employ *all* of these aspects in their own lives; rather, they were "claimed wholly by their environment and could imagine no other."[37] As an expres-sion of the enduring "self," Wright's black boy narrative was both an affir-mation of "self" over circumstance and a critique not only of the white world, but also of the kind of subservient blacks that were creations of this world.

Unlike his schoolmates, his family, his community at large, Wright ima-gined another world, another way of being and doing: he had cultivated a mood of hope. And, yet, this difference in choice could not be explained phenomenologically, at least not by Wright himself within the text; for exam-ple, his home life was no different than his classmates (perhaps even worse, even more stifling), his social and physical environment were theirs, he worked as other black boys had, but somehow, Wright, still, was different.[38] There was nothing ostensibly different about him other than that mysterious thing, that entity called the human personality, constituted not by the self-same unified subject, but by a plurality of social and historical forces acting upon and somehow belonging to one body, to one person.

Out of this confluence of forces, who and what we are, that is, the internal compulsion toward what we in the West call autonomy (*ipseity*)—that is, self-directed action[39] —Wright as "subject" was formed; this is what his black boy narrative added to the "given" racial narrative. Wright, himself, and perhaps, to his mind only him,[40] strove against the grain of the standing racial logic, inserting his *will*, his *desire*, that is, his sense of "self" *as* free-dom (*ipseity*) into a world replete with its own forces; a world whose logic challenged, whose force relations threatened "the varied forces that were making me reject the culture that had molded and shaped me."[41] And, yet Wright, almost inexplicably, strove; his desire for a free existence, his call forward toward an "impossible" humanity[42] ; his call to conscience would not let him be a genial or social slave,[43] or a dog, even if "to them [white folks], both of us *are* dogs."[44] Wright even surprised himself, not being able to account for the source of his own will and desire toward freedom.

> Well, I had never felt my "place"; or, rather, my *deepest instincts* had always made me reject the "place" to which the white South had assigned me. It had never occurred to me that I was in any way an inferior being. And no word that I had ever heard fall from the lips of southern white men had ever made me really doubt the worth of my own humanity.[45]

Perhaps it was all the suffering Wright experienced; perhaps the racism of the South and the waiting false sanctimony and disappointment(s) of the North were the sources of Wright as "subject" and "freedom." But neither (experiences in the South or the North) can fully explain Wright's "deepest instincts." Perhaps, then, it was the idea of what the suffering meant, what racism itself meant; what watching what both racism and suffering had done to other black folk, in particular his father and his mother, meant that held the key to understanding Wright's deepest instincts. It is this insight that gives Wright's black boy narrative existential and phenomenological texture—beneath the acts or experiences themselves an understanding of who and what we do lies; the phenomenological method revisited (making explicit what is implicit in experience). Maybe we have simply been looking in the wrong place all along. It is not the suffering *as such*, but a reflection into it that is truly the moment of transforming suffering and pain into a principle of life. Subject "wins its truth only when, in utter dismemberment, it finds itself."[46] On the precipice of collapse, on the verge of death (social and physical) Wright discovered freedom is located, freedom is found, and "transcendence" (if there is such a thing, or a need for such a word) is won.[47] It is a bitter victory and ironic, yet liberating. In this victory a kind of magic takes place; an incantation of the self toward possibilities, toward difference; the black self, while recognizing itself within a white society, still hails itself forth differently, not as the articulation (read: imago) of the white imagination, or the negative reaction of the black imago; not even through the evocation of that disastrous sublation of the dialectic,[48] but as a self straddling acceptance and rejection.[49] Wright laments, as much to himself as to us, this spurious and ironic freedom:

> Men should be able to confront other men without fear or shame, and that if men were lucky in their living on earth they might win some redeeming meaning for their having struggled and suffered here beneath the stars.[50]

We are reminded with Wright's *Black Boy* that suffering itself is just the *beginning* of consciousness, not its transcendence. One cannot be drawn into self-conscious reflection simply through suffering—if this *were* the case, the entirety of the black community would have exhibited existential clarity and certain freedom, both of which Wright thought they in fact lacked. But, like the risk of language—the possibility of never finding meaning, that is, building a bridge to others—what emerges out of suffering might be as much mouse as man. That is, for Wright suffering itself means nothing; what is required for freedom is a kind of reflection into the suffering and an understanding of the tenuous nature of freedom—one is always between accepting and rejecting. That is say, he was never able to fully articulate himself in the world as free, rather as freeing. What Wright sought, what we seek, was as much an explanation as an analysis of the fractured personality wrought with ontological despair. The racist and disappointing world that was before his eyes looked foreign to him because it *was* foreign; it *felt* alien to him because the world *was* alien to him. The presence of whiteness produced a disjointed view of the world. What remains to be seen is if he can ever make himself at home in the world amidst the pain and the suffering, the paradoxes and the ironies. That is the task of *Black Boy*. Yet, our task is a meta-theory of the possibility of such an openness. How can he make a home for himself in such an alien world? Our task is a phenomenological one engaging the interiority of a black human subject making sense of his being in a racist world and calling himself forward in such a world. Given this task, our question is loaded: *how* and *why* does Wright call himself forward in *Black Boy* as a black boy?

BLACK BOY: RICHARD WRIGHT'S EXISTENTIAL PHENOMENOLOGICAL NOVEL

For Wright, coming to terms with the transience and incongruity of black life in the South meant that black people could not, or should not, buy fully into the idea of blackness as a fixed ontological "project," (acceptance) nor should they think of it as a permanent character beyond whiteness (rejection), but in-between, in the liminal space of the in-between. Blackness, then, for Wright, operates as a historically contingent/situated reality which, because of its contingency, is "absolutely" free—that is, dislocated from an "essential" history or an essential mode of being—yet at the same time because of this same contingency it is a concrete facticity which, because of its real consequences of life and death, must be heeded as if it were an essential history or mode of being.[51] Formed within this liminality, Wright found himself, like many black folk in America, in an ambiguous position. While the history that was stretched before and mapped onto him (as belonging *to* him) was not his (he was, after all, not a nigger), he had to behave as if it was his on one level, all the while maintaining his own identity, which, on another level, had to reject this history.

What Wright offers us in *Black Boy* is not the subject of modern Western thought—the autonomous, reflective Cogito, or transcendental ego; or the categorical self—but a dispersed subject, constituted in and constituting multiple intersecting points (historicity, social, political, and economic environment[s], as well as physical geography). What is called the self in freedom (*ipseity*), the self of directed action, for modern thought, organized around a rationale pole that is not informed by one's environment, but *informs one's environment*, can no longer exist in Wright's black boy world.

There is nothing rational about Jim Crow—outside of Jim Crow's own internal logic—and the subjects—both black and white—that emerge out of this history are certainly not the Cartesian, Kantian, or even the Husserlian selves. Rather, in Wright's own black boy narrative, this self becomes a site of various moments, various experiences; freedom, thus, consists in not solely self-directed action, but is a conflation of various experiences centered around the vibration of a subject toward an impossible unity (neither acceptance nor rejection), and thus, ultimately, a paradoxical freedom—that is, the freedom of reconciling one's experiences to one's self, and the self to one's experiences. This freedom is paradoxical in that one can never choose one's environment, nor can one overcome or be reconciled to it. Rather, all one can do is mine/mind their environment and attempt to produce from it a liminal space between acceptance and rejection.

For example, Wright once wrote of the specious emergence of whiteness and white people for his emotional life, and the ambivalence it caused within him. Initially, Wright notes,

> Though I had long known that there were people called "white" people, it had never meant anything to me emotionally. I had seen white men and women upon the streets a thousand times, but they never looked particularly "white." To me they were merely people like other people, yet somehow strangely different because I had never come in close touch with any of them. For the most part I never thought of them. [52]

For Wright, white people initially "simply existed somewhere in the background of the city as a whole"[53] with the trees and the sidewalks, as part of the surrounding environment, as background, but *came* to have a specific emotional meaning for him through the black boy narratives of his own family and community members in which whites could and would capriciously violate the lives of black people. In one formative scene in *Black Boy* Wright recalls overhearing adults retell a story in which a black woman's husband had been lynched by a white mob, and how she, in taking revenge, killed many of the mob before being killed herself. Wright recounts his reaction to this story.

> I did not know if the story was factually true or not, but it was emotionally true because I had already grown to feel that there existed men against whom I was powerless, men who could violate my life at will. I resolved that I would emulate the black woman if I were ever faced with a white mob; I would conceal a weapon, pretend that I had been crushed by the wrong done to one of my loved ones; then, just when they thought I had accepted their cruelty as the law of my life, I would let go with my gun and kill as many of them as possible before they killed me. The story of the woman's deception gave form and meaning to confused defensive feelings that had long been sleeping in me . . .

These fantasies were no longer a reflection of my reaction to the white people,
they were a part of my living, of my emotional life; they were a culture, a
religion.[54]

What Wright expressed here is that whites, who were once only part of the
landscape of his life, his living order, emerged from this order, no longer
background, but foreground, through the *threat* of physical violence and
social death. Whites were no longer just "white" people, but those "men
against whom I was powerless, men who could violate my life at will."[55]
Men whose caprice could enter his life and remove him from it. And, yet, at
an early age Wright decided he was not going to let this threat enclose him,
that he would fight back with misdirection (as the old woman had). He would
"conceal a weapon, *pretend* that I had been *crushed by the wrong* done . . .
then, just when they thought I had *accepted* their cruelty as the *law* of my
life, I would let go with my gun." Wright's method, thus, involved a cunning
ruse in which he would give the appearance of clinging to life—pretending to
accept their cruelty as law—rather than risking annihilation; yet this appearance (of clinging to life) *was* a covert confrontation and a fundamental risk of
death. Wright's method, like the old woman's, is a parody of the life and
death struggle: he risked death while simultaneously feigning defeat. This is
a trickster element of Wright's narrative and captures the ambivalence and
irony of freedom in an anti-black racist world. Freedom is dissembled.
Wright's strength is his cunning, his freedom his deception.

The process of this freedom is paradoxical; it is a magical process involving
the will of the individual over and against (and *through*) exogenous forces.
The freedom of the black subject in the West is even more magical given that
their historical experiences (of anti-black racism) are infinitely reborn
through the repetition of rituals and the reinscription of social practices.[56]
Wright's ability to submerge, "conceal" and pretend, and then emerge was an
accomplishment of his will; and, what was accomplished was but an ambivalent and often contradictory "self." A "self" that neither fully accepted, nor
fully rejected its own history; a "self" that could not find solace in his own
family and community, and was also surrounded by the ominous force of
whiteness; a "self" that remained distant, alienated, conflicted; a "self" that
still strove toward that impossible unity of itself and the world, magisterially
rising, ambivalent and conflicted "*like a bird of flaming gold*"[57] liminally.

Is Wright then telling us that the "self" that is sure of its truth, its place
within the world and history is itself a joke, a false unity? What Wright's
usage of the liminal "self" helps us to see effectively is that the "self" of the
modern world—the autonomous and absolutely free self—is nothing other
than the will directing itself toward a unity that cannot actually exist; a unity
that is false, because the idea of rational, self-directed self itself is false.

What is this "self" that exists beyond experiences, that, in fact, unifies these experiences within itself; what is this core "self"? As a paradox, our experiences and our language to capture them is nothing other than the impossibility of reconciling our experiences to ourselves in total (and vice versa). And, Wright's *Black Boy* then stands out as a courageous gesture of the impossibility of writing down our experiences, much more so than *Native Son*'s Bigger Thomas, who, in stabbing air and smothering shadows, thought that he could escape his own reality with *action*, ultimately betraying his own ambivalence.

If we think of phenomenology as a method that calls forth the self out of ordinary experience, then we have to wonder what sort of phenomenological method is necessary for this dispersed self, and whether the traditional phenomenological system can, in fact, account for this ambivalent and contrary "self." What would it mean to call oneself into the clearing, if one is but a complex confluence of forces? What would it mean to write a narrative about such a person and to call such a narrative anything that approaches autobiography? And, yet we have Wright's *Black Boy*, a "record of childhood and youth" chronically the experiences of a black person, a black subject coming of age, coming into "consciousness" of the reality of the world, the anti-black world that has its own logic and structures waiting for him, always already, seemingly infinite. Wright's own words express the possibility and impossibility of such a novel, such an accomplishment as *Black Boy*:

> If I deal with racial problems, it is because those problems were created without my consent or permission. [58]

Black Boy on the surface is primarily about "race" and "racism" and their effects on a human being. *Black Boy* is also a novel concerned with the endurance of Wright, the individual, through the suffering at the hands of white society, the black community as a whole, and his own family in particular. But, it would be a mistake to reduce Wright's work to either of these: the former being the deterministic realism that brought out critics such as James Baldwin; the latter, an existential humanism that transcends differences and factual life for universal humanism (or, perhaps, the concrete universal). Wright's novel, though, was both, but neither one. There are moments where it seems Wright created characters that are but archetypes—proving the larger social issue of the deforming effects of racism on the human personality—but, there are times that his words sing and dance with the mystery of life itself and the ever unfolding landscapes of human meaning.

> Up or down the wet or dusty streets, indoors or out, the days and nights began to spell out magic possibilities.

If I pulled a hair from a horse's tail and sealed it in a jar of my own urine, the hair would turn overnight into a snake . . .

If I heard a voice and no human being was near, then either God or the Devil was trying to talk to me . . .

Anything seemed possible, likely, feasible, because I wanted everything to be possible . . . Because I had no power to make things happen outside of me in the objective world, I made things happen within. Because my environment was bare and bleak, I endowed it with unlimited potentialities, redeemed it for the sake of my own hungry and cloudy yearning.[59]

Wright's novel, though, is more than either of these. It is novel with " a conviction that the meaning of living came only when one was struggling to wring a meaning out of meaningless suffering."[60] When the term "existential phenomenology" is used here it is to highlight the confluence of these elements—the mysteries of life and the factual aspects of life—as they are present in black life, in Wright's black boy life. Reading Wright's novel as existential phenomenology is not to reduce it to a play of words or to another tradition by way of analogy. Rather, it is meant to locate certain qualities— hunger, dread, desperation, loss, and reconstitution—within the tradition of Fyodor Dostoevsky's *House of the Dead*, Andre Malraux's *Man's Fate* and H.L. Mencken's *A Book of Prefaces*, all of which Wright names as sources of "companionship";[61] it is to follow Wright's own deeper sentiments in his black boy life, "building bridges" across paradoxes—of language, of freedom; it is to explain, rather to exhort the spirit of black boy in the Memphis Public Library, with trickery and treachery, "pretending to be defeated," "concealing his weapon," "retrieving" books for a white coworker, a spirit that gave "insight into the sufferings of others, made me gravitate towards those whose feelings were like my own,"[62] a new way of "seeing and feeling" that would carve meaning "out of meaningless suffering." Claiming that Wright's *Black Boy* is existential phenomenology is to say that it was a mystery, a grand, ironic, and paradoxical accomplishment, as were the works of Dostoevsky, Malraux, and Mencken—though "the impulse to dream had been slowly beaten out of me by experience,"[63] it would surge up again.

To me, with my vast ignorance, my Jim Crow station in life, it seemed a task impossible of achievement. I now knew what being a Negro meant. I could endure the hunger. I had learned to live with hate. But to feel that there were feelings denied me, that the very breath of life itself was beyond my reach, that more than anything else hurt, wounded me. I had a new hunger.[64]

A hunger that was to "make me skeptical of everything while seeking everything, tolerant of all and yet critical."[65] A hunger that offered existential and phenomenological insights into suffering itself to give form, to stretch out of the page to others who suffered as he had, and yet endured to get it all down, to transform inner life and the factual world "feeling something new, of being affected by something that made the look of the world different."[66]

> Can't you see it
> Can't you feel it
> It's all in the air

> *I Just want to be* Known *in my Singularity*
> *I Just want to be* Thought *of, Regarded Singularly*
> *To hell with all this righteous formality*
> Race, *after all, is just a "Matter of Vocabulary"*
> *It is not* who *one really* is . . .
> "I am a human being before being an American;
> I am a human being before being a Negro."[67]

One can imagine Richard Wright struggling, suffering "in the blackest of southern nights," moving between affirmation and negation . . . dissembling. One can see Wright calling out from his dreamy landscape of *Native Son* or from his waking and walking nightmare of *Black Boy* (*American Hunger*). The cry is there, if you listen. Quietly. Shhh . . . you can hear Richard Wright crying out; you might even be able to see a man writhing. And what a sight, truly a sight it is. Our Grand Hero is crying out. Has his quest led us here? To his grandest defeat? What would lead us here? Why would Wright lead us here? To this place of desperation, of agony and pain? Where are we? Listen for an answer. Nigerian poet Ben Okri gives us a hint: "Living is a Cross / That any one of the rock-faces / Comprehends."[68] And what does this lead us to? Existential-phenomenological disclosure: the truth of one's life, as constituted by a constructed "self," is disclosed as one's own, as real to the extent that one finds his/her own cross, and bears it. Wright's cross was race (among other things). *A heavy burden to be disclosed as black for Wright.* And, still it *must* be more. (Could he get his experience all down if it was just his being a black, dirty nigger?) *Black Boy* is a narrative of his search for more: a search for place (no matter how fictional it may be), for a home, for being-in-the-world,[69] for a bosom like that of Abraham's to rock his weary soul (perhaps just an old black woman's breast to confess tears to).[70]

A Whisper: Men like Wright are not born, nor are they made—"*woven . . . out of a thousand details, anecdotes, stories.*"[71] Men like Wright *burst* forth on the scene[72] ; they *explode* from underground, from the viscous bile of hate and desire, love and repulsion—they emerge from/in the cracks of contradiction of American history; they are brought to the surface from underground to the scene from a series of historical forces. Neither fathers, nor mothers, nor sisters, nor brothers; neither aunties, nor uncles, nor cousins, they have a "strange birth" where all are related to red clay hills, deep and warm waters of swamps and marshes, signifying of slave churches and testimonials of field cries, dissemblance of broken tools and aborted fetuses.[73] In the cracks, Wright's voice whispers:

> The moments of living slowly revealed their coded meanings . . . the wonder I felt when I first saw a brace of mountainlike, spotted black-and-white horses clopping down a dusty road through clouds of powdered clay . . . the yellow, dreaming waters of the Mississippi River from the verdant bluffs of Natchez.[74]

Men like Wright come forth on the scene existentially as those beings who authentically come to live, come to have meaning in the bleakest of circumstances.[75] Can you hear Beethoven's Ninth Symphony in a Nazi prison?[76] Can you catch a note on the still, dead air of such a place? Or, is that the only way to *hear* at all? "*Because* my environment was bare and bleak," Wright whispers, "I endowed it with unlimited potentialities."[77] Wright's own "strange birth" as a being of the Jim Crow South told to us through his *Black Boy* narrative foregrounds his existential search to catch a note, to find a meaning, to hear an echo. And, Wright discovered that meaning in life itself was a battle to be won, an ironic battle for existence waged through human suffering.

Wright knew more than most men, at least more than most white men (and those men who pretended to be white, or at least, pretended *not* to be black) that suffering gave way to, that is, disclosed, acute consciousness, an acute awareness of the transience of life and the transience of, not only our desires and best laid plans, but our existence as human beings upon the earth. And, it was this realization that galvanized itself into a sort of mood, a way of *seeing* and *thinking* the world; this realization, for Wright, became a *disposition*.

CONCLUSION: PHENOMENOLOGICAL HORIZONS AND EXISTENTIAL CONTOURS

The original title for the second volume of Richard Wright's long, continued black boy saga *American Hunger*, *The Horror and the Glory*, captures both the struggle of his black boy existence, and his ironic triumph of creating meaning and order out of the suffering of his lived experience. What Ralph Ellison wrote of Wright's *Black Boy* is apropos: "Wright's most important achievement: He has converted the American Negro impulse toward self-annihilation and "going underground" into a will to confront the world."[78] That is, Wright's great achievement was that he managed to transform an invitation to death into a principle for life.[79] There is no doubt horror in Wright's collective saga, but there is also glory. Oh, the glory . . . *since I lay my burden down.*

There is something distinctly black about Richard Wright's *Black Boy.* It is about a boy who is black—cosigned under the *eidos* of the white imaginary—and it is the epistemological lens through which that black boy sees the world. The novel is black in both ways: it is at once a black epistemological novel and a narrative about being black. And, what is more, and perhaps which might be either illuminating or troubling depending on one's political view, *Black Boy* as a novel stands out as Richard Wright's blackest novel; the novel that only a black boy could write: it describes the world through the eyes of a youth, a child, a black *boy* in a way that only a *black* boy could see it, could understand it, and quite possibly, could interpret it.[80] And it is this which is philosophically of interest, the novel presents not only an epistemic gaze, but an existential outlook caged in phenomenological description. *Black Boy* is at once a narrative about a black boy and an episteme of a black boy, but, and what is more, it is an existential phenomenological work illuminating what it means to be a human being in the world, unveiling and reconciling oneself to the world and the world to oneself.

Black Boy is a narrative that rose out of the place of Wright's birth, a narrative as native to the land as the crops were to the region. Wright was very much a man *of* his times, that is to say, a man who sprang forth from his time, expelled, as it were, by the confluence of historical encounters and historical memories. Wright's narrative rose, not so much to be explained by such encounters, but that it itself may explain such encounters.

Black Boy is a phenomenological narrative wherein the "truth" of the world "as such" (that is, as lived, as experienced, as interpreted and apprehended) is disclosed through a black boy's suffering. As a phenomenological text *Black Boy* captures a narrative distinctly American and a phenomenological method distinctly black. Phenomenological disclosure in Wright's novel is not concerned with a transcendental ego or the general structures of human being per se, but with a specific narrative, about a black *boy*, that functions as universal discourse. Wright's black American phenomenological narrative gathers both the general and specific accounts and modes of being as human being as it tells of the human condition—the struggle to find meaning, to locate one's interpretation, to be in the world—heightened by the specific experiences of a black *American* child.

Richard Wright's *Black Boy* phenomenologically unfolds an existential narrative that, like Nina Simone's "Mississippi Goddamn," reads as a show tune for a show that has yet to be written, a show that he would spend the entirety of his life learning how to begin. How to talk about freedom, how to thinking freely, how to be what and who he is. Nina Simone's voice comes back, loud, that same searing blues angst, to take us away:

Everybody knows about Mississippi
Everybody knows about Alabama
Everybody knows about Mississippi Goddamn . . . That's it!

NOTES

1. Nina Simone, *Nina Simone in Concert* (Philips Records, 1964).
2. Richard Wright, *Black Boy* (New York: Harper & Brothers, 1945).
3. Wright's *Black Boy* reads as an ironic narrative filled with rhetorical gestures. In the text there are moments where Wright is elucidating larger metaphysical or ontological issues of race and human dignity; it is in these moments that it is not altogether clear who Wright is speaking to, himself in internal monologue, or his imagined audience—perhaps both. This is especially ambiguous at those moments where he is affirming his humanity or when he has discovered something of a secret to southern ways of living. Yet, it is clear in these moments that Wright wants the reader to take a journey with him, to be engaged and take a step out of the netherworld of benign race discourse, to take a critical step back to examine the kinds of beings—white and black—a southern reality creates. It is this manner of pulling the reader forward out of their passive receiving, crossing the private and the public, that *Black Boy* takes on a democratic mode of representing and participating in the world that is the tradition of "call and response."
4. Nina Simone, *Nina Simone in Concert*. Wright, reflecting on the tragedy of slow pace of social justice in *Black Boy*, writes: "'Maybe that's what's wrong with Negroes,'" I said, "'They take too much time'" (205). Wright often criticized other black boys, either openly or in his own mind, for their willingness to go along with the racial logic of the south and not be critically reflective—on its nature, its rule, and the absurdity of the whole structure; rather, they preferred to think themselves smart or clever, either staying alive or hustling underground, confounding whites and getting ahead. Wright recounts a particularly disturbing exchange with a black boy named Shorty, who allowed a white man to kick him in the rear end for a quarter. While Wright was confounded as to how he could let himself be kicked for a quarter, Shorty was confounded why Wright didn't understand how to work the racial system to get over and to make some money.

> "How in God's name can you do that?"
> "I needed a quarter and I got it," he said soberly, proudly.
> "But a quarter can't pay you for what he did to you," I said.
> "Listen, nigger," he said to me, "my ass is tough and quarters is scarce." (250)

For Wright, boys like Shorty inhabited the "do it slow" of Simone's song; in concrete terms that meant that neither they nor their world would ever be different than it currently was. They had accepted their lot in life, not in sober resoluteness, but wholly, utterly. "If a white man had sought to keep us from a job, or enjoying the rights of citizenship, we would have bowed silently to his power. But if he had sought to deprive us of a dime, blood might have been spilled" (251).
5. Charles Chestnutt, *The Marrow of Tradition* (Ann Arbor: University of Michigan Press, 1969).
6. Nina Simone, *Nina Simone in Concert*.
7. Nina Simone, *Nina Simone in Concert*.
8. Nina Simone, *Nina Simone in Concert*.
9. Though Simone was born in North Carolina and not Mississippi, this is but a biographical fact, and makes a deeper point about the placeness of Mississippi that transcends the geographical space of Mississippi proper. One need not be born and reared in Mississippi to understand Mississippi, to decipher its complex and nuanced social signifiers, and to be in the

presence of Mississippi, even as far away as North Carolina. To the transcendent quality of Mississippi for black Americans, one may look to the last lines of "Mississippi Goddamn": "Alabama's got me so upset / Tennessee made me lose my rest / And everybody knows about Mississippi Goddamn." This is an epistemological as well as a phenomenological statement in which the "knowing" is the transposition of history located in the air, in the water, in the soil, in the flesh of Mississippi. Mississippi, for *all* blacks, takes on a social and historical factness (in terms of significance) that is passed down, like recipes, from generation to generation and disclosed in such metaphysical statements as Simone's. One may note that "Mississippi Goddamn" was composed in response to the death of civil rights leader Medgar Evers, who both emerged from and was returned to that Mississippi land in the most violent of ways, shorn by a bullet. The death of Evers, along with less-high-profile cases of racial violence and discrimination became associated with the meaning Mississippi, its history brought forth into the present, and the racial oppression of the United States generally.

10. Wright notes in *Black Boy* of his personal resistance to and overcoming of the southern tradition of breaking black folk of wonder and desire, "I was building up in me a dream which the entire educational system of the South had been rigged to stifle. I was feeling the very thing that the state of Mississippi had spent millions of dollars to make sure that I would never feel; I was becoming aware of the thing that the Jim Crow laws had been drafted and passed to keep out of my consciousness; I was acting on impulses that southern senators in the nation's capital had striven to keep out Negro life; I was beginning to dream the dreams that the state had said were wrong, that schools had said were taboo . . . In me was shaping a yearning for a kind of consciousness, a mode of being that the way of life about me had said could not be, must not be, and upon which the penalty of death had been placed" (186–87).

11. This critique, that through philosophical introspection or through the analysis of the lives and experiences of others, one can develop an existential outlook, is one that Ellison, like Wright charged many of the European intellectuals of the 1930s and 1940s with. In a letter to Richard Wright, Ellison notes that it was black Americans and not French philosophers who possessed an experimental mood or attitude toward the world necessary for existential insight given that they (black Americans) lived and suffered under the social (read: ontological) conditions that the French philosophers could only write (and theorize) about. In his biography of Ralph Ellison, *Ralph Ellison: Emergence of Genius* (New York: Wiley & Sons, 2002), author Lawrence Jackson writes, "Ellison wrote to Wright in France that American blacks, living with the tension of horror and chaos enjoined to their most significant emotions and experiences, had a philosophical advantage over the French existentialists. The French had to dive from the height of their philosophy into the deep pool of reality; black Americans spent their day-to-day lives underneath the surface of the water" (340).

12. In his powerful book *Black Bodies, White Gazes* (Lanham, MD: Rowman & Littlefield, 2008) philosopher George Yancy argues that the black subject, vis-à-vis the black body, is not simply lost to itself in dealing with the white world, but is stolen from itself and returned to itself distorted, disjointed (see chapter 1, "The Elevator Effect"). It is in this manner that the self not only engages the world and its object, to rediscover itself in a new and more robust manner, but that the black self as ontologically stolen, relocates itself underneath, so to speak, things themselves. It is not the same manner of locating oneself in the objects of the world as their author (and vice versa), of locating spirit, but of reconstructing, from nothing, a self, a spirit which does not see itself reflected, but *makes* itself ex nihilo—this, of course, is not to discount the major impact of European language and thought, in addition to the American geographical location, to the creation of a new black cultural and spiritual self. Rather, as Ralph Ellison has pointed out in his essay "What America Would Be without Blacks," that black folk are a hybrid people. What makes this distinctive though, is that what they brought together was not just African and European as well as indigenous American experiences, but life and death; those elements that were made to destroy black folk were transformed into those elements that sustain them.

13. One is brought to mind of Michel Foucault's genealogical work on power in the ideas of vectors or forces acting upon the subject, or the subject acting upon the world. One may also bring to mind the work of Huey Newton and other Black Panther Party writings. For a fascinating article on Foucault's indebtedness to Newton, Clever, and Davis's work in his own theory

of power and forces see Brady Thomas Heiner, "Foucault and the Black Panthers," *City* 11, no. 3 (December 2007): 313–56. I would like to thank Dr. Tommy J. Curry for bringing this article to my attention.

14. We have to remember that Wright's *Black Boy* and his posthumous *American Hunger* (New York: Harper & Row, 1977) were written and published before civil rights legislation, which was seen as a symbol of freedom for black folk given legal, or de jeure, segregation was "ended." For Wright, though, segregation and Jim Crowism never ended in his own lifetime, making the idea of freedom simply that: an idea, or quite better, an ideal, but one he never quite achieved in his own writing. Rather, for Wright, his ideal was much more of an existential freedom and transcendence of the human subject, not the abstract subject of humanism, but one marked and scared by the factual reality of being black and American, black and Western, and never having seen the possibilities of ending the tension of these. And, while Reconstruction and the migration north promised change and freedom for Wright, neither achieved its goals systemically or personally; neither did his expatriation to Europe or Africa. Interestingly, Wright witnessed the independence of African and Asian nations, for example, the independence of the West African nation of Ghana in 1957, and not his own nation.

15. This is as much an epistemological claim as it is a phenomenological one. Wright often spoke of African American existence in the Jim Crow South in terms of a "strange birth." It was as if African Americans were not born in a natural sort of way, but were emergent and organic beings. African Americans, on this reading, don't have (natural) parents per se, rather, their parents are historical, social, political, and economic forces. As if this group were not and could not exist in the "normal" world where people come to be—that is, develop over periods of time both individually and socially—African Americans emerged grown, emerged fully formed and ready, as it were, to contend with and to be contended with in the Jim Crow South. There was no coming of age or into consciousness; African American youth *were* always already grown, and it made no sense to speak of African Americans in terms of *Bildungsroman*, a certain type of narrative form in which the protagonist learns, develops, and grows into consciousness and unveils the world, as it were. For examples of this epistemological and phenomenological position in Wright's work see "How Bigger was Born" in *Uncle Tom's Children* (New York: Harper & Brothers, 1940); *12 Million Black Voices* (New York: Thunder Mouth Press, 1941); "The Ethics of Living Jim Crow," reprinted from *Black Boy*; *Rite of Passage* originally published in *The Richard Wright Reader* (New York: Harper Perennial, 1978).

16. Richard Wright, *Black Boy*, 274.

17. Richard Wright, *American Hunger*, 135. Although originally intended to be paired with *Black Boy* in a two-volume work titled, *The Horror and the Glory*, *American Hunger* was published posthumously in 1977. The Library of America has recently restored, unexpurgated, the original version.

18. Maurice Merleau-Ponty, *The Visible and the Invisible* (Evanston, IL: Northwestern University Press, 1968, [1964]), 3.

19. Richard Wright, *Black Boy*, 284. Wright finds himself wrestling with a paradox familiar in existential phenomenological writing: he must leave the South to find the *meaning* of the South for his own life. In order for us to examine the everyday of our lives, experiences we are too close to understand and properly place philosophically, we must paradoxically create space between ourselves and our experiences. Yet, it is in and through these very everyday encounters that we are seen to implicitly understand our own lives illuminated in our handling and interpreting the world. What we want to accomplish philosophically, then, is an explicit articulation of our already implicit understanding.

20. The concept of flight is being used here in two ways: On the one hand, the idea of flight is parallel to the existential concept of bad faith, where one flees personal responsibility by allowing others to decide for them their projects, meaning, and purpose. On the other hand, the idea of flight is one of a necessary creation of distance from the everyday for personal reflection.

21. Richard Wright, *Black Boy*, 284.

22. This is a reversal of the famous lines of Franz Fanon's *Black Skin, White Masks* (New York: Grove Press, 2008) where he writes, "Sealed into that crushing objecthood, I turned beseechingly to others. Their attention was a liberation . . . and by taking me out of the world, restoring me to it" (109). Wright's argument, here, is that by placing himself in another environment, but not taking him out of the world, he may flourish; one doesn't need the other to release them from the world, one simply may need the correct environment for flourishing. Though the North had(s) its shares of racial problems, it symbolized for Wright a different *space* and *place* from the South, both in terms of concrete matters such as the customs and rituals for humiliating black people and of a shift in the physical geography.

23. Richard Wright, *Black Boy*, 284.

24. This is a reference to Ralph Ellison's review of Richard Wright's *Black Boy* in which he claims that Wright had produced a blues novel—or, at least a novel in the blues tradition; the blues defined in the quoted portion. Ralph Ellison, *Shadow and Act* (New York: Vintage Books, 1972), 78.

25. This explains how Wright could discover his southernness by leaving the South, his Americanness by leaving America.

26. This is a classical rehearsal of the phenomenological understandings of the black subject and the black body. In this reading, a black person's self-conception is distorted, their body image is handed back to them as something they do not recognize (that is, cognize), but, due to oppressive circumstances, *have* to understand, still, as somehow theirs and somehow constitutive of who and what they in fact are. For examples of this classic phenomenological argument see Franz Fanon's *Black Skin, White Masks* (1952); Charles Johnson's article "Phenomenology of the Black Body" (*Michigan Quarterly Review* 32, no. 4 [December 1993]: 595–614), originally published in the winter 1976 issue of *Ju-Ju Research Papers in Afro-American Studies*; Thomas F. Slaughter's "Epidermalizing the World: A Basic Mode of Being-Black" (*Man and World* 10, no. 3 [September 1977]); and, more recently, George Yancy's book *Black Body, White Gazes* (Lanham, MD: Rowman & Littlefield, 2008).

27. Franz Fanon, *Black Skin, White Masks*, 110.

28. This is the classic argument found, or thought to be found, in slave and ex-slave narratives: if the "object" of the interrogation comes out to be a non-human, how, then, does a non-human come to engage in the very human activity of existential, that is, philosophical interrogation of writing about one's own life? Of course this is the irony of race and racism in the West: the denial of that which is affirmed—that is, to deny one's human is to affirm one's humanity.

29. This reversal is not simply a changing of terms, or a denial of factual reality, but an insight into reality itself that gives one a perspective that G. W. F. Hegel gestured toward in *Phenomenology of Spirit* (Oxford: Oxford University Press, 1977): what is thought to be opposite, or contrary exists within what is affirmed—and carries within it its opposite and the seeds for its reversal. That is to say, white racism carries within it the signs and seeds of its own negation as "blackness"—that very negative term—carries within it the sign and seed of its own reversal: humanity.

30. Thomas F. Slaughter, "Epidermalizing the World: A Basic Mode of Being Black."

31. Richard Wright, *Black Boy*, 45.

32. Richard Wright, *Black Boy*, 45.

33. Ralph Ellison, *Invisible Man* (New York: Vintage Press, 1952), 94.

34. Franz Fanon, *Black Skin, White Masks*, 116.

35. One can look to Wright's characters Bigger Thomas and Cross Damon—in addition to "The Man Who Killed a Shadow," and "The Man Who Lived Underground"—to discover a theme in his work. Murder, revenge will not bring forth redemption, nor will it call forth one into the clearing of being to be born again into truth (*aletheia*). It will take something more than mere *resentment* to bring forth the kind of being which does not only assert or negate, but does *both*. But, as one can see in *Native Son*, *Black Boy*, *American Hunger*, and *The Outsider*, Wright had not quite figured out how a black person could call him or herself forward as active—the yes as well as the no. In his later travel writings and lectures, *White Man, Listen!* (New York: Anchor Books, 1964), Wright gives us a more complex diagnosis of the problem of racialization, but here too he stops short of assigning value, of figuring out what to do. The

best approximation, for me, comes at the end of *American Hunger* where he writes, "I would hurl words into this darkness and wait for an echo, and if an echo sounded, no matter how faintly, I would send other words to tell, to march, to fight, to create a sense of the hunger for life that gnaws in us all, to keep alive in our hearts a sense of the inexpressibly human" (135). Perhaps this is a deliberate existential ploy not to give answers to the difficulties of living; perhaps this is simply Wright coming to terms with the difficulty of racialization, segregation, and colonialism.

36. Ralph Ellison, "Change the Joke, Slip the Yoke," in *Shadow and Act* (New York: Vintage Books, 1972), 49. In this fascinating passage, Ellison evokes Wright's *Black Boy* to speak of the power of the phobic object and the release of the psyche through its sacrifice. In this way the "blackness of things black" is both a metaphorical and literal sacrifice of the black just as the "yessah boss" or the phenomenological apperception of the southern Negro involves self-humiliation/self-annihilation.

37. Richard Wright, *Black Boy*, 115–16.

38. Perhaps one could point to Wright's home life to offer an explanation of Wright's isolation and difference from the black boys of his community. Richard Wright's home life was drastically different from other black boys. His grandmother's constant demands of his time, his behavior, the contest over his very "soul" meant that Wright was kept from doing and being with other black boys, creating in him a sense of distance between himself and other black youth his own age. In *Black Boy* Wright notes, "I was reserved with the boys and girls at school, seeking their company but never letting them guess how much I was *being kept* out of the world in which they lived, valuing their casual friendships but hiding it, acutely self-conscious but covering it with a quick smile and a ready phrase" (139; emphasis added). But, there were other black boys who had similar experiences as Wright but did not turn out as Wright had. One explanation that has been offered is that Wright himself had lied in *Black Boy*, and that he in fact was not exceptional, and while this thesis is interesting and important, for this essay, which is phenomenological in nature, it is not important what the facts are, but what Wright *believes* them to be, and how he approaches translating and transferring them into his narrative. For a good essay on Wright's *Black Boy* being less than truthful, see Timothy Adams, "I Do Believe Though I Know He Lies: Lying as Genre and Metaphor in Richard Wright's *Black Boy*," *Prose Studies* 8, no. 2 (September 1985): 172–87.

39. This is both a political (social) and ontological argument. In social/political philosophy, on both the analytic and continental sides, the claim of freedom is concerned, whether implicitly or explicitly, with an idea of personal sovereignty and agency (also known as autonomy, or self legislation, self-given law), whether we are critiquing or affirming this idea. Wright, too, utilizes the idea of freedom in both the social and political sense as well as the ontological sense. One can see this in his work *American Hunger*, the title Wright wanted for the whole of *Black Boy*, where "hunger" was understood both a political concept and as an ontological longing, a fracture of the subject that caused a need for discovering the self through self-directed action. This, for Wright, becomes a problem for black people, or in his case, a black boy in a racist society that wants to not only control black bodies politically and socially, but also ontologically in terms of their humanity.

40. Wright's *Black Boy* can be read as a narrative concerning an existential individual confronting an everyday world with trappings of conformity and belonging. The sort of individualism Wright discovered in himself is echoed in the existential philosophical conceptions of *the* individual presented by both Søren Kierkegaard and Friedrich Nietzsche synthesized in a single quotation by Karl Jaspers: "Like a lonely fir tree, egotistically isolated, looking toward something higher . . . throwing no shadow, only the wood dove building its nest in my branches" ("Existenzphilosophie," in *Existentialism from Dostoevsky to Sartre*, ed. Walter Kaufmann [New York: Meridian, 1975], 204). An individual such as Wright, and Kierkegaard and Nietzsche for that matter, finds himself alone, that is, isolated—either by choice or by circumstance—unable to convince himself to "fit in" everyday pre-reflective life. And, what is more, for Wright, given his blackness—the coloration and metaphysics adjoined to his being—the need for his individuation is accelerated by his lack of social freedom. Wright's *Black Boy* fought social and communal pressures on many fronts: his family, the black community, the white community, and, when he migrated to Paris, the intellectual, dogmatic scene. Wright's

blackness confronted the general desire in America for conformity and in the specific case of his own family and community, both of which sought to conquer his industrious and adventurous spirit by constructing around him a scaffold of culture and ritual at once concerned with religion and trade as with surviving whiteness and white people. The conflict of the individual and the community intraracially was Wright's first encounter with the tension that would frame his life. The white world at large sought to define and enforce its definition of blackness, whiteness, human being, and Being generally with violent force. More can and needs to be said of Wright's existential individual that often springs up in characters and themes throughout much of his work. For good essays on Wright's individualism see Carla Capetti's "Sociology of an Existence: Richard Wright and the Chicago School," in *Richard Wright: Critical Perspectives Past and Present*, ed. Henry Louis Gates and K. A. Appiah (New York: Amistad Press, 1993); Nina Kressner Cobb's "Richard Wright: Exile and Existentialism," *Phylon* 40, no. 4 (1979): 362–74; Abdul JanMohamed's "Negating the Negation: The Construction of Richard Wright," in *Richard Wright: Critical Perspectives Past and Present*, ed. Henry Louis Gates and K. A. Appiah (New York: Amistad Press, 1993).

41. Richard Wright, *Black Boy*, 281.

42. To cloud the waters more, it can be said that in Wright's work, the idea of humanity is an ever-expanding concept, one that can never be filled or completed concretely. It is, rather, an idea—while at the same time not being a regulative ideal—that we strive toward, ultimately failing, giving us new possibilities, new concepts, new language, and new ways of interacting with one another. If this is true for Wright, then, what do we say about his critique of modernity and whiteness? If humanity is ever expanding and receding, like the horizon, then how do we say anything about our contemporary construction/situation? Can one critique without offering (alternative) solutions or programs? And, should we be looking for solutions at all? Or, should we be looking for new ways to think our present situation to complicate it? In a series of lectures, *White Man, Listen!* Wright addresses this concern "with a degree of frankness that I [Wright] rarely, in deference to politeness, permit myself" (xvii). He writes,

> When one is rash enough to commit oneself publicly upon issues as large and weighty as those contained in these lectures, one is naturally confronted with a cry for specifications, programs, platforms, and solutions; particularly is this comfort demanded with insistence by those who live uneasy lives in vast industrial civilizations where a hysterical optimism screens the seamier realities of life, hiding quicksands of cataclysmic historical changes . . . I'm much more the diagnostician than the scribbler of prescriptions. (xvi)

43. Richard Wright, *Black Boy*, 276.

44. Richard Wright, *Black Boy*, 264; emphasis added.

45. Richard Wright, *Black Boy*, 283; emphasis added. Wright does not account for the development of a predilection toward certain ways of being, though he does account for the ways one is in the world, once a predilection is set in place. For him, there was not much explanation given as to why he resisted communal being—blackness or whiteness—and why he was ensconced in individualism. Further he writes, "From where in this southern darkness had I caught a sense of freedom? . . . The external world of whites and blacks, which was the only world that I had ever known, surely had not evoked in me any belief in myself. The people I had met had advised and demanded submission" (282). Wright's development of personality takes on a metaphysical quality; he existence has a gossamer texture as only an intuitive being can.

46. G. W. F. Hegel, *Phenomenology of Spirit*, 19.

47. This perhaps explains the difference between Wright and many of the other black folk in his community. Wright was willing to face death, while others were unwilling to give up the very thing, which, ironically held them as slaves: life. In facing death, Wright was able to overcome his oppressive situation—a condition for his freedom.

48. The purposive activity and movement of consciousness is simply a philosophic mode of translating from the night of the absolute some universal claim of existence and does not address *the* issue of existence, namely, black existence: alienation and suffering. The sundering

of the "self" of consciousness in philosophic speak offers us nothing other than the self of an anti-black racist *culture* (that is, the white "self" dialectically building and being built within the *lebenswelt* of Western modernity), and thus does not aid Wright in his analysis of his own suffering, and the suffering of "many thousand gone" lost within the cycle of history or the unfolding of Spirit, nor with his reconciliation of the weight of his own suffering—the history of his black body and that slow crushing, a stone slab on the chest of racialized ontological sundering. If one remains unconvinced of the danger of philosophic dialectical thinking for black modern subjects, one need only to gaze at Jean-Paul Sartre's essay "Black Orpheus" (1948) to see what happens with blackness when affected within dialectics of revolution: blackness is washed away for the larger project of the "human" without adequately losing itself "in the night of the absolute," the only condition for consciousness of self, as Fanon would go on to write (1967; 133). Thus, the negative moment of consciousness, the night of the absolute, for the black modern subject is not an externalization that returns into the self as *self*-consciousness, but a condition where one is driven out of oneself only to "return" when the self is no longer black, a condition that can never lead to *self*-consciousness, rather an unhappy consciousness (which is but a racial stoicism). It is no wonder Fanon was a fan of Wright's Bigger Thomas (139) and *12 Million Black Voices* (222).

49.   Phenomenology offers Wright an absurd victory, an absurd freedom. "What I know, what is certain, what I cannot deny, what I cannot reject—this is what counts. I can negate everything of that part of me that lives on vague nostalgias, except this desire for unity, this longing to solve, this need for clarity and cohesion. I can refute everything in this world surrounding me that offends or enraptures me, except this chaos, this sovereign chance and this divine equivalence which springs from anarchy . . . And these two certainties—my appetite for the absolute and for unity and the impossibility of reducing this world to a rational and reasonable principle—I also know I cannot reconcile them" (Albert Camus, "Absurd Freedom," in *The Myth of Sisyphus and Other Essays* [New York: Vintage International, 1983], 51). What, then, is left for Wright called forth as an absolute nothing (as black) but "to tell, to march, to fight," and what does this bring to Wright? In a word: clarity. All we can ask for, Wright discovered, is clarity. And, this is what Wright sought: the reasons for the things, not necessarily their solutions, but a clear and sober articulation.

50.   Richard Wright, *Black Boy*, 285.

51.   A worthwhile example of this occurs in Wright's short story "The Ethics of Living Jim Crow," which appeared, in an extended version in *Black Boy*, but was also published in his collection of short stories, *Uncle Tom's Children*. In the story Wright is confronted with his own desire to serve in combat against white people and, at the same time, must face the reality that this sort of combat could result in his very death. In a scene from the story Wright recounts how he has suffered injury from fighting with the white boys from across the train tracks, and coming home expecting to be nursed and congratulated by his mother for his heroic action. What he is confronted with is an education of growing up Jim Crow. He writes of their exchange, "I never fully realized the appalling disadvantages of a cinder environment till one day the gang to which I belonged found itself engaged in a war with the white boys who lived beyond the tracks . . . During the retreat a broken milk bottle caught me behind the ear, opening a deep gash which bled profusely . . . I sat brooding on my front steps, nursing my wound and waiting for my mother to come from work. I felt that a grave injustice had been done me . . . I raced down the street to meet her. I could just feel in my bones that she would understand. 'How come you didn't hide?' she asked me. 'How come yuh always fightin'?' I was outraged, and bawled . . . She grabbed a barrel stave, dragged me home, stripped me naked, and beat me till I had a fever of one hundred and two . . . She would . . . impart to me gems of Jim Crow wisdom" (247–48).

52.   Richard Wright, *Black Boy*, 30–31.

53.   Richard Wright, *Black Boy*, 31.

54.   Richard Wright, *Black Boy*, 83–84.

55.   Richard Wright, *Black Boy*, 85.

56. *Black Boy* can, in fact, be read as a chronicle of the repetition of rituals and the re-inscription of social practices from both white and black people. Wright tells us the experiences he suffers from whites constantly reaffirming their dominance through violence (literal and metaphorical) and from blacks reaffirming their powerlessness at the hands of whites.

57. Ralph Ellison, "Flying Home" (1944) reprinted in *Flying Home and Other Stories* (New York: Vintage Books, 1996), 173.

58. Richard Wright, Interview in *L'Express*, 1960.

59. Richard Wright, *Black Boy*, 81–83.

60. Richard Wright, *Black Boy*, 112.

61. Fyodor Dostoevsky, *The House of the Dead* (New York: Penguin Books, 1985). Wright notes, "I read Dostoevsky's *The House of the Dead*, an autobiographical novel depicting the lives of exiled prisoners in Siberia, how they lived in crowded barracks and vented their hostility upon one another. It made me remember how Negroes in the South, crowded into their Black Belts, vented their hostility upon one another, forgetting their lives were conditioned by the whites above them. To me reading was a kind of remembering" (Richard Wright, *"Black Boy* and Reading" in *The Lexington Reader*, ed. Lynn Bloom [Lexington, MA: D.C. Health, 1987], 101–2; reprinted in *Conversations with Richard Wright*, ed. Keneth Kinnamon and Michel Fabre [Oxford: University of Mississippi Press, 1993], 81–82).

Andre Malraux, *Man's Fate* (New York: Vintage Press, 1990). Wright wrote of Malraux's importance: "Already on the Left there are tendencies to frame the goal of writing in terms of a New Humanism, such as that which guides the work of Andre Malraux. It was Malraux who provided a framework in which the problem could be conceived in psychological terms. Malraux contended that men were most human when they were engaged in a conflict which called forth all their qualities of hope and courage; it was he who first introduced the highly intelligent and self-conscious character in revolutionary fiction" (Richard Wright, "Writing from the Left," *Biblio.*, 170 (74), Wright Misc. 812, 8, reprinted in *Richard Wright: Books and Writers*, ed. Michel Fabre [Oxford: University of Mississippi Press, 1990], 103).

H. L. Mencken, *A Book of Prefaces* (New York: Knopf, 1917). In *Black Boy* Wright mentions Mencken's text as "fighting with words . . . Yes, this man was fighting with words. He was using words as a weapon, using them as one would use a club" (272). This aspect of Mencken's work spoke to Wright who sought to overcome the "bewilderment and fear" that "made me mute and afraid" (Richard Wright, *"Black Boy* and Reading," 101) so that he, too, could use words to fight, create a new world.

It is important to note that Wright sought out and found in others companions to his own suffering. In these texts, among many, Wright found voices that, too, "suffered beneath the stars" (285). This desire for companionship followed Wright throughout his life and can be witnessed in his many affiliations, especially those that crossed racial and national borders.

62. Richard Wright, *Black Boy*, 112.

63. Richard Wright, *Black Boy*, 272.

64. Richard Wright, *Black Boy*, 274.

65. Richard Wright, *Black Boy*, 112.

66. Richard Wright, *Black Boy*, 272–73.

67. 70. Richard Wright, *L'Express*, 1960.

68. Ben Okri, "Living is a Fire," in *An African Elegy* (London: Johnathan Cape, 1992), 46–47.

69. It is in this way that *Black Boy* can be thought of as more than just Wright's own story, but a story of a *black* boy, who is also a black *boy*—both universal and particular—a narrative of growing up, or coming of age, for black persons, especially black boys in the South. In this sense, *Black Boy* is not just Wright's story, but the story of *all* black boys.

70. This is a reference to Wright's novella *Right of Passage* (New York: Harper Trophy, 1995) in which the lead character, Johnny, is pushed into a life of street subsistence after he feels himself rejected by normativity and society as a whole—he discovers he is adopted, a revelation that causes him to "run off." In the streets he joins a gang of black orphan boys who steal for their life and sustenance. Yet, Johnny does not want to steal for his sustenance. Rather, he wants a normative home of a mother and father, sister and brother (in fact, all the boys in the story want this, too), but having been "lied" to, he feels he must run off. Yet, he still yearns for

comfort, which he identifies with an old black woman in whose breasts he can bury his head and tears and be taken out of the street world (101–2). The character of "Johnny" can be seen as a metaphor for Wright's own feelings of abandonment and his inability to "run off" in *Black Boy*, and also Wright's own sociopolitical statement on black truancy and the perils of growing up black boy—the search for normativity and affection only to find rejection.

71. Franz Fanon, *Black Skin, White Masks*, 111; emphasis added.

72. An extrapolation of the Sartrean-borrowed Heideggerian phrase of anonymous emergence onto the plane of human existence. From nothing (the non-being of the not-yet existent) to existence (the being of human being) one comes forth, naked and empty into a world drawn up, carved out, participating in a world of meaning and production. Wright's extrapolation is that his emergence is less anonymous and accidental, and more of a force of history itself unfolding given his peculiar existence as black. Wright is not simply on the plane where there is only man; he is on a plane where there are only black men and white men, a different plane and place than Heidegger's existential Dasein or Sartre's man peeking into a keyhole. Wright's emergence is specious and marks, not the emergence of human consciousness, but a *Break* in human consciousness.

73. That is to say, the economic and concomitant political (or, is it vice versa?) realities of black life in America from chattel slavery to Jim Crow segregation to our contemporary post-raciality necessitated and continues to necessitate different family structures than those articulated, or theorized, in white communities—patriarchical structures, nuclear families, etc.—and necessitated by white norms. For Wright, this difference took on a more nuanced role in that the black community became for him something that was imposed upon individual persons thought of (by white people) as black and, thus, thrown together into community living. For Wright, the problem of the non-normative family and community became a distorted version of itself: his mother never took on the traditional mother role, his father was not the traditional father; the same can be said of his aunts and of his grandmother. For an explication of this in Wright, see Richard Wright, "Blueprint for Negro Writing," in *The Portable Harlem Renaissance Reader* (New York: Penguin Books, 1995), 194–205; and also, *12 Million Black Voices* (New York: Thunder Mouth Press, 2002), especially part 1, "Our Strange Birth," and part 4 "Men in the Making."

74. Richard Wright, *Black Boy*, 14.

75. Similarly, Ralph Ellison calls these sort of folk, those who are born of, yet outside of "history," men in transition, outside of the groove of temporality. Ellison writes of these men in *Invisible Man*, "What was I in relation to the boys, I wondered. Perhaps an accident, like [Frederick] Douglass. Perhaps each hundred years or so men like them, like me, appeared in society, drifting through, and yet by all historical logic, we, I, should have disappeared around the first part of the nineteenth century, *rationalized* out of existence. Perhaps like them, I was a throwback, a small distant meteorite that died several hundred years ago and now lived only by virtue of the light that speeds through space at too great a pace to realize that its source has become a piece of lead" (442). The same can be said of Wright, and those of whom Wright writes, especially in *12 Million Black Voices*.

76. Ralph Ellison, "Richard Wright's Blues," in *Shadow and Act*, 82.

77. Richard Wright, *Black Boy*, 81–83.

78. Ralph Ellison, "Richard Wright's Blues" in *Shadow and Act*, 94.

79. Albert Camus wrote the following to both understand and describe man's absurd condition: "By the sheer activity of consciousness, I transform into a rule of life what was once an invitation to death" (Albert Camus, *The Myth of Sisyphus and Other Essays*, 64).

80. Though it is true that the title is meant to reflect the historical fact that *boy* is meant to reflect a racist culture which deems all black men "boys," I think that phenomenologically considered, the "boy" of black boy also takes on an epistemological tone: it is a story told through the insights of youth, as a black boy comes of age learning what he has already seemed to know—was, as the old folks say, born knowing—about himself and society, and himself in society. Given this phenomenological take on the text, *Black Boy*, then, is *about* a boy, told *by* a boy, who is also a "boy." It is apropos to quote Claude McKay who wrote in his poem, "The Negro's Tragedy,"

So what I write is shot out of my blood.
There is no white man who could write my book
Though many think the story can be told
Of what the Negro people ought to brook.
Our statesmen roam the world to set things right.
This Negro laughs, and prays to God for Light! ("The Negro's Tragedy" ll. 9–14)

Chapter Three

Experiencing Existentialism through Theme and Tone

Kierkegaard and Richard Wright

Desirée H. Melton, College of Notre Dame of Maryland

> The Hero I can *think* myself *into* . . . but not Abraham.
> —Søren Kierkegaard, *Fear and Trembling*

Søren Kierkegaard's existentialism develops in response to, among others, G. W. F. Hegel's dialectical rationalism. Where Hegel thought that increasing clarity of concepts and categories would unfold under rational scrutiny, Kierkegaard asserts that human life is by nature ambiguous, and thus beyond the guise of rationalistic order. As such, he does not put much faith in reason to guide us practically. Rather, he focuses on moods and feelings—that is, states of being, such as anguish, despair, dread, and freedom—as markers of our ambiguous lived situation. These moods and feelings often surface as a sort of "fuzzy" unease, one that we cannot quite pinpoint or clearly articulate—and one that reason cannot help to explain away or give us tools to cope. Such is the concrete nature of the human condition.

Kierkegaard draws from many different methods to explain this new philosophy.[1] He uses parables and writes under pseudonyms in lyrical prose. He writes traditional philosophical theory as well but he seems to appreciate that non-traditional methods of theorizing suit existentialist philosophy best because it is concerned with concrete, subjective human lived existence not easily explained merely by abstract, philosophical theory alone. The most well-known existentialists who succeeded Kierkegaard also found literature (and literary technique) to be an invaluable medium of expression. Albert

Camus, Jean-Paul Sartre, and Simone de Beauvoir among others found that existential concerns like freedom, choice, despair, anguish, etc. lend themselves quite naturally to literary treatment because novels vividly convey these moods in a way that abstract theory cannot. Literature, though, is not always an effective means of presenting the human condition in a way that makes it accessible. How successful a work will be is largely a matter of its tone. Indeed, some literary works are widely considered existential precisely because they strike the right tone. Among some of the most well known (for their tone) are those of Dostoyevsky, Tolstoy, Chekhov, Ellison, Morrison, Baldwin, and Wright. I suggest that for a literary work (particularly fictional literature) to be existential it is not enough to draw on existential themes, it also must strike what I call "an existential tone."

Remarkably, existential writers and their critics have largely ignored the role of tone in existentialist literature. Instead, they have focused their attention on thematic content alone—to such an extent that the "existentialist hero" has turned into a cliché. In this essay, I draw due attention to the role of tone in existential literature and theorize its significance for communicating existential themes. To this end, I will analyze Johannes de Silentio's *Fear and Trembling* and Richard Wright's *Native Son* and *The Outsider*.

I begin with an analysis of *Fear and Trembling*; I show the importance of theme and tone in de Silentio's exploration of faith and resignation through the Old Testament story of Abraham and Isaac. Though *Fear and Trembling* does not take the form of a novel, its lyrical quality places it closer to literature than traditional philosophical theory. Its tone, as well as the concerns taken up, brings the reader closer to experiencing the existential moods and feelings de Silentio struggles to articulate. I suggest that an existentialist *tone* that captures and conveys the paradoxes of existence in a profound way allowing the reader to *experience* it is crucial to existentialist fiction.

I then turn to Wright's *Native Son* and *The Outsider*, specifically noting how the differences in tone make one novel existentialist and the other not. Fiction should reach the reader in some way, draw the reader in, and elicit a response. I suggest that this is no less true for existentialist fiction. It is perhaps more important given the kind of concerns existentialism takes up. The task of existential theory is to present existential notions. It does not have to affect the reader in any deep way, although of course, it can. Existential novels have a more significant task. They must take the reader *into* existential issues in such a way that lets the reader *experience* them because the existential issues are not static concepts; they are part of a lived experience and are best understood through feeling them.

EXISTENTIAL TONE IN *FEAR AND TREMBLING*

The Old Testament story of Abraham and Isaac is well known. After waiting for a son for many years, God blesses Abraham and his wife Sarah with a child when they are seventy years old. They treasure and adore Isaac. Then one day God commands Abraham to sacrifice his beloved son. Abraham is to pack a mule with enough provisions for several days and travel with his son to Mount Moriah where he is to kill him. Abraham never has to go through with this sacrifice, (though Abraham does not know this at the time) because as he is about to kill Isaac, an angel appears and offers a lamb for Abraham to sacrifice instead. The story is about faith; Abraham proved his faith in God by his willingness to follow God's command (against his own desires and without any understanding of the necessity of the action itself) and sacrifice his beloved son.

It is difficult to understand how a father can do what Abraham was prepared to do. Kierkegaard notes that it is far easier to "think" ourselves into the situation of a tragic hero like Brutus, for example, who must punish his child to fulfill his ethical obligation, than to understand Abraham. De Silentio writes,

> When a son forgets his duty, when the State entrusts the father with the sword of judgment, when the laws demand punishment at the father's hand, then it is with heroism that the father must forget that the guilty one is his son. Nobly will he hide his pain, but in the nation there will be not one, not even the son, who fails to admire the father. [2]

If Brutus fulfills his obligation we praise him for his courage to set aside his personal desires and do what is required of him for the good of the nation. Abraham's test is different, however. The state does not require him to sacrifice Isaac. There is no competing universal moral demand.

To appreciate why Abraham is the father of faith rather than just a tragic hero, one must intimately engage with Abraham's experience of faith as he lived it. One must consider what happened after God commanded Isaac's sacrifice. Abraham packed provisions to last through the journey; he gathered up his son; "He mounted the ass. He rode slowly down the path." One cannot fully understand what faith means for the individual by thinking about what it means to believe in God's love. De Silentio comes to know what faith is through imagining Abraham's experience, as Abraham must have experienced it. He writes, "If I myself were to talk about him I would first depict the pain of the trial. I would remind people that the journey lasted three days and well into the fourth; yes those three and a half days should be infinitely longer than the two thousand years separating me from Abraham."

De Silentio comes to see that faith in God requires an unintelligible belief in God's grace. Abraham's faith must enable him to believe that God would make it so that he would be with Isaac again in this life. Not that he will be reunited with Isaac again in eternity or that God will change his mind but that he will have Isaac again in *this* life. This is what faith requires—and de Silentio struggles to understand Abraham's faith through a passionate engagement with Abraham's situation. De Silentio ultimately concludes that he cannot.

> It is said to be hard to understand Hegel . . . but when I have to think about Abraham I am virtually annihilated. I am all the time aware of that monstrous paradox that is the content of Abraham's life, I am constantly repulsed, and my thought, for all its passion, is unable to enter into it, cannot come one hair-breadth further. I strain every muscle to catch sight of it, but the same instant I become paralyzed. [3]

The tone of *Fear and Trembling* is like a focused dialogue between de Silentio and Abraham, a committed attempt to understand another in his particularity. And one can *feel* de Silentio struggling to understand Abraham. His struggle to understand Abraham is even more important since Abraham "cannot speak." Abraham's inability to speak is twofold. First, Abraham cannot explain his absolute duty to the Absolute without resorting to the ethical because he has an absolute relation to the Absolute. Ethical language, though, fails him; and, as such Abraham cannot express his particularity in terms of ethical universals. Yet, ethical language is all he has so he must keep silent. Second, Abraham's faith cannot be expressed fully to another person because it is a state of being, a feeling, an experience. It is as challenging to explain faith as it is to explain love. Nevertheless, de Silentio tries to connect and understand Abraham's personal conflict the only way he can—through trying to understand the particulars of Abraham's individual situation, not through an abstract description of the notion of faith, but by getting inside Abraham's experience to understand faith as it is lived through Abraham the individual.

Kierkegaard and others have theorized utilizing existential concepts, yet because these concepts emerge *from* lived experience they, like the experience(s) they illuminate, are not static and are best understood through feeling them rather than explaining them within abstract theory. These existentialists must approach existential concepts in such a way that how they bear on a human life can be felt. This existential approach is quite different than that taken when explaining ethical concepts that appeal to universal morality, for example. We are able to explain how competing interests tear us apart and how difficult it is to be good; desires we do not think we should indulge, our misguided passions and inappropriate behavior easy enough because they can be understood in terms of and within our ethical concepts and in terms of our ethical language. However, something like faith is exceedingly difficult to express. It is more of a feeling or state of being than a definable concept or notion. Literature or literary techniques, like the lyrical prose of *Fear and Trembling*, is the approach that expresses existential notions in the way that lets us experience them. In experiencing them, we not only get a clearer sense of existential themes better than reading abstract theory, but we are also able to connect to the Other *in* their particularity.

THE OUTSIDER

> When learning how to make swimming movements, one can hang in a belt from the ceiling; one may be said to describe the movements all right but one isn't swimming.
>
> —Kierkegaard, *Fear and Trembling*

Richard Wright fails to strike a tone of intimate, experiential engagement with his character Cross Damon in his novel *The Outsider*. Wright follows Cross Damon through a series of events meant to show how out of place he feels. We find out that Damon is separated from his wife and they have three young sons. He wants a divorce but she refuses to give him one even when she finds out his underage mistress is pregnant with his child. Early in the novel, Damon is involved in a subway accident where a dead passenger is mistaken for him. He sees his chance to start anew, free from the responsibilities of his boring job, wife, children, mistress, and mother and takes it. From there, Damon leaves town, changes his name several times to keep up the charade, kills a coworker whom he happens upon in a dive motel, gets involved with communists, kills three of them, and indirectly causes the suicide of his lover before he is in turn killed. Wright focuses more on his protagonist's response to situations, rather than the situations themselves, making the novel a rather loosely connected chain of events in the life of Cross Damon.

Consider how Cross describes his initial attraction to Gladys:

> While holding her in his arms on the dance floor that desire for her leaped in him and it carried an extra urge to bind her to him and make her feel her humanity; he hungered for her as an image of woman as body of woman.[4]

And Cross with a hooker: "He was suddenly hungry for her; she was woman as body of woman."

Or Cross reflecting on the longing for understanding:

> Panic drapes the look of the world in strangeness, and the more one stares
> blankly at that world, the stranger it looks, the more hideously frightening it
> seems. There is then born in one a wild, hot wish to project out upon that alien
> world the world that one is seeking. This wish is a hunger for power, to be in
> command of one's self. [5]

The explicit development of traditional existential themes like dread, despair,
and death in *The Outsider* is a limitation, but not its foremost limitation. The
narrator's explicit description of Cross Damon's particular situation dooms
the novel far more than the "clump[y]" themes that give it a choppy feel. His
emotional clarity just does not ring true.

> His sense of despair deepened and he yearned for the first time to be free of
> this circling, brooding that filled his skull, this elusive shadow of himself that
> tortured him. . . .
>
>   His mood of self-loathing, a mood that had been his longer than he could
> recall, a mood that had been growing deeper with the increasing complexity of
> the events of his life. He knew himself too well not to realize the meaning of
> what he was feeling; yet his self-knowledge born of a habit of incessant reflec-
> tion, did not enable him to escape the morass in which his feelings were
> bogged. His insight merely augmented his emotional conflicts. [6]

But how much insight does Cross Damon have? Like faith, true self-hatred,
despair, and dread are difficult to articulate. Moreover, any actions one takes
while in one of these emotional states often escapes awareness. In C. Stephen
Evans's understanding, "Kierkegaard thinks that human beings hardly ever
make choices with full consciousness of what they are doing. Lack of clarity
about what one is doing is the rule, not the exception, in the Kierkegaardian
picture of the personality." The narrator, however, clearly explains Cross's
sense of dread and despair through self-reflection and is fully aware of the
reasons behind the awful actions he takes. The language is existential but it
lacks an existential tone.

An existential tone is what primarily contributes to our understanding of
Abraham, however. If Abraham is not properly understood, one could find
his willingness to kill his son deplorable. As de Silentio points out, "The
ethical expression for what Abraham did is that he was willing to murder
Isaac; the religious expression is that he was willing to sacrifice Isaac."
Abraham could not speak because he did not have the language to explain
himself. How could he explain that God commanded him to sacrifice Isaac in
faith to Him after he waited a lifetime for him? How could he explain that he
had faith that God would return Isaac to him in this life? To understand the
full meaning of the religious expression, one has to experience God's command as Abraham experienced it. De Silentio's tone—his manner of engagement—demonstrates that he does.

Unlike the dialogue between de Silentio and Abraham that creates an intimate tone, the dialogue between the reader and the narrator in *The Outsider* sets a rather detached tone. The reader cannot experience Cross's crisis because the narrator merely employs existential terminology to describe Cross's situation rather than inviting us into Cross's life so we can experience it. The reader is given no means to begin to understand Cross's particularity. As a result we do not feel how torn Cross is by his desire for both freedom and human connection, thus, we cannot get a real sense of his dread or despair. The reader fails to connect with him because the tone of the novel does not allow or enable such a connection. I do not think it is the case that the reader feels distanced from Cross because he is unpleasant—although he is. The distance from Cross is a result of the reader's inability to experience the character all together; the non-existentialist tone of the novel—despite the explicit existentialist terminology—simply does not allow us to.

NATIVE SON

> That sorrow can make one demented may be granted and is hard enough; that there is a strength of will that hauls close enough to the wind to save the understanding, even if the strain turns one slightly odd, that too may be granted.
>
> —Kierkegaard, *Fear and Trembling*

Wright's second novel tells the story of Bigger Thomas, a poor twenty-year-old man living in a Chicago tenement with his mother and younger siblings. The novel opens as Bigger and his family are just beginning what seems to be another miserable day. After Bigger kills a large rat that has managed to evade capture for some time, he leaves the house in a huff, annoyed by his mother's constant nagging. She wants him to stop hanging out with his hoodlum friends and get a job to support the family. Eventually Bigger takes a job as a chauffer to a rich white family headed by Mr. Dalton, a philanthropist who gives to black schools and supports black education. Bigger, in fact, is to replace a black driver who left Dalton's employ only after getting an education and a government job. One of Bigger's first assignments is to take Mr. Dalton's college-age daughter, Mary, to a university lecture. Instead of attending the lecture, however, Mary arranges for a furtive meeting with her boyfriend, Jan. Jan tries to win Bigger's confidence quickly, telling him his interest as a communist in helping blacks gain freedom. He then suggests they all have dinner at a soul-food restaurant in Bigger's neighborhood. They all drink heavily through the meal and Mary passes out. At Jan's insistence, Bigger drops off Jan, leaving Bigger to carry Mary into the house late at night on his own. He places her on her bed moments before her blind mother enters the room. A black man in a young, drunken white girl's room, Bigger is afraid Mary will give his presence away with her mumblings; he covers her face with a pillow only to discover that he has killed her. He decides to dispose of the body by cutting her into pieces and burning the remains in the furnace. An investigation begins into Mary's disappearance and Bigger is standing by when the police find bits of bone and Mary's earring in the furnace. Scared, he gives himself away by taking off. Later, after his girl-friend, Bessie, figures out what he has done and is reluctant to escape with him, he rapes her. Moments later, when she is sound asleep in the abandoned building where they are hiding out, he bludgeons her to death with a brick and disposes of her by throwing her down a freezing elevator shaft. Bessie eventually dies of her wounds and exposure. Bigger is sentenced to death for Mary's murder and dies by electric chair.

Cornel West sees Bigger's actions as a result of self-destructive behavior brought about by the white hatred that surrounds and ultimately consumes him. The effect of white supremacy on Bigger is the "psychic terror and physical violence" meted out against Bessie and Mary. Bigger feels a strong hatred for whites because of the limited way he is forced to live his life while whites enjoy many freedoms he can only dream of. I would go further, however, and suggest that Bigger is in despair, *revealed* through his self-hatred in response to white supremacy. Wright never uses the word "despair" but Bigger's existential struggle is apparent nonetheless. Bigger does not concretely articulate his despair either—because, like Abraham he cannot, for he lacks the language (and his own language has failed him)—but he gestures toward it in recognizable ways: in Bigger's search for an escape, some distraction from his miserable life.

> Bigger felt an urgent need to hide his growing and deepening feeling of hyster-ia; he had to get rid of it or else he would succumb to it. He longed for a stimulus powerful enough to focus his attention and drain off his energies. He wanted to run. Or listen to some swing music. Or laugh or joke. Or read a *Real Detective Story Magazine*. Or go to a movie. Or visit Bessie. [7]

After he kills Bessie he tries to understand what drives him to do it, but finds that despite his attempts, his condition is unintelligible even to himself.

> But what was he after? What did he want? What did he love and what did he hate? He did not know. There was something he knew and something he felt; something the world gave him and something he himself had; something spread out in front of him and something spread out in back; and never in all his life, with this black skin of his, had the two worlds, thought and feeling, will and mind, aspiration and satisfaction, been together; never had he felt a sense of wholeness. [8]

By anyone's account Bigger is a deplorable character, but he is also a sympathetic character, primarily because of the way Wright presents him to the reader. The reader senses Wright's engagement with Bigger Thomas as a character in conflict. Bigger, like Abraham, is affected by a *force* that is difficult for him to articulate. Abraham is under the power of faith and Bigger is crushed by despair over oppression and discrimination. And like de Silentio in *Fear and Trembling*, Wright enables us to come close to experiencing Bigger's particular predicament as he experienced it. Wright does not tell us Bigger is in despair but we feel it.

> "Goddammit!"
> "What's the matter?"
> "They don't let us do *nothing.*"
> "Who?"
> "The *white* folks."
> "You talk like you just now finding that out," Gus said.
> "Naw. But I just can't get used to it," Bigger said. "I swear to God I can't. I know I oughtn't think about it, but I can't help it. Every time I think about it I feel like somebody's poking a red-hot iron down my throat. Goddammit, look! We live here and they live there. We black and they white. They got things and we ain't. They do things and we can't. It's just like living in jail. Half the time I feel like I'm on the outside of the world peeping in through a knot-hole in the fence."[9]

We can feel Bigger Thomas's experience as a young black man living under oppression in a miserable tenement with a new job that makes him feel more powerless than before because Wright describes Bigger in a way that lets us step into his life and experience it. Bigger's inability to speak—to pinpoint and articulate exactly what is bothering him—makes him genuine. How can he clearly explain what it is like to live with near constant humiliation? How can he explain that rather than feeling doomed to freedom he aches to be free but has no sense of what freedom will mean for him? Wright captures Bigger in his particularity and takes us through his experience without resorting to the distracting existentialist terminology that contributes to *The Outsider*'s artificial feel.

I am not suggesting, however, that Bigger Thomas is akin to Abraham. Abraham is the father of faith. Bigger is not. There are similarities, though, in Kierkegaard's and Wright's approaches toward their subjects. Johannes de Silentio passionately tries to understand Abraham in his particularity and Wright develops Bigger Thomas in such a way that his reader tries to understand him in his particularity. Bigger's inability to convey his despair is similar to Abraham's inability to speak about his faith in God. Abraham did not have the language that could convey his relationship to the Absolute because it is above the ethical and the ethical is the only language he has. I suggest that Abraham is silent also because of his inability to explain how faith feels. He cannot explain his total belief in God because the feeling cannot be put into words, ethical or otherwise. Bigger is also at a loss for words. He cannot pinpoint the despair he feels under oppression. Living under oppression gives him a general sense of unease that he finds difficult to sort through and convey. The best he can do is to express a hazy anxiety that the reader still manages to recognize. Like a real-life individual troubled by the alienation he experiences simply because he exists, compounded by the alienation he experiences as a victim of oppression, Bigger finds it difficult to give voice to exactly what is bothering him. Nevertheless, Wright does not let him convey his unease in abstract terms like "alienation," "despair," and "anguish." He rather describes Bigger's unease by letting Bigger tell us how alienation, despair, and anguish *feel*, and this is what makes him a believable existentialist character.

There is a well-established tradition of existentialist fiction that asks us to identify with the experiences of characters rather than presenting existentialist notions couched in stilted existentialist language. Existentialism is visceral, embodied, and living. We feel Sethe's pain at the prospect of her daughter facing a life of slavery in Toni Morrison's *Beloved*. We feel the Underground Man's alienation in Dostoyevsky's *Notes from Underground*. We feel Ivan's despair at the inevitability of death and the absurdity of trying to make sense of one's life in Tolstoy's *The Death of Ivan Ilyich*. These works are existential because they vividly and honestly illustrate existential notions through creating fictional characters with concerns that readers recognize and invite the reader to *experience* them.

CONCLUSION

> We do not choose [our] caretakers and therefore do not choose the fundamental influences that mold our lives. We inherit personality traits, abilities, and defects, opportunities and deprivations that largely make our lives what they are, and our capacity for altering any of those capacities and traits is very limited.
>
> —Richard Schmitt, *Alienation and Freedom*

As Schmitt seems to suggest, there are elements of our situation that are no doubt ours, yet somehow not within our direct control: we are born into families, nations, genders, and races—that is, whole matrices of social and historical positioning—not of our own choosing; and, existentially speaking, we often have to make decisions without any practical guidance of what we should decide and without foreknowledge of how our decisions will turn out. And, though we prize our freedom, we dread it at the same time because we know that with the freedom to choose comes responsibility for the choices we make—even if we are not directly responsible for the conditions out of which we have to choose. Still, decisions are a part of life and we must make them. Freedom and the responsibility we bear for our freedom results in anxiety, dread, despair, and anguish.

These traditional existentialist themes are very difficult to theorize. They have been, though, through the works of Sartre, Beauvoir, Nietzsche, and Kierkegaard. But abstract theory alone is inferior to the experience of these conditions, which do not reside in a textbook; rather, they are lived and experienced by actual humans and come to constitute what it means to be human. Kierkegaard understood, perhaps better than any other existentialist philosopher, that to fully understand notions like faith or anguish one must get inside the experience of the person who is going through it.

In *Fear and Trembling*, de Silentio sets out to understand Abraham, the Other, in his particular situation with the Absolute. He wants to appreciate his personal crisis in a way that labels like "Father of Faith" fail to capture. To appreciate and begin to understand Abraham's struggle and the measure of faith involved in his willingness to sacrifice Isaac, Kierkegaard intimately engages with Abraham's encounter with the Absolute as *Abraham experiences* it, giving his work an existential tone. There is no other way to fully capture Abraham's trial other than trying to step into it and feel it as Abraham does.

The Outsider is widely regarded as a work of existential literature. On the surface, it seems to fill all the requirements of existentialist literature: the protagonist feels isolated from society as he is torn by his desire to have both freedom and deep human relationships. Wright adopts the appropriate terminology, giving his chapters titles like "Dream," "Dread," and "Despair." The tone of the novel, however, is not existential. In contrast, Wright did not intend his most well-known novel, *Native Son*, to be an existential novel; nevertheless, I suggest that the theme and tone make it far more existential than *The Outsider*. It invites the reader into Bigger Thomas's lived experience. The reader comes to not only understand traditional existential concerns but also what despair is like *for Bigger*, what anguish is like for him, such that we appreciate his subjective existential crisis and even empathize with him despite the awful things he does—much like we excuse Abraham for the awful thing he is willing to do. In *Native Son*, Wright leaves the "concept" of despair, anguish, dread, etc., aside and focuses on how those conditions are actually lived by the human who experiences them. In doing so, he carries on the spirit of Kierkegaardian existentialism.

NOTES

1. Existentialism was coined many years after Kierkegaard's death. It is only in retrospect that he is regarded as the first existentialist.

2. Soren Kierkegaard, *Fear and Trembling*, ed. Howard V. Hong and Edna H. Hong (Princeton, NJ: Princeton University Press, 1983), 87.

3. Soren Kierkegaard, *Fear and Trembling*, 63.

4. Richard Wright, *Native Son* (New York: Mileston Editions, 1940), 66.

5. Richard Wright, *Native Son*, 196.

6. Richard Wright, *The Outsider* (New York: Harper Perennial Modern Classics, 1953), 21, 318.

7. Richard Wright, *Native Son* (New York: Harper Perennial, 2003), 31.

8. Richard Wright, *Native Son*, 225.

9. Richard Wright, *Native Son*, 23.

Part II

Richard Wright's Philosophical Imagination

Chapter Four

Fear, Trembling, and Transcendence in the Everyday of Richard Wright

A Quare *Reading*

Victor Anderson, Vanderbilt University

Quare Etymology (with apologies to Alice Walker)

> *Quare* (kwár), n. 1. Meaning queer; also opp. of straight; odd or slightly off-kilter; from the African American vernacular for queer; sometimes homophobic in usage, but always denotes excess incapable of being contained within conventional categories of being; curiously equivalent to the Anglo-Irish (and sometimes "Black" Irish) variant of queer, as in Brendan Behan's famous play *The Quare Fellow*.
> —adj. 2. A lesbian, gay, bisexual, or transgendered person of color who loves other men or women, sexually and/or nonsexually, and appreciates black culture and community.
> —n. 3. One who *thinks* and *feels* and *acts* (and sometimes, "acts up"); committed to struggle against all forms of oppression—racial, sexual, gender, class, religious, etc.
> —n. 4. One for whom sexual and gender identities always already intersect with racial subjectivity.
> 5. Quare is to queer as "reading" is to "throwing shade."
>
> (E. Patrick Johnson, 2006, 125)

READING WRIGHT

Hong and Hong begin their translation of Søren Kierkegaard's *Fear and Trembling* and *Repetition* with this astute observation from his *Two Ages* (1846), namely, that these texts "exemplify Kierkegaard's view of the optimal relation between a writer's experience and his writings."[1] They quote Kierkegaard:

> The law manifest in poetic production is identical, on a smaller scale, with the law for the life of every person in social intercourse and education. Anyone who experiences anything primitively also experiences in ideality the possibilities of the same thing and the possibilities of the opposite. These possibilities are his legitimate literary property. His own personal actuality, however, is not. His speaking and his producing are, in fact, born of silence. The ideal perfection of what he says and what he produces will correspond to his silence, and the supreme mark of that silence will be that the ideality contains the qualitatively opposite possibility.[2]

So it is with Wright. Experience and silence mark off the *biopoetics* (the concept of which I take up later) of a life burdened by the repetition of fear and trembling, of hunger and dread, and of unquenchable loathing of self and of community. His is a silence that marks him a *quare kid* within his own racialized community of southern blacks, who are themselves signified by and signifying on the *talkativeness* of the everyday. "Having grown taller and older, I now associated with older boys, and I had to pay for my admittance into their company by subscribing to certain racial sentiments," says Wright, continuing, "The touchstone of fraternity was my feeling toward white people, how much hostility I held toward them, what degree of value and honor I assigned to race. None of this was premeditated, but sprang spontaneously out of the talk of black boys who met at the crossroads."[3]

In this speech situation, Wright bargains his own sense of individuality to gatekeepers of black acceptance, black boys, the loitering gang, demanding for the price of acceptance, namely, the negation of silence. In Wright's biographical writings, silence does not denote mere shyness, although this trait is referenced by Wright throughout his biographical writings. Silence performs a critical posture. It signals a delay within signifying practices validating intersubjective normativity and rendering by simmering down "excess," which in the black vernacular—his *quareness*—is suspended in counter-memory and biopoetics.

Of an afternoon when school had let out I would saunter down the street, idly kicking an empty tin can, or knocking a stick against the palings of a wooden fence, or whistling, until I would stumble upon one or more of the gang loitering at a corner, standing in a field, or sitting upon the steps of somebody's house.

"Hey." Timidly.

"Your eat yet? Uneasily trying to make conversation.

"Yeah, man, I done really fed my face." Casually.

"I had cabbage and potatoes." Confidently.

"I had buttermilk and black-eyed peas." Meekly informational.

"Hell, I ain't gonna stand near you, nigger!" Pronouncement.

"How come?" Feigned ignorance.

"Cause you gonna smell up this air in a minute!" A shouted accusation.

Laughter runs through the crowd.[4]

In the back and forth between interlocutors, silence, timidity, meekness, feigned ignorance give way to jest, or boy talk about farting, which is a subject among boys that is always ripe for a joke, that doubly signifies the everydayness of race consciousness in Wright's *Black Boy.*

"Nigger, your mind's in a ditch." Amusingly moralistic.

"Ditch nothing! Nigger, you going to break wind any minute now!" Triumphant pronouncement creating suspense.

"Yeah, when them black-eyed peas tell that buttermilk to move over, that buttermilk ain't gonna wanna move and there's gonna be war in your guts and your stomach's gonna swell up and bust!"

Climax.

The crowd laughs loud and long.[5]

The normal play of signifying jest establishes a field of mutuality, of reciprocity among interlocutors, opening each to the free play of fantasying and projection, against which the white presence is transcended in imagined defeat of black over white.

"Man, them white folks oughta catch you and send you to the zoo and keep you for the next war!" Throwing the subject into a wider field.

"Then when that fighting starts, they oughta feed you on buttermilk and black-eyed peas and let you break wind!" The subject is accepted and extended.

"You'd win the war with a new kind of poison gas!" A shouted climax.

There is high laughter that simmers down slowly.

"Yeah maybe poison gas is something good to have." The subject of white folks is associationally swept into the orbit of talk.

"Yeah, if they hava race riot round here, I'm gonna kill all white folks with my poison." Bitter Pride.

Gleeful laughter. Then silence, each waiting for the other to contribute something.[6]

An early writer on Wright's corpus flags the manner in which silence recoils throughout biopoetic counter-memory operating and reconstructed by Wright. Robert Bone (1969) comments lead easily to a *quare* reading of the text as silence maneuvers to contain the excess of Wright's unconventional *quare* being:

> Wright's response to the straitened circumstances of his life was implacable rebellion. The more his society insisted on setting artificial bounds on his experience, the greater his compulsion to trespass, to taste forbidden fruit. The more his society conspired against his human weight and presence, the more determined he became to assert himself, to compel the recognition of his individuality. Hence, his urge to write, which was born of a fierce desire to affirm his own reality. What obsessed him was a fear of nothingness, of becoming in the end what the white South proclaimed him to be: a non-man. The linguistic equivalent of nothingness is silence. Throughout *Black Boy*, we can observe Wright's obsessive fear of speechlessness: "I was frightened speechless; I wanted to speak, but I could not move my tongue."[7]

Co-present in Wright's experience of captive subjectivity, over-determined as it is under the all purveying oppressive gaze of white supremacy, silence breaks through in the power of signifying humorous protest with the boys, throwing shade: "5. Quare is to queer as "reading" is to "throwing shade." However, the stultifying power of speechlessness does not only operate in relation to the white presence. As Wright knows all too well, it even operates in a feedback loop within his own racialized community. Wright describes this circulatory effect in his account of going to school in West Helena and being asked to write and spell his name on and at the blackboard. He knows his name and address, and he knows how to write, and spell. However, his quareness marks him indubitably as the subject of laughter, positioning him within the spectacle of a standup comedy that articulates him, in counter-memory, "the laughingstock of the classroom," as he stands, frozen by internalized silence produced by the spectator gazes of his black schoolmates "looking at my back." The excerpt below highlights the interlocking relation of the linguistic feedback loop, between the power of "speech and naming," on the one hand, and "speechlessness and laughter," on the other, circulating within the biopoetics of Wright's racially constructed identity.

> "Write your name," the teacher called to me.
>   I lifted the white chalk to the blackboard and, as I was about to write, my mind went black, empty; I could not remember my name, not even the first letter. Somebody giggled and I stiffened.
>   "Just forget about us and write your name and address," the teacher coaxed.
>   An impulse to write would flash through me, but my hand would refuse to move. The children began to twitter and I flushed hotly.

"Don't you know your name?" the teacher asked.

I looked at her and could not answer. The teacher rose and walked to my side, smiling at me to give me confidence. She placed her hand tenderly upon my shoulder.

"What's your name?" she asked.

"Richard," I whispered.

"Richard what?'

"Richard Wright."

"Spell it."

I spelled my name in a wild rush of letters, trying desperately to redeem my paralyzing shyness.

"Spell it slowly so I can hear it," she directed me.

I did.

"Now, can you write?"

"Yes, ma'am."

"Then write it"

Again I turned to the blackboard and lifted my hand to write, then I was blank and void within. I tried frantically to collect my senses, but I could remember nothing. A sense of the girls and boys behind me filled me to the exclusion of everything. I realized how utterly I was failing and I grew weak and leaned my hot forehead against the blackboard. The room burst into a loud and prolonged laugh and my muscles froze.

"You may go to your seat," the teacher said.[8]

In Wright's experience, this moment of being and nothingness, of fear and trembling, which is described by Bone, articulates Wright's *Black Boy*. After many years of reflexive musings, Wright's existential grasping of the non-resolvability of silence, naming, speech, and laughter are produced and re-produced in the temporal flow of Wright's memory, finding relief in Wright's counter-memory. Counter-memory, here, signifies the non-resolvability of the "passing" of the past into the "presentness" of the present, being re-presented by the counter-memory in Wright's *re-memberings*. The representational force of being and nothingness, silence and naming, of being frozen and sitting replicate by repetition in Wright's counter-memory.

This circuit of counter-memory moves throughout the solitary, no I should say, the silences afforded Wright in reading and writing, which are displays of transcendence in the everyday of Richard Wright, even as his hunger remains unquenchable. The hunger is sometimes physical; it is not a metaphor. It is real hunger, the kind that physically aches and makes one violently self-preoccupied with its satiation, even to the point of narcissism. Days and nights he sleeps with an under-fed belly, feeding on crumbs from whites folks' tables, hoping, as he watches them from the kitchen, that they will leave just a little meat on their plates for him to consume. Wright's hunger sediments, giving form to rage that waits to explode like buttermilk and black-eyed peas churning in the belly.

After his father abandons the family and his mother's social situation changes for the better from abject poverty, for the first time Wright can remember, there is plenty to eat. Still, in this possible ideality, its opposite actualizes in narcissistic hunger accompanied by rage, which will come to signify his entire relationship to the gate-keepers of black respectability, the black preacher and good church-going folk. On a particular Sunday, Wright's mother invites the "tall Black preacher" to dinner along with several neighbors. Wright remembers himself excited, and happy in anticipation of satisfying his everyday hunger by the consumption of golden-brown fried chicken at the center of the table, which appears to him boundless. He notes that as soon as the preacher arrived, "I began to resent him, for I learned at once that he, like my father was used to having his own way." It is time to eat, the table is set. He finds himself silently sitting "wedged at the table between talking and laughing adults." However, before he can satisfy his narcissistic hunger with the fried chicken, he must overcome the soup. Sized up by comparison of anticipated satisfaction with the bowl of soup, which pales compared to "the crispy chicken," the golden brown fried chicken wins-out.

> The others began to eat their soup, but I could not touch mine.
> "Eat your soup," my mother said.
> "I don't want any," I said.
> "You won't get anything else until you eat your soup," she said.
> The preacher had finished his soup and had asked that the platter of chicken be passed to him. It galled me. He smiled, cocked his head this way and that, picking out choice pieces. I forced a spoonful of soup down my throat and looked to see if my speed kept up with that of the preacher. It did not. I tried eating faster, but it was no use; other people were now serving themselves chicken and the platter was more than half empty. I gave up and sat staring in despair at the vanishing pieces of fried chicken. "Eat your soup or you won't get anything," my mother warned.
> I looked at her appealingly and could not answer. As piece after piece of chicken was eaten, I was unable to eat my soup at all. I grew hot with anger. The preacher was laughing and joking and the grownups were hanging on his words. My growing hate of the preacher finally became more important than God or religion and I could no longer contain myself. I leaped up from the table, knowing that I should be ashamed of what I was doing, but unable to stop, and screamed, running blindly from the room.
> "That preacher's going to eat all the chicken," I bawled.
> The preacher tossed back his head and roared with laughter, but my mother was angry and told me that I was to have no dinner because of my bad manners.[9]

The scene signifies Kierkegaard's dialectics of a possible ideality and its opposite in actuality. Paradox is not perhaps at issue here in Wright's *quare* counter-memory. Moreover, I do not think that the vignette's representational force concerns distributive justice or fairness. At least as far as justice is concerned, all have equal access to the same meal of soup and plenty of chicken. However, the story does highlight in Wright's *quare* counter-memory the tenuous connection between respectability and acceptance and nonconformity and exclusion. The relation appears an overlay on the circuit between silence and speech, discussed above, and the manner in which nonconformity, Wright's *quareness* as a *quare kid*, brings him under the discipline and punishment, exclusion from the table, of the black community's gate-keepers of respectability and cultural normativity. Here, *quare* behavior signifies "acting out" or "acting up" or even "reading and throwing shade." It falls under Johnson's *quare* connotation: "—n.3: One who *thinks* and *feels* and *acts* (and, sometimes, "acts up"); committed to struggle against all forms of oppression—racial, sexual, gender, class, religious, etc." Wright's *quare* behavior, in turn, brings him under the spectacle of the comedic at the table gate-keepers of black cultural normativity, good church folk, just as his *quare* behavior at the blackboard is punished by the signifying laughter of black children. *"The preacher tossed back his head and roared with laughter, but my mother was angry and told me that I was to have no dinner because of my bad manners."*[10]

Wright's *quareness* recoils in discipline and punishment. For his predecessors, conformity is a life-saving coping practice, which is preparatory for successful black cultural compliance to the expected norms of white domination. *Quare* behavior, failure to comply, is death dealing, marking the subject, by what literary critic Abdul R. JanMohamed describes as the "death-bound-subject." *"The death-bound-subject's life is thus defined by the need to avoid the possibilities of life as well as the possibility of death.* This is the aporetic zone occupied by bare life, a zone between the status of 'flesh' and that of 'meat,' neither quite alive nor quite dead"[11] Under the shadow of Wright's southern nights, acting *quare* results in beatings, exile, and the ultimate signification of the death-bound-subject: lynching.

Black gay literary critic and poet, Essex Hemphill describes, in his now-classic *Brother to Brother: New writings by Black Gay Men* (1991), this circuit between social conformity and *quare* behavior.

> I approached the swirling vortex of my adolescent sexuality as a wide-eyed scrawny teenager, intensely feeling the power of a budding sexual drive unchecked by any legitimate information at home or on the streets. I had nothing to guide me except the pointer of my early morning erection, but I was not inclined to run away from home to see where it would lead. I could not shame my family with behavior unbecoming to an eldest son. I had the responsibility of setting an example for my younger siblings, though I would have preferred an older brother to carry out that task, or a father to be at home.
>
> There would have been one less mask for me to create when long ago it became apparent that what I was or what I was becoming—in spite of myself—could be ridiculed, harassed, and even murdered with impunity. The

male code of the streets where I grew up made this very clear: sissies, punks, and faggots were not "cool" with the boys. Come out at your own risk was the prevailing code for boys like myself who knew we were different, but we did not dare challenge the prescribed norms regarding sexuality for fear of the consequence we would suffer. [12]

In the *quare* counter-memory of *Black Boy*, the reciprocating experience of violence and death, of fear and trembling in the everyday, are not without moments of transcendence that for instance the finite province of fantasy and projecting provides. Alfred Shutz and Thomas Luckmann describe its dynamics:

> Projection is Utopian: in a performance of the fantasying consciousness I envision a condition that has not yet occurred . . . What and how I fantasy is stamped by the past through overlayings of my lived experiences and encounters. I can fantasy something that I know with certainty (or assume with the utmost probability) will never happen (even if I wanted it to—and when I fantasy something, this is far from saying that I really want it to happen). Moreover, I can in fantasy anticipate something that I expressly do not want, but rather whose occurrence I fear. Unlike dreaming, the project of an act is characterized above all by my assumption at the moment of projection that the project will be realizable. [13]

Designating fantasying as a finite province of conscious life points out that as a projection of the conscious life, what is projected, enjoyed, played out, in what one loses oneself in and invites others into the fantasized world as intersubjective play of ideality, such a finite province of conscious life, as is fantasy and projection, is disrupted by the actuality of everyday time. Everyday time renders such fantasying moments of transcendence *momentary*.

> My fantasies, of course, had no objective value whatever. My spontaneous fantasies lived in my mind because I felt completely helpless in the face of this threat that might come upon me at any time, and because there did not exist to my knowledge any possible course of action which could have saved me if I had ever been confronted by a white mob. My fantasies were a moral bulwark that enabled me to feel I was keeping my emotional integrity whole, a support that enabled my personality to limp through days lived under the threat of violence. [14]

In Wright's counter-memory, fantasy is the "ideality" of a finite province of conscious life that is broken, precisely as Kierkegaard suggests, by its opposite within the "actuality" of living, of being alive, and of behaving *quare*.

> These fantasies were no longer a reflection of my reaction to the white people, they were a part of my living, of my emotional life; they were a culture, a creed, a religion. The hostility of the whites had become so deeply implanted

in my mind and feelings that it had lost direct connection with the daily environment in which I lived; and my reactions to this hostility fed upon itself, grew or diminished according to the news that reached me about the whites, according to what I aspired or hoped for. Tensions would set in at the mere mention of whites and a vast complex of emotions, involving the whole of my personality, would be aroused. It was as though I was continuously reacting to the threat of some natural force whose hostile behavior could not be predicted. I had never in my life been abused by whites, but I had already become as conditioned to their existence as though I had been the victim of a thousand lynchings. [15]

It would not be long, however, in the actuality of Wright's everyday that the possible ideality offered by fantasy would substantiate its opposite. Wright precariously finds himself the victim of white violence on a lonely road after making a delivery.

The story follows a particularly gruesome scene in which Wright takes a job as a porter for a clothing store selling cheap goods to blacks on credit. He describes the attitudes of the white owner, his son, and the clerk as contemptuous and brutal toward black patrons: "The boss, his son, and the clerk treated Negroes with open contempt, pushing, kicking, or slapping them," Wright says. Within his quare counter-memory, he asserts his inability to "get used to it." And disdain reciprocates between both the store owners and the patrons, whom he astonishingly asked himself as he recalls, "How can they accept it?" Wright himself is self-disciplined by silencing his feelings while internalizing "guilt and fear" as he labors under the surveillance of "the boss" who "suspected that I resented what I saw." While polishing brass outside the store, Wright sees the owner and his son dragging and kicking a black woman into the store. In silence, he continues his polishing. Suddenly he hears "shrill screams coming from the rear room of the store; later the woman stumbled out, bleeding, crying, and holding her stomach, her clothing torn." She is then carted off by a white policeman to jail under charges of public intoxication. Entering the rear of the store, Wright observes the boss and his son washing their hands, looking at him, laughing nervously. "The floor was bloody, strewn with wisps of hair and clothing," Wright recalls. Stunned, he is reassured by his boss that he has nothing to fear but as a lesson to him, he assures him, "Boy, that's what we do to niggers when they don't pay their bills." [16]

This scene of white violence exacted of a black woman is then juxtaposed to white violence on a black boy, himself. Within the episteme of white supremacy, all black bodies are "flesh"; all are "meat." Offered a cigarette by the boss's son, Wright recalls: "This was a gesture of kindness, indicating that, even if they had beaten the black woman, they would not beat me if I knew enough to keep my mouth shut." [17] However, Wright's failure to learn this white supremacist episteme, a signification of his *quareness*, subject-positions him precariously between the "feigned ignorance" displayed in the signifying jest of black boys talking "smack," or in *quare* vernacular, "throwing shade," and the deadly ignorance of having not acquired the life-saving practices of speaking and silence that Negro buffoonery performs in the white presence.

While he is returning from a drop-off in the suburbs on his bicycle, Wright's tire is punctured. He begins walking back to town on a hot dusty road, sweating and walking his bicycle by the handle bars. A car pulls up to him and slows next to him. The white driver asks, "What's the matter there, boy?" After Wright explains the problem, the driver offers him aid by suggesting that he "hop on the running board" of the vehicle, while holding his bicycle.

> "All set?"
>   "Yes, sir."
>   The car started. It was full of young white men. They were drinking. I watched the flask pass from mouth to mouth.
>   "Wanna drink boy?" one asked.
>   The memory of my six-year-old drinking came back and filled me with caution. But I laughed, the wind whipping my face.
>   "Oh, no!" I said.
>   The words were barely out of my mouth before I felt something hard and cold smash me between the eyes. It was an empty whisky bottle. I saw stars, and fell backwards from the speeding car into the dust of the road, my feet becoming entangled in the steel spokes of the bicycle. The car stopped and the white men piled out and stood over me.
>   "Nigger, ain't you learned no better sense'n that yet?" asked the man who hit me. "Ain't you learned to say *sir* to a white man yet?"[18]

In Wright's counter-memory, *quare* behavior performs on the precariousness of the everyday, circulating throughout the dysfunctions of a family's nomadic lifestyle, brutal beatings, fear and trembling. Its grotesquery circulates in intermitting schooling, endless physical hunger, the stinging laughter of a dead-beat father, the snickering of black school children, the gloating laugher of a cocky black preacher. *Quare* counter-memory as dangerous memory recoils in feigned or real ignorance, awkward speechlessness, and inhuman silence while internalizing disdain of white brutality on a helpless black woman. *Quare* counter-memory takes up into relief, Wright's non-compliance of black cultural life saving wit in the white presence. "'Nigger, ain't you learned no better sense'n that yet?' asked the man who hit me. 'Ain't you learned to say *sir* to a white man yet?'"

The *quareness* of Wright's biopoetics positions him within JanMohamed's aporetic tensions of the death-bound-subject. As in Wright's counter-memory, so in the counter-memory of many black same sex–same gender loving people, their *quare* idealities and fantasies of self-assertion, self-reclamation mark off for them transcendence in the everyday over the threat of violence and death and of being and nothingness accompanied with its opposites in the actuality of their lived experiences. *Quare*, as Johnson conceives it, operates as a trope playing on the performance of counter-memory, producing and reproducing dangerous and precarious memories of fear, trembling, and transcendence in the everyday of Richard Wright.

In Wright's *quare* counter-memory articulated in *Black Boy (American Hunger)*, the new heaven and a new earth, the heavenly vision of the North and the celestial city of Chicago provide the possible ideality of his enduring childhood and youthful fantasies. Fantasying this possible ideality becomes consuming and implosive over against the stark realism of southern violence, immanent death, and the all-pervasive threat of nothingness, which hovers as what is of Ultimate Concern, religiously determining and directing black bodies and black experience. Such conditions literally give "definition," as in texture, to the felt qualities of black fear, trembling, and hunger. As Shutz and Luckmann propose, in fantasying and projecting, fear, trembling, and hunger simultaneously form the background conditions to the sense of transcendence within the everyday absurdities of southern life. In the *quaring* of Wright's counter-memory, fantasy and projecting conspire in a formation of action, as in "gotta get out of here."

> I dreamed of going north and writing books, novels. The North symbolized to me all that I had not felt and seen; it had no relation whatever to what actually existed. Yet by imagining a place where everything was possible, it kept hope alive in me. But where had I got this notion of doing something in the future, of going away from home and accomplishing something that would be recognized by others? I had, of course, read my Horatio Alger stories, my pulp stories, and I knew my Get-Rich-Quick Wallingford series from cover to cover, though I had sense enough not to hope to get rich; even to my naïve imagination that possibility was too remote. I knew that I lived in a country in which the aspirations of black people were limited, marked-off. Yet I felt that I had to go somewhere and do something to redeem my being alive. [19]

Wright arrives in his New Jerusalem, but his *quare* imaginings are met with cynicism, distrust, suspicion, disappointment, alienation, and disillusionment with black heaven, Chicago's South-Side slums, the Relief Center, and the Communist Party. Each moment marks *Black Boy (American Hunger)*. However, as much as fear and trembling recoil at every stage of Wright's counter-memory and *quare* biopoetics, each moment is also almost always presented in Wright counter-memory with an unquenchable hunger for transcendence beyond limiting conditions of summer nights and while in Chicago, the bare necessities for a place to live, food, education, work, and sleep. Every page of *Black Boy (American Hunger)* turns on the ubiquity of unresolved fear, trembling, hunger, and futility all mixed up with the nagging sense and possibility of transcendence from and in the everyday. This indeterminate hunger is qualitatively different from the finite physical hunger of the everyday. It is a hunger satiated in reading, where in the *quaring* of Wright's counter-memory, "reading" is the clue to the satisfaction of a more basic hunger, writing, as in "Mama, I wants to be a writer, a poet." But write about what? This is an existential question that for Wright is always open to the future of actualized projections of action and being alive. As Kierkegaard warns, "The ideality contains the qualitatively opposite possibility." In the everyday of Richard Wright, the ur-experiences of fear, trembling, and hunger follow as unwelcomed company into the "actuality" of Wright's "ideality" of black heaven, Chicago's South Side. In Wright's new geopolitical situation, they perform the non-resolvability of horror and the glory.

READING *QUARE*

My *quare* reading of Wright's biopoetics is mostly interested in the unresolved determinacy of hunger (finitude) and hope (transcendence) as they recoil in the everyday actuality of Wright's "being alive." It is very tempting, although misguided, to take up these moments in Wright's biographical writings under sometimes too simple and reductive interpretative schemes, schemes such as a native son, self-hating and self-loathing Negro, misogamist peddler, leftist, communist intellectual, anti-communist existentialist, post-Freudian compilation of eight men, and death-bound-subject. My *quare* reading displays no interest in such reading practices. To what extent each of these reading schemes or types captures something significant about Wright, I am well content to leave to critics most at home in Wright Studies.

As for my own reading, no judgment is made of the course of Wright's journey, or of the family into which he is born, the community into which he was reared, the friends and enemies against which he measured himself, the teachers or bosses by which he was disciplined and punished, the women whom he greeted with affection and those he objectified; no judgment is made of his relation to fellow workers, black, white, or Jew against which he compared himself, whether in the labor market or in the Communist Party. All such moments are substantively embodied in Wright's *quare*, ambiguous life. Each moment is volleyed about, as it were, in the back and forth of the finitude of fear, trembling, and hunger, and the transcendence of hope, fantasying, projection of plans, and action. Each moment illumines throughout the biopoetics of Wright, the sense of life, the coming into being of his personality. They also highlight the sense of self-reclamation in the everyday of Richard Wright.

Biopoetics: My *quare* reading employs three symbols to capture the texture, that is, the *feel* of or *felt quality* of his biography. The operational symbols are biopoetics, counter-memory, and *quare, quaring, quareness*. I used biopoetics not in the interest of playing on "postmodern jargon" coined to render what is taken for granted obscure. Rather, I wanted a word that signifies the active, on-going, signifying processes of counter-memory in the production and reproduction of Wright's biographical writings. I wanted a word that creates empathetic understanding between me as a contemporary reader and Wright as a predecessor. Autobiography is miserably inadequate for this existentially, reflexive purpose. By framing my *quare* reading of Wright's biographical writings by the word *biopoetics*, I wanted a word that also flags the active impulses of cultural forces that contribute to Wright's counter-memory of childhood and youth, of southern nights and of the God that failed him in the New Jerusalem, the Communist Party.

The word *biopoetics* foregrounds formative moments in the production of Wright's biography, while holding back closure (as in "This is my life's story" or "This is the meaning of my life"), which all too often is signified by autobiography. This concern was also paramount to Wright's own ambivalent relationship to autobiography, according to one of his biographers, Constance Webb:

> Putting down a letter he had just read from his agent, Paul R. Reynolds, Jr., in early 1940, Richard was astonished, then alarmed and finally curious. Paul tentatively suggested that sometime in the future he should consider writing an autobiography . . . "Hey! Whoa! I'm only thirty-two! I've got a lot of years ahead before I'm ready to sum up the meaning of my existence" was Richard's initial reaction. A second emotion came crowding into his mind with a powerful urge to write and find out what was going on deep down inside but with it a warning that it was dangerous to probe into oneself too intensely . . . Richard was compelled to turn it over, back and forth in his mind. Perhaps he would write such a book when he had completed a third work of fiction, on which he was working. An inner distaste toward revealing in first person instead of through a fictitious character the dread and fear and anguish self-questioning of his life was a temporary dam and he preferred not to use the term autobiography.[20]

Counter-memory: Joined to biopoetics has been the symbol, "counter-memory." It stands in place of autobiography. Together, the biopoetics and counter-memory signify an interpretative loop or circuitry. Biopoetics signify an identity in becoming, highlighting the precarious and capricious cultural determinacy of life options in the making, the coming into being, of Richard Wright. Counter-memory signifies the ambiguous texture of Wright's biographical consciousness, the meaning structure of his conscious attention to the course of his beginnings and life journey. Counter-memory captures the messiness of black life in the United States, whether in the South or North. It recognizes that one's life is a work in progress. It is closed off neither by moments passed nor by the immediacy of moments now being experienced. Both the past and present, in reflexive understanding and re-membering, produced in Wright a counter-memory within the biopoetics of a life open to the future of what Kierkegaard proposed in the dialectics of possible ideal-ities and their possible opposites. Wright's biopoetics and its articulated counter-memory delay and resist interpretative moves that establish and set-tle the author's identity, whether of Wright or of another, by treating what is signified by autobiography, closing an account, reconciling, and settling a life lived and being lived in and through the everyday.

Quare: The hermeneutical moves which I have been describing are per-formed in my *quaring* of Wright's biographical writings. This is not to mark Wright with a queer identity, which is a hotly contested description when assigned to straight or same-sex–same-gender loving black writers or people. *Quare* does not stand in for an identity at all. As Johnson constructs it, it destabilizes identity in order to foreground difference, while articulating identities in their fluent, responsive, engaged, recoiling, messy, and "slightly off-kilter" displays. Johnson derives his *quare* episteme from its black cultu-ral and familiar vernacular roots. He explains:

> I remembered how "queer" is used in my family. My grandmother, for exam-ple, used it often when I was a child and still uses it today. When she says the word, she does so in a thick, black, southern dialect: "That sho is a 'quare' chile." Her use of queer is almost always nuanced . . . My grandmother uses "quare" to denote something or someone who is odd, irregular, or slightly off-kilter—definitions in keeping with traditional understanding and uses of "queer." On the other hand, she also employs "quare" to connote something excessive—something that might philosophically translate into an excess of discursive and epistemological meanings grounded in African American cultu-ral rituals and lived experience.[21]

My *quare* reading of the everyday of Richard Wright does not signify a fixed, stable identity. It highlights critical, interpretative moves, in the prac-tices of reading and writing, from an empathetic standpoint of a life in mo-tion and nomadic, as it were, questioning and shy, speaking and silenced, understood and forgotten, restless and "boundaryless." My *quare* reading of Wright's biopoetics and counter-memory screens-in the agency by which Wright takes ownership of his life. Wright overcomes, ambiguously, fear and trembling, dread and futility, and aching hungers by hope, fantasying, pro-jecting options, and other forms of transcendence of the everyday through African American cultural rituals and lived experience.

Robert Reid-Pharr's (2001) conception of boundarylessness articulates best the *quare* significations of Wright's biopoetics and counter-memory on which my reading depends—even if not made explicit. For Reid- Pharr, "restlessness" is too passive. "Boundarylessness" is active, moving, traveling. He says in his seminal essay on black queer theory, "Tearing the Goat's Flesh," that "I was receiving many more invitations to speak at queer events, to appear on queer panels, to comment on queer papers than to demonstrate my expertise in (Black) American literature and culture. Thus, as the saying goes, 'as all roads lead North, I head North.'"[22] From the South to the North, whether it is Wright or Reid-Pharr, geopolitical forces on race and identity enter into the biopoetic flow of time-consciousness articulated as counter-memory in biography. This boundarylessness between race and identity, being and belonging, or the "crossroads" as Wright describes the geopolitical location of his hanging out with the boys just talking, performs on the unresolvable play of significations between "nigger vs. negro," "black youth vs. black boy," "field hand vs. porter, dish washer, or street cleaner," "post-office clerk vs. artist, writer" and "party buffoon vs. humanist, intellectual." Reid-Pharr illuminates:

> My interest in queer theory, and indeed all the theoretical apparatuses from which I borrowed, stems not from an interest in producing positive images of black gays and lesbians. Instead, I am more concerned to mark the incredible slippage in meaning that necessarily accompanies even the most progressive articulations of modern identity. You say black gay, I hear nigger fag. "Tearing the Goat's Flesh" is best understood, then, not as evidence of a burgeoning black queer theory but instead as an effort on my part to affect the corrosion of the easy manner in which we talk about all identities, to demonstrate the funky, messy underside of the brave new world that some of us hope to fashion.
>   I argue in this work that the black gay stands in for the border crossing and boundarylessness that has so preoccupied contemporary Black American intellectuals in particular. I argue that black gay men represent in modern American literature the reality that there is no normal blackness, no normal masculinity to which the black subject, American or otherwise, might refer. [23]

Wright's *quare* biopoetics and counter-memory on childhood (*Black Boy*) and adult maturity (*American Hunger*) signify a boundarylessness that is as substantially complex as it is indeterminate. They bring into focus Wright's own ambiguous life: as a black boy, read a "dumb little nigger" refusing to sell his poodle for three cents short of a dollar (his asking price), although he is achingly hungry[24]; as a buffoon, read six-year-old drunken laughingstock of the saloon[25]; as a man of integrity, read whistle-blowing snitch "spilling the tea" on the cook for spitting in the restaurant's food[26]; as an avant-garde artist, read Uncle Tom writer or "a white man's nigger" conspiring with a Jewish director to provide black actors with black scripts purporting to reflect black realities. [27]

On my reading, the boundarylessness, which in the biopoetics and counter-memory of Wright's *quare* consciousness, recoils on a negro in America who can write, the American negro writer, the negro communist pamphleteer, the anticommunist negro, and the race-transcending negro humanist. The boundarylessness of Wright's biopoetics and counter-memory do not display the sense of a meandering, wandering, and aimless life. Rather, what is accented in Wright's *quare* boundarylessness is a nomadic existence, traversing geopolitical borders of race and identity. Still, *quaring* Wright's biopoetics and counter-memory reveals at every turn the tragic dialectic installed on them by Kierkegaard's dictum that every *possible ideality* invites its *possible opposite*.

To conclude, in *quaring* fear, trembling, and transcendence in the everyday of Richard Wright, I am most aware of myself as having also been "read." This recognition does not identify Wright's biopoetics and counter-memories with either mine or for that matter anyone else's biography. My *quare* reading aims to create a path toward empathetic understanding through the intersubjective textuality, the boundarylessness of the social life-world inhabited by Wright, which cross-pollinates in the intertextuality of the boundarylessness of race and identity that informs my contemporary *quare* existence.

> Although I frequently do the talking, you my dear reader (for you understand the interior psychic states and emotions, and that is why I call you "dear"), will nevertheless be reading about him on every page. You understand that variety of the transitions, and even if now and then you wonder a bit at suddenly getting a shower bath of moods, you nevertheless will subsequently realize how everything is variously adapted, the one mood to the other, so that the particular mood is fairly correct, which is a primary point here where the lyrical is so important. Sometimes you may be distracted by an apparently pointless witticism or an idle defiance, but later you perhaps will be reconciled to these things.
>
> Your devoted,
> Constantin Constantius. [28]

NOTES

1. Soren Kierkegaard, *Fear and Trembling, Repetition*, ed. Howard V. Hong and Edna H. Hong (Princeton, NJ: Princeton University Press, 1983).
2. Soren Kierkegaard, *Fear and Trembling*, ix.
3. Richard Wright, *Black Boy (American Hunger): A Record of Childhood and Youth* (New York: HarperCollins Publications, [1945] 1989), 78.

4. Richard Wright, *Black Boy (American Hunger): A Record of Childhood and Youth*, 78–79.

5. Richard Wright, *Black Boy (American Hunger): A Record of Childhood and Youth*, 79.

6. Richard Wright, *Black Boy (American Hunger): A Record of Childhood and Youth*, 79.

7. Robert Bone, *Richard Wright* (Minneapolis: University of Minnesota Press, 1969), 14–15.

8. Richard Wright, *Black Boy (American Hunger): A Record of Childhood and Youth*, 75–76.

9. Richard Wright, *Black Boy (American Hunger): A Record of Childhood and Youth*, 25–26.

10. Emphasis added.

11. Abdul R. JanMohamed, *The Death-Bound-Subject: Richard Wright's Archeology of Death* (Durham, NC: Duke University Press, 2005), 19; emphasis added.

12. Essex Hemphill, ed., *Brother to Brother: New Writings by Black Gay Men* (Boston: Alyson Publications, 1991), xv.

13. Alfred Shutz and Thomas Luckmann, *The Structures of the Life-World*, vol. 2 (Evanston, IL: Northwestern University Press, 1983), 22.

14. Richard Wright, *Black Boy (American Hunger): A Record of Childhood and Youth*, 74.

15. Richard Wright, *Black Boy (American Hunger): A Record of Childhood and Youth*, 74.

16. Richard Wright, *Black Boy (American Hunger): A Record of Childhood and Youth*, 180.

17. Richard Wright, *Black Boy (American Hunger): A Record of Childhood and Youth*, 180.

18. Richard Wright, *Black Boy (American Hunger): A Record of Childhood and Youth*, 181.

19. Richard Wright, *Black Boy (American Hunger): A Record of Childhood and Youth*, 168–69.

20. Constance Webb, *Richard Wright: A Biography* (New York: G. P. Putnam's Sons, 1968), 197–98.

21. E. Patrick Johnson and G. Mae Henderson, eds. *Black Queer Studies: A Critical Anthology* (Durham, NC: Duke University Press, 2005), 125–26.

22. Robert Reid-Pharr, *Black Gay Man: Essays* (New York: New York University Press, 2001), 101.

23. Robert Reid-Pharr, *Black Gay Man: Essays*, 103.

24. Richard Wright, *Black Boy (American Hunger): A Record of Childhood and Youth*, 68–71.

25. Richard Wright, *Black Boy (American Hunger): A Record of Childhood and Youth*, 20–21.

26. Richard Wright, *Black Boy (American Hunger): A Record of Childhood and Youth*, 273–77.

27. Richard Wright, *Black Boy (American Hunger): A Record of Childhood and Youth*, 364–66.

28. Søren Kierkegaard, *Fear and Trembling, Repetition*, 231.

Chapter Five

Specularity as a Mode of Knowledge and Agency in Richard Wright's Work

Abdul R. JanMohamed, University of California, Berkeley

In 1986, when David Lloyd and I organized a conference on "The Nature and Context of Minority Discourse" at the University of California, Berkeley, I commenced a debate with my late colleague, Barbara Christian, about the nature of "theory," more specifically about the differences between what is formally designated as (Western) "theory" in the academy and the theoretical content of African American and other "ethnic" literatures. She argued, in part, that

> people of color have always theorized—but in forms quite different from the Western form of abstract logic. And I am inclined to say that our theorizing (and I intentionally use the verb rather than the noun) is often in narrative forms, in the stories we create, in the riddles and proverbs, in the play with language, since dynamic rather than fixed ideas seem more to our liking . . . My folks, in other words, have always been a race for theory—though more in the form of the hieroglyph, a written figure which is both sensual and abstract, both beautiful and communicative. [1]

The debate between us was mostly about what constituted the definition of "theory" rather than about the deep, subtle, and profound understanding contained in African American literature about the effects of slavery, racialization, genderization, and the various modes through which these coercive formations could be best resisted, and so on. We both agreed that African American literature contained and articulated knowledge about the predicaments and experiences of oppression that far surpassed the knowledge about these matters contained in abstract "theoretical discourse" derived from

Western philosophy. While Barbara was content to use the term "theory" for the form of knowledge contained in "minority" literature, I felt, at that time, that the term "theory" ought to be limited to designate a mode of thought that was abstract, systematic, and that proceeded fundamentally via deduction. I felt that knowledge contained in figurative writing, i.e., in literature (which was quite the opposite of the abstract, systematic, and deductive), however superior it may be to that abstract, "theoretical" knowledge, ought to be designated by a different term or articulated via a different category of knowledge. I was content, for the time being, to call this knowledge contained in literature "wisdom" as opposed to "theory," without knowing quite what I meant by "wisdom," though it was clear to me even then that "wisdom" could be defined as a form of knowledge that is simultaneously "theoretical" and "practical" in that it not only adequately understands the phenomenon at stake but also includes a practical plan for actually coping with the sociopolitical dilemmas created by that phenomenon.

It is only now that I begin to understand that "wisdom" is a form of knowledge that, to use J. L. Austin's "theoretical" terminology, is simultaneously "constative" and "illocutionary."[2] It is constative in that, like "theory," it contains, or at least strives to contain, an accurate description and a supposedly "objective" understanding of the reality on which it focuses, and it is illocutionary in that it enjoins one to act in certain ways. The illocutionary function of this kind of knowledge can be mapped, as Frederic Jameson has done, in macro-theoretical terms; the function of all works of art, according to Jameson, being to provide imaginary resolutions for real social contradictions that cannot be resolved in actuality. Each literary or artistic text, according to this formulation, is a symbolic act.[3] But I would like to propose that this is also the case at the micro level: that what Barbara Christian calls the "hieroglyph," the figurative language being used to construct a narrative, can be an act of resolution; an attempt to formulate an accurate "constative" description of phenomenon or event can itself be a form of resolution, an illocutionary act. This is, at this point, still a relatively crude formulation, one in need of substantive elaboration and clarification. It is, however, a view that I am putting forward because I have been led here by my attempt to understand more fully Richard Wright's struggle to articulate his experience of Jim Crow society as accurately as possible and to overcome, through the process of accurate articulation, its determining power over his formation as a "black boy." If we treat Wright's work as at once theoretical and practical, constative and illocutionary, then we can map his philosophical contributions, his "theoretical" insights about racialization, etc., that are embedded within his fiction. Wright's philosophical views contained in his fiction are far more profound, it seems to me, than those articulated more explicitly in a theoretical vein. I would like to explore in this chapter some examples of

Wright's embedded theoretical insights, which, it must be emphasized, have to be excavated from the deep structures of his fictions and autobiographical texts.

An apposite example is provided by the revisions that Wright was forced to undertake at the behest of the Book of the Month Club, which published the first edition of his autobiography, *Black Boy*. The racialized prurience of the editors at the Book of the Month Club obliged Wright to make a series of revisions. Among the changes, there is a fascinating substitution of the threat of death for the threat of castration. In both the original and the Book of the Month versions the fundamental situation remains the same. Wright, having been given a chance by a benevolent owner of an optical factory to learn a trade, is eventually forced to resign from his apprentice position by his two southern white supervisors who threaten to kill him if he insists on acquiring any of the skills in the optical trade, skills that are considered the racial prerogatives of white people.[4] The final outcome or "resolution," that is, Wright's humiliation and resignation from his job, is identical in both versions. However, Wright was forced to revise one of the conversations/confrontations between him and his white supervisors that preceded the resignation. The revision replaces a conversation that symbolically castrates young Richard with one that threatens him with death.[5] And the enormous coercive power of the *threat* of death, rather than death itself, must be emphasized here: the threat, as a promise of violent action, lies precisely between two forms of coercion, between what Antonio Gramsci identifies as "dominance" and "hegemony"; as a verbal enunciation the threat belongs in the hegemonic realm of coercion and yet it promises coercion via (non-symbolic) violence if the victim does not submit to hegemonic coercion. For Gramsci hegemony is sufficiently sutured in place when the oppressed have internalized the values, practices, and most importantly the rules articulated by the oppressors.[6] In this context, oppressed individuals like Wright are obliged to incorporate the threat of death into the fundamental structures of their psyche. They have to police and contain their own desires and aspirations with their fear of dying. The threat of death is in this sense more fundamental than the threat of castration, though it must be remembered that in Jim Crow society the lynchings of black men were often preceded by literal castration.

In the original version the symbolic castration is articulated in the following conversation:

> "Richard, how long is your thing?" he asked me.
> "What thing?" I asked.
> "You know what I mean," he said. "The thing the bull uses on the cow."
> I turned away from him; I had heard that whites regarded Negroes as animals in sex matters and his words made me angry.

"I heard that a nigger can stick his prick in the ground and spin on it like a top," he said, chuckling. "I'd like to see you do that. I'd give you a dime if you did it." [7]

Under pressure from the editors at Book of the Month Club, Wright changes this conversation to the following:

"Nigger, you think you'll ever amount to anything?" he asked in a slow, sadistic voice.
     "I don't know, sir," I answered, turning my head away.
     "What do you niggers think about?" he asked.
     "I don't know, sir," I said, my head still averted.
     "If I was a nigger, I'd kill myself," he said.
     I said nothing. I was angry.
     "You don't know why?" he asked.
     I still said nothing.
     "But I don't reckon niggers mind being niggers," he said suddenly, and laughed. [8]

At first sight the revision seems incongruous; on the face of it there is neither a clear principle nor a specific form of equivalence between the two remarks (the castrating injunction to demean himself by [impossibly] demonstrating his super-masculinity, on the one hand, and the injunction to commit suicide, on the other hand) that would explain the unconscious logic that makes the substitution possible. On the constative register, that is, on the register that accurately and honestly describes the event and the conversation between Wright and the two white supervisors, the substitution is radically incongruous; it raises questions regarding the veracity of Wright's description of his life: it makes us question whether Wright is writing an autobiography, in which the dialogue cannot be altered so dramatically, or a work of fiction, in which such substitution would be entirely permissible. However, if we treat both dialogues as illocutionary, performative events and explore them as invitations or impositions of certain injunctions and identifications, then the underlying logic that defines their equivalence begins to emerge. The veracity of Wright's representation of his life experience consists in the structural isomorphism of two descriptions, that is, in the similarity of the illocutionary injunctions embedded in the dialogues.

     The underlying, illocutionary logic of the injunction in the first description, which endows Richard with a super-human prick, contradicts itself and puts Richard in a double bind. The contradiction consists of two moments that are virtually simultaneous. The first moment endows the black male with hyper-masculinity, just so that it can, in the second moment, be abbreviated, cut off, castrated by the very remark that endows the subject with hyper-masculinity. And this symbolic castration is enacted by putting Richard in a double bind. There are only two ways out of the predicament in which

Richard has been placed: either he can directly challenge the insulting, castrating remark, in which case he risks being killed (a very real danger from Wright's viewpoint and experience), or he can "refute" the castrating injunction by demonstrating the hyper-masculinity that he supposedly possesses, in which case he would succumb to a total debasing of himself. Whether he tries to fight with them, whether he tries to prove his masculinity, or whether he simply succumbs in silence to their insults, the end result is either his symbolic castration or his literal death. This injunction endows him with super-human powers only in order to demonstrate his immediate powerlessness; or, to put it the other way around, it enjoins him to demonstrate his power in a manner that would totally debase and negate his humanity.

The structural, illocutionary logic of the second version, which enjoins Richard to committee suicide, is fundamentally identical to that of the first one. However, because it is articulated as an unequivocal injunction, it further clarifies the underlying forms of subjection and identificatory investments involved in the process of racialized construction of the emasculated subject. In the first place the injunction implicitly invites a form of subjective identification ("If I was a nigger") between the powerful white subject and the powerless black object. This identification, like spinning on one's prick, is also an impossible feat in the Jim Crow context. The injunction also implies that the only form of agency that Richard can possess as a subject would constitute itself in the act of committing suicide; that the only way in which he can demonstrate his power as a subject is by killing himself. Thus it is being suggested to Richard that, rather like the anorexic, the only way in which he can demonstrate control over his own life is by ending that life. Once again, as with the sexual, castrating remark, he is being offered a form of power that can only result in his total disempowerment.

Thus the two versions of the same "event" have a common articulation of the fundamental component of the mode of "dis-empowerment" of black men in Jim Crow and slave societies. Both versions reveal that it is not sufficient for white society to render black men entirely "powerless." To be sure, in both cases Richard is being forced into silent acquiescence of his humiliation, and being subjected repeatedly to such acquiescence is a clear sign of his utter powerlessness. However, in both cases Richard is also being invited to "empower" himself: suicide empowers the subject to become the *agent* (in a context otherwise devoid of agency for that subject) of an action that ends his/her life. Suicide is always a profoundly illocutionary statement. Similarly, if Richard were able to show them that he could spin like a top on his prick, then he would be demonstrating super-human power; by spinning like that he would be "empowering" himself. But, of course, his "success" would totally dehumanize him and thus once again contribute to his powerlessness. In both cases, the implication is that the enslaved, black subject is allowed to possess power only if he will turn that power against himself to further debase or destroy himself. In Foucauldian terms one can say that the only form of power allowed for such a subject is that found in self-subjugation; subjectification is possible only through self-subjugation. Or to put it differently, this subject is enjoined, by the deployment of massive "external" violence, to turn all reactive violence against himself. Such a subject is trained, from a very early age, to internalize violence when faced with external aggression; he is trained not just to be acquiescent and compliant, but also to become an *active* agent of the external violence that is forming him.

Wright's fiction provides, among other things, a remarkable series of meditations about the psycho-political processes through which this internalization takes place as well as about the ways in which the repression or denial of the internalization of violence has to be forced to come to consciousness for the subject to be liberated. The meditations are in fact diegetic rehearsals or experiments designed to show how certain individuals behave under various oppressive conditions and to probe the structures and meanings of that behavior. As Wright says in the preface to *Native Son*, he consciously and deliberately sets up his fiction as an experimental laboratory, a space within which he can arrive at a better understanding of the nature and structure of various sociopolitical oppressive apparatuses:

> So, with this much knowledge of myself and the world gained and known, why should I not try to work out on paper the problem of what will happen to Bigger? Why should I not, like a scientist in a laboratory, use my imagination and invent test-tube situations, place Bigger in them, and, following the guidance of my own hopes and fears, what I had learned and remembered, work out in fictional form an emotional statement and resolution of this problem?[9]

I would like to emphasize several aspects of Wright's procedure. First, he clearly thinks of his fiction as a diegetic thought-experiment designed to acquire knowledge about how to "resolve" the aporetic contradictions that constitute individuals like himself (and his fictional avatar, Bigger) who grew up in Jim Crow society; the fundamental telos of Wright's fiction is epistemologically inflected. Second, in this thought experiment Wright's meditational or epistemological procedure consists of specular self-reflection, i.e., infusing Bigger (and his other characters) with his own emotional experiences and making them think and behave in various ways so that Wright himself can better understand their as well as his own subject formation. As he says elsewhere in that preface: "The extension of my sense of the personality of Bigger was the pivot of *my life*; it altered the complexion of *my existence*. I became conscious, at first dimly, and then later on with increasing clarity and conviction, of a vast, muddied pool of human life in America. It was as though *I* had put on a pair of spectacles whose power was that of an x-ray enabling me to see deeper into *the lives of men*."[10] Wright is clearly establishing a complex mirror relationship between himself and Bigger, one that may have been influenced by (and one that is certainly amenable to a fruitful analysis via) Jacques Lacan's theorization of the "mirror-stage" in general and more specifically via a dialectical exploration of two modes of identification entailed in the mirror relation, that between *constituting* identificatory subjectivity and *constituted* identificatory subjectivity. To gloss this briefly and roughly, one can say that the former is characterized by an identification with the subject of the gaze, who is an active agent of the process of seeing, while the latter is characterized by an identification with the object of the gaze, who "allows" himself to be passively formed by the telos of the gaze. This, as we will see later, overlaps in interesting ways with the Foucauldian notion that subjection consists of subjectification, on the one hand, and subjugation, on the other, and with Austin's differentiation between illocutionary and constative utterances.

These meditations on the process and effects of the internalization of violence are ubiquitous in Wright's work, and their specular structuration becomes progressively pronounced. It is instructive to juxtapose an early and a late version of Wright's specular meditational investigation in order to understand his epistemological project of coming to consciousness about the role of self-abjection in the formation of a racially oppressed subject.

Like the forced substitution of the passage in his autobiography, the earlier example, drawn from *Native Son*, is caught up in a dialectical oscillation between castration/rape and death. Early in the novel an episode in which Bigger beats up and humiliates his friend Gus demonstrates, I would like to suggest, that the symbolic rape of Mary and the subsequently literal rape of Bessie are preceded by this scene of homosocial rape/castration, which constitutes a powerful example of specular self-subjugation. Afraid to cross the racial border in order to rob Blum's store but equally afraid to show his fear, Bigger projects his fear onto his friend Gus and taunts him to decline participation in the robbery. If Gus declines, then Bigger can use it as a convenient excuse for aborting the plan. When Gus refuses to decline, Bigger picks a fight with him and in the process commits his first "rape." After kicking him in the rear, then tripping him when he tries to get up, Bigger finally mounts Gus with his knife open and ready to penetrate Gus's body. Instead of doing that, however, he forces Gus to lick the knife several times and then finally, in a mock ritual, pretends/threatens to cut out Gus's belly button.[11] The narration of this episode is compulsively insistent about the specular nature of this mock rape/castration. The narrative describes Bigger's projection of his fears onto Gus a total of six times within a span of three pages. It is worth citing one of these six instances because it connects in an uncanny fashion with the racist injunction about suicide ("If I was a nigger, I'd kill myself"). According to the narrative, Bigger "had transferred his fear of whites to Gus. He hated Gus because he knew that Gus was afraid, as even he was; and he feared Gus because he felt that Gus would consent and then he [Bigger] would be compelled to go through with the robbery. *Like a man about to shoot himself and dreading to shoot and yet knowing that he has to shoot and feeling it all at once and powerfully, he watched Gus and waited for him to say yes.*[12] Given the narrative insistence that Bigger's gun and knife are phallic symbols that he uses to compensate for his sense of castration, what Bigger does to Gus clearly amounts to symbolic castration and rape at once. And that castration/rape comes to be equated, as in *Black Boy*, to suicide.

What needs to be emphasized here is that because of the insistently specular nature of the relations between Bigger and Gus, what Bigger does to Gus, he does to himself. The implication thus is that Bigger rapes and castrates himself in order to prevent himself from crossing what appears to be a relatively mundane racial border. However, according to Wright's prefatory essay, this and all other racial borders are metonymically linked with the crossing of the "ultimate taboo," the rape of a white woman. Thus rather than violate this metonymically charged prohibition, Bigger is willing to castrate/ rape himself symbolically, an act which fully clarifies the nature of his cleaved subjectivity. His actions bifurcates his subjectivity in such a manner that one part of him collaborates with the racializing structure against the other part that is potentially rebellious. If we map this in terms of Bigger's agency, it becomes clear that in his capacity as the castrator of Gus, Bigger identifies with the white paternal subject-position, the constituting position of power from which he is seen as castrated and from which his castration is enforced and policed. However, as a castrated subject, he identifies with the pathetic figure of Gus, whom he has just constituted by beating, emasculating, and humiliating. Bigger thus occupies both positions: constituting and constituted identities. Furthermore, this diegetic exploration brilliantly clarifies that Bigger can empower himself only by *constituting* himself as the defeated, disempowered, *constituted* victim of his own actions. Bigger's subjectivity is deeply cleaved: on the one hand, he identifies with his castrators, with those who hold the power, on the other hand, he identifies with the castrated, with those already subjugated by the prevailing power. There are, it seems to me, at least two quite disturbing implications of this formation. To the extent that this entire specular episode is presented as a fight, it would seem that two halves of the oppressed are structured to remain in a perpetual war with each other. Second, such a subject is trained, through this perpetual war, to police the boundaries of his own subjectivity; he is granted agency only on the condition that he deploy it against his own desire for agency. Gramsci persuasively argues that "hegemony" is effectively constituted when the oppressed have internalized the assumptions, values, behaviors, practices, etc., of oppressors. And he adds that such hegemony is always attended by the threat of violent oppression if the hegemonic rules are disregarded. It would seem that through his diegetic "theorizing" Wright views it somewhat differently. What we can add to Gramsci's formulation, coming at it from Wright's explorations, is that the space between hegemony and violent dominance is sutured not just the oppressor's threat of violence. Rather, it is sutured predominantly by the habitual deployment of internalized violence; it would seem that hegemony authorizes the oppressed person to develop a form of agency that is trained to police and violently repress the oppressed subject. Hegemony trains the oppressed to use violence against themselves in order to contain or repress their own desire and aspirations.

Throughout his fiction Wright never stopped exploring the complex, labyrinthine structures that constitute self-subjugation or the unconscious collaboration of the subject in his/her own oppression. An example from his late fiction clearly demonstrates the evolution of Wright's understanding of this phenomenon. After exploring various permutations of such unconscious collaboration, Wright arrives, in his last published novel, *The Long Dream*, at a pristine formulation. While all the other explorations of self-subjugation are articulated via the interactions between various characters, the formulation in *The Long Dream* is stripped down to a single act and a single enunciation that distill the essence and structure of all other versions. Two young black boys get into an argument about their racial identities, and the argument quickly degenerates into a physical fight, which ends with each boy calling the other a "nigger" and threatening to lynch him. Utterly drained and dejected by this fight, Fishbelly, the young protagonist, broods over the incident quietly in isolation in his darkened bedroom. Eventually, the narrative tells us, he

> crossed to the dresser and snapped on the light and stared openmouthed at the reflection of his tear-stained black face in the mirror. He grimaced at that reflection, then sucked a volume of hot liquid from his saliva glands and spat, spattering the glass.
> "Nigger," he whispered in a voice that was like an escaping valve. [13]

Through his friend, Frantz Fanon, Wright may well have been aware of Lacan's description of how the subject is constituted in infancy by passing through the mirror stage. And if Wright was aware of that theory, he may well have been exploring how that stage functioned in a racialized society.

According to Lacan, when the young child, roughly between the age of one and two, sees and recognizes himself for the first time in a mirror he forms his initial imago or his ideal ego. For that young child who does not yet have a coherent sense of self, the image in the mirror provides the first complete experience of a coherent subject. Yet this is a paradoxical and aporetic moment; it is simultaneously a moment of self-recognition and self-alienation. It provides self-recognition to the extent that the mirror presents a complete image of the self. However, that image is also alienating to the extent that the "real" identity of the subject is thrown into deep structural ambiguity: is the "real" subject the one on this side of the mirror, the one who is putatively the constituting subject, or is it the one on the other side, the constituted subject who is "coherent" in contrast to the not yet fully coherent or sutured child on this side; is the imago or the ideal ego a capture of the subject such that the subject will always be chasing after its own perfect image? In Wright's rearticulation of this mirror-stage, he taints the mirror with racism; what happens, he seems to be asking, when the mirror held up to the child is racialized. In the first place it is obvious that imago of a racialized child is a totally negative one; it is the exact opposite of what an ideal ego ought to be. Second, and more disturbing, is the fact that that imago is captured entirely by the infinite negative attributes that are packed into that one self-identificatory utterance: "nigger." Third, the act of Fishbelly spitting at himself in the mirror is utterly horrifying because it simultaneously constitutes an act of projection and introjection. The constituting identity of the subject projects everything negative about itself onto the constituted identity of the subject; yet to the extent that Fishbelly is spitting at *himself* he is also the recipient of the projection; he is in effect introjecting all the negativity contained in the word and in the act of spitting. The act of spitting and calling himself a "nigger" is a powerfully specular act that binds and sutures Fishbelly in a state of total abjection; and he is both the agent and the victim of that act of bondage. Yet this act of self-constitution is not deemed entirely effective as long as the subject remains conscious about it. Consequently, the narrative later casually informs us that the next morning Fishbelly had totally forgotten this entire episode. In other words that episode and the act of self-abjection and self-subjugation has been quickly repressed into the unconscious, from where, like ballast in a ship, it will continue to exert a powerful influence on all of Fishbelly's future actions, conscious or unconscious.

Clearly Wright is deeply preoccupied with exploring and unearthing the role of specularity in the production of the oppressed, abjected subject. And to the extent that he is successful, he is able to generate penetrating knowledge regarding the negative role of specularity in the mechanism of the subject's forced obligation to constitute himself via abjecting himself. Yet horrifying as this revelation is, specular reflection is also an even more powerfully liberating modality of knowledge. For we must remember that the entire dyadic, "dialectical" relationship of self and the Other, from Hegel's mapping of the master-slave relationship to Lacan's mapping of the mirror-stage, is not in fact dyadic; it is always triadic. The observer—the philosopher, the writer, the analyst, etc.—always constitutes the third apparently invisible or unacknowledged member who is describing the dyad. Indeed, one can say that the relationship between the dyad, on the one hand, and the observer, on the other hand, itself constitutes a specular relationship. In the process of staging and observing the specular relation between self and Other, the observer or author is trying to gather knowledge about the ways in which the various positions of the actors might reflect his own options. The staging of the specular relation is itself a mirror for the author/observer. And in that capacity, specularity can generate knowledge that can liberate one from the capture by the specularity involved in the processes of racialization. While Wright does not pursue these connections "theoretically," he is perfectly well aware of them; indeed his career as a writer was profoundly motivated precisely by the challenge of generating potentially liberating knowledge from subjecting himself to specular reflection. When Wright is fleeing from the Deep South to Chicago, he is quite clear about his motives:

> I was leaving the South to fling myself into the unknown, to meet other situations that would perhaps elicit from me other responses. And if I could meet enough of a different life, then, perhaps, gradually and slowly I might learn who I was, what I might be. I was not leaving the South in order to forget the South, but so that some day I might understand it, might come to know what its rigors had done to me, to its children. I fled so that the numbness of my defensive living might thaw out and let me feel the pain—years later and far away—of what living in the South had meant.[14]

Wright's strategy is to establish some temporal and spatial distance between himself and the context that formed him so that he could have a better perspective on his own identity and formation. Wright's entire literary career, it would seem, consists of a specular examination of his own formation: the focus of the project to know and understand what the South had done to him, "to its *children*," is clearly announced in the title of his first major publication—*Uncle Tom's Children*—and in the name of the protagonist of *Native Son*, Bigger Thomas, who is after all also a young son, a child of Tom.

Wright's entire literary project thus comes to be specular, a turning and an examining of himself as a product of a racialized culture. It is a project that aims to generate knowledge about self and society partly by staging a series of specular confrontations, from Bigger's fight with Gus to Fishbelly's spitting at himself in the mirror. Wright's frequent, if not obsessive, recourse to this strategy of generating knowledge from the staging of specular scenes raises a question about the reasons for the privileging of this particular epistemic modality. It is privileged, I would like to propose, for two reasons. First, because the specular production of knowledge holds an intrinsically crucial position in the structure of epistemology itself; and second, because it provides a structural guarantee for one's political freedom. Epistemology is by definition a specular endeavor to the extent that epistemology consists of the attempt to understand and know the very processes of knowledge itself: in this sense epistemology is nothing other than knowledge examining itself. But on a sociopolitical register the role of reflexivity in the production of knowledge also becomes crucially important in guaranteeing the very possibility of political freedom. If my past experience as a child forms me in ways that I could not control at that time, even if the past is one that is totally determining, the possibility that I can always turn around and examine that past, i.e., the possibility that I can perform a specular examination of myself, becomes structural guarantee of the possibility of my freeing myself more or less from the determining power of that past.

Because specular self-examination provides the fundamental ground for generation of knowledge as well as the structural guarantee of one's potential political freedom, slave societies as well as colonial occupations prohibited the acquisition of literacy or, at least, made it virtually impossible. So many slave narratives as well as literary depictions of Jim Crow and colonized societies abound in articulations of the struggles over the acquisition and control of literacy. And these struggles permeate a range of sociopolitical sites as literary forms and styles; they permeate everything from political and financial struggles over access to adequate education, at the macro-structural end, to the politics of style and syntax, at the micro-structural end.

It is instructive, perhaps, to conclude by contrasting two instances of the micro-structural struggle. The first instance has already been cited at the beginning of this chapter, but it may be useful to reproduce it once again in order to clarify the point. Here once again is the second version (with emphasis added) of the conversation between Wright and the white man determined to prevent Wright from learning the optical trade, that is, from acquiring any kind of knowledge that might change his economic and political predicament:

> "Nigger, you *think* you'll ever amount to anything?" he asked in a slow, sadistic voice.
>
>   "I *don't know*, sir," I answered, turning my head away.
>
>   "What do you niggers *think* about?" he asked.
>
>   "I *don't know*, sir," I said, my head still averted.
>
>   "If I was a nigger, I'd kill myself," he said.
>
>   I *said nothing*. I was angry.
>
>   "You *don't know* why?" he asked.
>
>   I still *said nothing*.
>
>   "But I don't reckon niggers *mind* being niggers," he said suddenly and laughed. [15]

If we emphasize the *acts* of "thinking," "knowing," "speaking/saying," and "minding," then it becomes clear that even the specific modality of harassment in this episode takes the form of a struggle over what kinds of knowledge can be spoken or admitted into existence and what kinds need to be repressed or otherwise denied. Because Wright grew up with these kinds of attempts to prevent him from thinking, knowing, and speaking he overcomes these attempted limitations precisely by submitting them to reflexive, specular analysis. He uses a modality of knowledge to overcome the attempt to prevent him from having access to knowledge. He submits the racist injunction against knowledge to epistemic and political scrutiny and thereby overcomes the injunction.

It is fascinating to see this kind of micro-structural struggle over epistemological control manifest itself in a very different time and place and in a different stylistic form. Following are the first three sentences of Frederick Douglass's autobiography:

> "I was born in Tuckahoe, near Hillsborough, and about twelve miles from Easton, in Talbot County, Maryland. I have no accurate *knowledge* of my age, never having seen any authentic record containing it. By far the larger part of the slaves *know* as little of their ages as *horses know* of theirs, and it is the wish of most masters *within my knowledge* to keep their slaves thus ignorant" [16]

I have analyzed elsewhere in greater length the linkage between literacy and death in Douglass's struggle for liberation. [17] Suffice it to point out here that these sentences contain a series of concentric circles designed to contain and negate knowledge. At the center lies a circle of non-knowledge—Douglass's lack of accurate knowledge of his age and, more generally, the notion that slaves are as ignorant as horses. Whereas a horse's capacities are innate, those of a slave have been artificially and forcefully limited by the master; in other words, the non-knowledge of the slave has been deliberately produced, contained, indeed "bound" by the circle of the master's knowledge, through which he has formulated the hegemonic and violent apparatuses designed to contain and negate the humanity of the slave. However, the third and final circle ("the wish of most masters *within my knowledge*") defines Douglass's knowledge of the political purposes of the master's knowledge; in other words, Douglass's knowledge contains and negates the master's knowledge, which was designed to contain and negate the possibility of Douglass's knowledge. Similarly, Wright's knowledge contains and defines the attempts by Wright's two white supervisors to confine Wright's knowledge and to insist to him that he should remain in the realm of non-knowledge.

In conclusion I would like to emphasize that both Douglass's and Wright's modality of knowledge takes a form other than that of a straightforward epistemic formulation. It is a mode that is simultaneously constative and illocutionary. It is constative in that it proposes to provide a clear descriptive account of an event or a dialogue. However, given the sub-textual staging of the politics of knowledge, this mode is simultaneously illocutionary in that it is, in the very moment of utterance, a symbolic act of containing and negating a preceding act of containment and negation. It is a mode of knowledge that defines epistemology as a specular endeavor and simultaneously defines specular knowledge as a liberating practice.

NOTES

1. Barbara Christian, "The Race for Theory," in *The Nature and Context of Minority Discourse*, ed. Abdul JanMohamed and David Lloyd (New York: Oxford University Press, 1990), 28.

2. J. L. Austin. *How to Do Things with Words* (Oxford: Oxford University Press, 1975).

3. See the first chapter of Fredric Jameson, *The Political Unconscious* (New York: Cornell University Press, 1982).

4. For a somewhat different analysis of this, see chapter 3 of my *The Death-Bound-Subject: Richard Wright's Archaeology of Death* (Durham, NC: Duke University Press, 2005).

5. In the following analysis I will use the name "Richard" to designate the young man in *Black Boy* and the name "Wright" to designate the author of *Black Boy*.

6. Antonio Gramsci, *The Prison Notebooks*, ed. and trans. Quintine Hoare and Geoffrey Nowell Smith (London: Lawrence and Wishart, 1971), 28ff.

7. Richard Wright, *Black Boy*, *Later Works* (New York: Library of America, 1991), 180.

8. Richard Wright, *Later Works*, 877.

9. Richard Wright, *Early Works*, 867.

10. Richard Wright, *Early Works*, 860–61; emphasis added.

11. Richard Wright, *Early Works*, 479.

12. Richard Wright, *Early Works*, 468; emphasis added.

13. Richard Wright, *The Long Dream* (Boston: Northwestern University Press, 2000), 37.

14. Richard Wright, *Later Works*, 879–80.

15. Richard Wright, *Later Works*, 877; emphasis added.

16. Frederick Douglass, *Autobiographies* (New York: Library of America, 1996), 15; emphasis added.

17. See "Between Speaking and Dying: Some Imperatives in the Emergence of the Subaltern in the Context of U.S. Slavery," in *Can the Subaltern Speak? Reflections on the History of an Idea*, ed. Rosalind Morris (New York: Columbia University Press, 2010), 139–55.

Part III

Richard Wright Today

Chapter Six

"The Uses and Hazards of Expatriation"

Richard Wright's Cosmopolitanism in Process

Alexa Weik, University of Fribourg, Switzerland

"I'm a rootless man," Richard Wright declares boldly in *White Man Listen!* "but I'm neither psychologically distraught nor in any wise particularly perturbed because of it."[1] In this and in many other statements, Wright claims for himself, and decidedly embraces, the status of the rootless cosmopolitan, the man who does "not hanker after, and seem[s] not to need, as many emotional attachments, sustaining roots, or idealistic allegiances as most people."[2] This radically solitary position, Wright "confesses" to his (presumably American) reader, "is no personal achievement of mine . . . I've been shaped to this mental stance by the kind of experiences that I have fallen heir to."[3] His historical situatedness, Wright suggests, as a black man in the racist United States, as an American who does not "belong" to the American community, and as a foreigner experiencing the French and African political climates of the 1950s, produced in him an outlook that rejects tradition and community in favor of what we might call a *Cynic* cosmopolitanism. After all, it was Diogenes the Cynic who first called himself a *kosmopolitês*, a "citizen of the world," and who famously refused, as Martha Nussbaum explains in her controversial essay "Patriotism and Cosmopolitanism" (1996), "to be defined by his local origins and group memberships . . . instead, he defined himself in terms of more universal aspirations and concerns."[4] In a similar spirit, Wright declared that he was perfectly able and happy to "make [him]self at home almost anywhere on this earth."[5] Fulfilling this capacity, however, turned out to be more difficult than he had hoped.

To aspire to cosmopolitanism, as Wright's life demonstrates, is to set one's self a demanding task, to invite failure. Nevertheless, it is precisely from both his successes and his failures that we can learn valuable lessons about the development of a cosmopolitan outlook. Wright's life and work show that the rootless, detached—Cynic—brand of cosmopolitanism that he passionately proclaimed in several of his writings is hard, if not impossible, to sustain in lived experience. Even more interesting, however, is that Wright's actions and writings were inconsistent with his proclamations of radical independence. Despite his occasional Cynic outbreaks, overall, he embraced a much more *Stoic* brand of cosmopolitanism, one that, starting from a necessarily specific geo-historical position, continues to strive for human solidarity across national and racial boundaries. Rather than condemning the resulting inconsistencies as failures or evidence of dishonesty, deceit, or disingenuity, we might consider them a necessary and nearly inevitable part of the cosmopolitan endeavor.[6]

As Kwame Anthony Appiah asserts in his *Cosmopolitanism: Ethics in a World of Strangers*, "There's a sense in which cosmopolitanism is the name not of the solution but of the challenge."[7] While Appiah is well aware of the challenges that cosmopolitanism poses to the individual, and stresses the centrality of the *conversation* (in its widest sense) in facing or overcoming those challenges, nowhere does he fully clarify how we should lead such conversations—itself a difficult theoretical and practical issue. Richard Wright's life and writings yield insight into the difficulty of being truly cosmopolitan; they reveal how we can, if not remedy, at least alleviate that difficulty. Read through theories of *intercultural hermeneutics* provided by German philosopher Hans-Georg Gadamer, theories that stress historical situatedness and the significance of the prejudice for (intercultural) understanding, Wright's writings insinuate an "in-process" approach to cosmopolitanism that favors the process of becoming a world citizen over its final outcome. Cosmopolitanism is understood here, then, as a complex dialogical *practice* in which the cosmopolitan ideal figures permanently as a yet-to-be accomplished and yet-to-be-fully-defined utopia.[8] The question thus becomes how individual persons can act toward the creation of conditions that would allow for the development of such a utopia.

As an African American in twentieth-century America, Wright occupied an outsider-insider position in his home country; he cultivated what he called his "double vision," a DuBoisian double consciousness, a power that facilitated his cosmopolitan development. Wright's painful location both inside and outside of American society—to say nothing of the larger Western world—prepared him for the kind of "border thinking" that Walter Mignolo considers prerequisite to a cosmopolitanism not determined by the hegemonic center. According to Mignolo, border thinking allows for "the recognition and transformation of the hegemonic imaginary from the perspectives of people in subaltern positions."[9] Wright's life and work occasion a reconsideration of cosmopolitanism from the position of border thinking, however. In addition, because the writer deserted the United States to declare himself a citizen of the world with a radicalism paralleled by few other American intellectuals, he illustrates the in-process nature of cosmopolitan practice.

COMING TO TERMS WITH COSMOPOLITANISM(S)

In the ancient Greek usage, a *kosmopolitês*, or "citizen of the world," was generally a man who valued the idea that all human beings belong to a single community. Defining cosmopolitanism in the *Stanford Encyclopedia of Philosophy*, Pauline Kleingeld and Eric Brown differentiate between two consecutive stages in Greek thought on cosmopolitanism, each of which drives this premise to a different conclusion. In the Cynic tradition, which dates back to Diogenes of Sinope, the cosmopolitan rejects all communal responsibilities by claiming to be a natural citizen of the cosmos—and nothing else. This cosmopolitan outlook is therefore framed by a *negative* claim, a rejection of all concrete allegiances.[10] The Stoic philosophers developed Cynic thought on world citizenship further and differently. Rather than rejecting all allegiances, the Stoic sees himself as a man whose primary allegiance is to a global community of human beings, while simultaneously allowing himself special loyalties to local or more specific communities. This claim is thus *positive*, emphasizing a proliferation of attachments.

Most current discussions of cosmopolitanism trace their lineage from the Greek Stoics and/or Cynics through Immanuel Kant's famous (and deeply Eurocentric) essay *Perpetual Peace* (1795). They often emphasize, however, as do those by Bruce Robbins and Pheng Cheah, that we can no longer assume a single version of cosmopolitanism[11] and should instead work with pluralistic "cosmopolitanism(s)."[12] How we define the supposedly universal values that define these cosmopolitanism(s), they argue, is based on our perspectives, and those perspectives are conditioned by our specific historical/geographical situatedness. In short, what we value depends largely on the cultural-ideological formations in which we participate. The problem with the multiple cosmopolitanisms referenced by Robbins and Cheah is that some persons are more likely to be heard than others—the "center," or the dominant of any given culture, tends to shape values such that the cosmopolitanism that emerges risks silencing the very Others it claims to recognize. This likelihood is why Mignolo insists that what he calls "critical"—read non-hegemonic—cosmopolitanism can only be (re)conceived from the perspective of the "hidden face of modernity": coloniality.[13] In Mignolo's view, "cosmopolitanism today has to become *border thinking*, critical and dialogic, from the perspective of those . . . that had to deal all along with global designs."[14] Only the perspectives of the marginalized and oppressed, he argues, can at this point offer visions of what it might truly mean to be world citizens. Otherwise, we are going to fall back into the same trap again and again, just as Kant did, and what we believe to be cosmopolitanism will end up being a justification of the inequalities of the world as it is.

Wright's double vision, born out of the dubious privilege of being an outsider-insider to U.S. society and Western modernity as a whole, seems to exemplify Mignolo's notion of border thinking. While Wright's border thinking initially resulted from subjection to American racism, his life as an expatriate outsider in French and, to some extent, Ghanaian and other societies placed him on new margins. The border thinking inherent in Wright's marginalized perspective within the United States was amplified by his repeated dislocations and resulting exposure to European and African cultures. His expatriation also distanced him further still from U.S. society, including the black community with which he still felt some identification and which now saw him, by and large, as having abandoned the struggle.[15] Thus, his marginalization was both deepened and broadened, as he became ever less a part of his "own" society, and a part—but only in part—of ever more societies.

RICHARD WRIGHT'S COSMOPOLITAN CONTRADICTIONS

Weary of the increasingly hostile U.S. racial climate, Wright and his family accepted a 1946 invitation by the French ministry of culture to spend a year in Paris. After his marriage to a white, Jewish woman led to more racist harassment at home, in 1947 Wright decided to move his family permanently to the French capital; in his own words, Paris was characterized by "such an absence of race hate that it seem[ed] a little unreal."[16] Soon Wright was joined in Paris by other African Americans, many of them ex-soldiers taking advantage of the GI Bill. He became one of the leading figures of this "new lost generation" that included James Baldwin, Chester Himes, Olli Harrington, and many other popular African American writers and artists.[17] All of them were fleeing a U.S. social climate poisonous with racial discrimination anti-communist propaganda and persecution. In Paris, they were able to escape such harassment, while immersing themselves in one of the major contact zones of the Pan-African movement that, as Brent Hayes Edwards shows in *The Practice of Diaspora* (2003), "allowed boundary crossing, conversations, and collaborations that were available nowhere else to the same degree."[18] Wright was very much part of these conversations and collaborations, which were deeply concerned with the joint struggle of black and

African people against Western oppression. However, as Kevin Gaines observes in a 2001 article, Wright's position in the Pan-African movement was complicated by his rejection of "Negritude, the politically charged assertion by some Francophone African nationalists of a transhistorical, transnational black cultural unity."[19] Wright rejected such black essentialism in favor of "modern" (non-primordial) political coalitions, and, in the same vein, formed at times close relationships to the (white) intelligentsia of France, which further disconcerted his black peers.

Wright's sudden and premature death in 1960 at the age of fifty-two gave James Baldwin reason to speculate about "the uses and hazards of expatriation." Some of Wright's former friends in the expatriate community in France, Baldwin argues, felt that he had perhaps been away from "home" too long such that he had made a mistake by "cut[ting] himself off from his roots."[20] Many of them, including Baldwin himself, "distrusted his association with the French intellectuals, Sartre, de Beauvoir, and company," because it seemed to them "that there was very little they could give him which he could use."[21] Rather, the French existentialists were thought to corrupt, if not destroy, the authenticity of Wright's (black) vision. Wright's declarations of (racial) rootlessness in his later writings certainly did not help things. Baldwin remembers that an African had once told him "with a small, mocking laugh, 'I believe he thinks he's white.'"[22]

What alienated Wright's friends in Paris made his critics in the United States even more uneasy. Cut loose from his original concerns and context, they argued, Wright had become intellectually homeless, a lonely wanderer in a strange world to which he did not belong. Later critics, such as Appiah, joined that chorus. Wright's trip to the Gold Coast, Appiah argued in 1987, was "yet another quest for a place of his own," a quest that failed miserably.[23] Wright's rejection of "a racial explanation," Appiah wrote, made it impossible for him to go to Africa on grounds of racial commonality, and without those grounds, he fell pray to a "paranoid hermeneutics": the need to distance himself from the black "natives" in Western (white) arrogance, embracing thereby the logic of his own oppressor. Between then and now, the dismissal of *Black Power* and others of Wright's later works has often been challenged. Defenses of Wright's later works date back at least as far as Cedric Robinson's 1983 claiming of Wright as a major thinker within the Western Marxist tradition (see *Black Marxism*). Most current defenses, however, build on Paul Gilroy's assertion in *The Black Atlantic* (1993) that Wright was a major thinker of Western modernity, seeking "complex answers to the questions which racial and national identities could only obscure."[24] Kevin Gaines reconsiders Wright from the perspective of diaspora, urging a view of Wright as a proponent of a black diaspora that is not to be understood in the more "conventional usage" of "describing a state of alienation resulting from a physical exile or displacement from an ancestral homeland."[25] Instead, Gaines suggests, Wright's discussion of anticolonialism in *Black Power* and *The Color Curtain* (1956) "recasts diaspora as the mobilization of black modernity toward a transnational and transracial community of struggle."[26] Although he follows Gilroy in stressing the transnational and transracial aspects of Wright's thinking, Gaines does not take up Gilroy's claim, expressed in both *The Black Atlantic* and *Against Race*, that Wright's outlook was cosmopolitan, preferring instead the concept of black diaspora explicated in Brent Hayes Edward's work.

While diaspora and cosmopolitanism share some overlap in their positions relative to the nation, both suggesting the transcendence of national boundaries in favor of broader solidarities, they also signify very different concepts. Diaspora, as Edwards explains it, "raises issues of *community* beyond the nation-state which are unavoidably fractured by difference."[27] Cosmopolitanism, on the other hand, constitutes, in its ideal form, a global and indiscriminate solidarity that is not defined by any specific *community*, instead reaching out to every human being inhabiting the cosmos. Cosmopolitanism, then, is a more abstract solidarity, one that asks us to empathize with and stand by Others with whom we have (or seem to have) very little in common. This empathy is why it is imperative, as Ross Posnock reminds us in "The Dream of Deracination: The Uses of Cosmopolitanism" (2002), that we recognize that the Other is not nearly as other as it might seem. "By making recognition of one's common humanity, rather than recognition of difference, the goal of a just social order," Posnock argues, "a post-identity cosmopolitanism is an ideal that extends freedom within modernity, especially to those who have been branded as scapegoats, as exotics, as modernity's Other."[28] And we can add, with Walter Mignolo, that to accomplish this ideal, modernity must first start listening to those Others.

In his later work, Wright was interested in exactly this project: extending freedom within modernity to modernity's Others by engaging with them. His own marginalized position within U.S. society had early led him to think through and speak loudly about questions of race and nation. With his departure from the United States, he continued to expand his thinking, looking for political allies in his struggle against racism and imperialist oppression outside of America's borders. To do so, it seems, he decided it necessary to be radically free, free to choose his own way to live as well as his allies and comrades. His bold declarations of Cynic cosmopolitan detachment, accompanied by his official abandonment of both the United States and the Communist Party, suggest a desire to transcend the constraints imposed on him by (U.S.) history. If he described himself in *White Man Listen!* as a "rootless man," he renounced his belonging even more radically in *Pagan Spain* (1957): "I have no religion in the formal sense of the word . . . I have no race except that which is forced upon me. I have no country except that to which I'm obliged to belong. I have no traditions. I'm free. I have only the future."[29] Wright's perspective parallels that of Cross Damon, the black antihero in his novel *The Outsider* (1953), who, after a freak accident in the Chicago subway, takes on the identity of one of the fatalities and decides to leave everything that previously determined his life behind: religion, social responsibilities, and, almost absurdly, even race. Quite unlike Wright, however, Damon, whose nihilistic worldview attributes godlike power to his own person, ends up killing four people and causing the suicide of the women he—against his will and determination—loves. After being mortally wounded, Damon realizes that he can transcend neither his race nor his human condition.

It seems bizarre that Wright would reward Damon's perspective with such a terrible epiphany, only to proclaim four years later his own radical independence from all markers of belonging: religion, nationality, traditions, and even, as in Damon's case, race. This bizarre situation, however, seems also symptomatic of Wright's central dilemma, as it appears in *The Outsider* and Wright's later nonfiction books, and also much earlier in *Native Son* (1940), the naturalistic framework of the first two books and the existentialist tone of the third of which have been oft-noted.[30] Wright seems torn between a sociohistorical and determinative view of the individual as without power and agency, and an existentialist view that gives the individual full agency and freedom, as well as the associated responsibility. Whenever he adheres to one of these two philosophies, the other is guaranteed to intrude sooner or later.

Why, then, would Wright place himself at one extreme—that of total freedom from attachment—despite his awareness of the difficulty, if not impossibility, of such a project? Perhaps because he believed that his double vision as an outsider-insider made him a man "ahead of his time." Looking at his statement in *Pagan Spain*, one could conclude that, like Cross Damon, Wright thought that he could or even had to use this "privileged" vision to free himself from all sociohistorical as well as biological determinations. It seems that after a lifetime of racialized discrimination, he wanted to break free from all constraints and attachments, like Diogenes the Cynic. Like Cross Damon, however, he remained forever shaped and inhibited by them—and this characteristic, too, he seems to have recognized.

No work of Wright's better exhibits his contradiction than *Black Power*. Wright's travelogue about his trip to the British Gold Coast impressively exposes not only his failure to deliver a politically correct narrative about Africa, but also—less frequently observed—his inability to live up to his own claim to be a rootless man, at home in the world. Subtitled *A Record of Reactions in a Land of Pathos*, *Black Power* is exactly that: a record of Wright's own awkward relationship to the challenge of his "African heritage." Confronted with "fantastic scenes"[31] filled with "half-nude black people," "monstrously swollen legs," "monstrously unbiblical hernias," and other monstrosities,[32] Wright constantly interrogates himself, trying to assess how and whether he can or must relate to the Africans he encounters. And, more often than not, he shudders with Western distaste and delicacy. He cannot come to terms with the sight of publicly exposed black breasts, refers again and again to those "long, fleshy, tubelike teat[s]," "some reaching twelve or eighteen inches . . . hanging loosely and flapping," which African women "do not bother" to give their babies in front of men.[33] Nor can he, an atheist, accept tribal rituals or superstitions. He perceives them as examples of pre-modern irrationality that make the Gold Coast "pathetic," inferior to the Western rationality he knows. Life in Accra turns out to be overwhelming and nauseating:

> The kaleidoscope of sea, jungle, nudity, mud huts, and crowded market places induced in me a conflict deeper than I was aware of; a protest against what I saw seized me. I waited irrationally for these fantastic scenes to fade; I had the foolish feeling that I had but to turn my head and I'd see the ordered, clothed streets of Paris.[34]

Such passages have attracted the ire of Anthony Appiah and others. The introductory scene of *Black Power*, in which Wright ponders his possibly "strange and disturbing" racialized relations to Africa, "evokes nothing so much as Conradian dread," according to Appiah, "a dread, intensified, no doubt, by the thought that Wright, the Afro-American, already has the horror stirring 'in the depths' of him, even in the tranquility of Paris."[35] Appiah apparently refers to Joseph Conrad's 1900 novel, *Heart of Darkness*. And conceived superficially, Wright's travelogue does invite the sort of criticism that Chinua Achebe heaped on Conrad in his 1975 lecture "An Image of Africa: Racism in Conrad's *Heart of Darkness*." Appiah executes virtually the same movement as Achebe, and moreover, emphasizes as most unforgivable that Wright, unlike Conrad, is black himself. The parallels between Wright's and Conrad's texts are indeed striking. Both books present first-person narrators who depart from England for West Africa, on uncertain (albeit different) missions. Both texts are at least partly autobiographical; Conrad fictionalized his experiences in the Belgian Congo, and Wright admittedly used fictional techniques to embellish the chronicle of his trip to the Gold Coast and throughout Ghana. In both cases, also, an unreliable narrator tells the story. Conrad filters his story of Marlowe and Kurtz through two layers of narration, one unnamed, and one—Marlowe—obviously unreliable since he merely repeats hearsay from an untrustworthy original source.

The narrator of Wright's "record of reactions" is clearly Wright himself. However, as James T. Campbell proves in *Middle Passages* (2006), "as an imaginative artist, steeped in Conrad, [Wright] inherited an image of Africa as a dark mysterious place."[36] Furthermore, Campbell argues, "when reading his travel diary, one is chiefly struck by Wright's own psychological instability. He had always been volatile, but never were his mood swings more extreme and seemingly erratic than during his time in Africa, where the combination of heat and unfamiliarity appears to have produced a kind of emotional meltdown."[37] Given that "most of *Black Power* was assembled by cutting and pasting from his travel diary,"[38] readers must expect to confront an unreliable narrator in this text, too—although the unreliability in *Black Power* is much less controlled and deliberate than in Conrad's novel. This important difference notwithstanding, several scholars, among them Ngwarsungu Chiwengo and S. Shankar, have recently explored the interesting similarities between the two works.[39] Both *Heart of Darkness* and *Black Power* offer similarly vivid descriptions of a West African climate that seems to be almost unbearably brutal—and sickening—for a Westerner. While this similarity may seem inconsequential, one might not expect the text of a Polish white man in the service of the British Empire to coincide with the account of an African American visitor theoretically *not* writing about a people under well-entrenched colonial rule, but instead depicting a nation at the height of its liberation struggle.[40]

Achebe complains frequently about Conrad's extensive use of blackness and of *pars pro toto* in his depictions of Africans, offering only speechless, fragmented black limbs and "gleaming white eyes" in some wild, uncontrolled frenzy. Wright, in turn, as Appiah and other critics have pointed out, offers accounts of "a swirling knot of men and women; they were dancing in a wide circle barefooted, shuffling to the demonical beat of drums."[41] And when he leaves the dancing crowd, puzzled and estranged, he states, "I had understood nothing. I was black and they were black, but my blackness didn't help me."[42] If Achebe complains that "*Heart of Darkness* projects the image of Africa as 'the other world,' the antithesis of Europe and therefore of civilization,"[43] one could certainly argue that Wright is guilty of the same projections, not least in his repeated expressions of indignation over bare breasts and public urination.

S. Shankar reaches conclusions similar to Appiah's in his more textured reading of *Black Power*, where he claims that "by rendering the Gold Coast 'pathetic,' [Wright] assimilates the country and its inhabitants to a powerful Western discourse of alterity."[44] Wright sees himself as a Western stranger in the Gold Coast, a cultural outsider who is different as well as distant. Throughout the text, he defines himself as *American* by nationality, and as *Western* by culture. Regardless of skin color or racial heritage, he is a Western intellectual raised and (self-)educated in the cultural realm generated by Christianity and Enlightenment, and therefore an outsider to African society. That he is an outsider to Western society as well—a second-class citizen at best—gives him a particular perspective on this cultural heritage, but does not alter the fact that his value system is thoroughly Western. As James T.

Campbell puts it in *Middle Passages*, "Even 'open-minded' travelers . . . view the world through specific cultural and historical lenses . . . The fact that some travelers possess black skin does not necessarily inoculate them against this influence, though it often complicates their reactions."[45] This complication perhaps explains the astonishing parallels between *Black Power* and *Heart of Darkness*. The cultural commonalities between Conrad and Wright are far more substantial than their national, temporal, and racial differences. Read this way, Wright not only falls short in the eyes of critics like Appiah, for whom he has surrendered "racial authenticity," but, more important in our context, he also fails utterly to follow through on his proclaimed severing of all attachments. Firmly tied to the Eurocentric worldview of the West, he is not, after all, the rootless Cynic cosmopolitan that he declares himself to be.

Two lessons emerge from Wright's failure here, on which I elaborate in the following section. The first lesson is that the position of a Cynic, rootless, and detached cosmopolitan is not only ethically problematic, but also highly impracticable. Human beings cannot, by sheer willpower, disconnect ourselves, our acting, our thinking, our feeling, from our *historical situatedness*—the historically conditioned character of our understanding. Such a step presupposes an autonomy of identity that we do not seem to have.

Wright's apparent failure further teaches, however, that his audacious declarations of rootlessness in *Pagan Spain*, and, partly, in *White Man Listen!* while effectually radical for shocking the (U.S.) public, do not comprise the limits of his actually existing cosmopolitanism. Rather, they might better be understood as part of his cosmopolitan process. While he was painfully aware of the complex entanglements that tied him to his historical situatedness, Wright was committed, in these texts and elsewhere, to the difficult endeavor of transcending these constraints, and he used the most radical rhetoric to underline this commitment. Wright's statements declare his intention to pledge his primary allegiance to no government, religion, or racial community. That he did pledge his allegiance to a much greater community becomes clear when one reexamines the philosophical shift that occurs at the end of *The Outsider*.

In Cross Damon, Wright creates a hero who desperately tries to transcend his particular historical situation and racial boundaries in an existential search for identity. Regarding race as a social construct rather than a predetermined essence, Damon not only violently confronts the normative power of a racialized U.S. society; he also believes that he can exist as an outsider to society in general. By making Damon's struggle for absolute autonomy a failure, however, Wright seems to argue that such autonomy is both inhuman and impossible. As is often observed, while Kierkegaardian dread characterizes the larger part of the novel, it is a decidedly humanistic version of existentialism that the novel acknowledges in the end, comparable to (and perhaps directly influenced by) Jean-Paul Sartre's position as he articulates it in *Existentialism and Humanism* (1945). On the last pages of *The Outsider*, Wright has Cross Damon openly renounce his nihilism, realizing that he needs the recognition of others as well as solidarity with them to constitute a meaningful identity:

> I wish I had something to give the meaning of my life to others . . . To make a bridge from man to man . . . Men hate themselves and it makes them hate others . . . Man is all we've got . . . I wanted to be free [but] the search can't be done alone . . . Alone a man is nothing . . . Man is a promise that he must never break.[46]

An excerpt from Sartre's *Existentialism and Humanism* reveals the parallels between Damon's final epiphany and Sartre's plea for a humanist existentialism:

> The man who becomes aware of himself through the cogito also perceives all others . . .The other is indispensable to my own existence, as well as to my knowledge about myself . . . We want freedom for freedom's sake and in every particular circumstance. But in wanting freedom we discover that it depends entirely on the freedom of others, and that the freedom of others depends on ours.[47]

According to Sartre, this intersubjectivity is what constitutes the *humanism* of existentialism. While each individual is free and therefore fully responsible for his or her actions, he or she is at the same time also dependent on the recognition of others and responsible for the consequences that chosen actions have for others. This realization is exactly the one that Damon makes at the end of his life: other humans matter, regardless of nation or race, and the building of a meaningful life cannot be accomplished alone. While *The Outsider* is, on the one hand, a novel about the very specific historical situation of the African American male in the mid-twentieth-century United States, Wright made clear, on the other hand, that his hero "could be *of any race*," and, presumably, of any nationality.[48] What Wright sought to depict was the problem of human existence as such.

Undoubtedly an *African American* novel, *The Outsider* is at the same time "an elaborate body of philosophically informed reflection on the character of western civilization and the place of racism within it," as Paul Gilroy puts it.[49] Wright is, indeed, concerned with a problem, and with solidarity that transcends race as well as nation. Like Damon, Wright himself yearns for ties based on insight, bonds open to individuals of every ethnicity or nationality. In *Black Power*, Wright repeats a speech that he gave during one of Nkrumah's political rallies, in which he claimed that the specific "heritage" of African Americans "has brought us a sense of unity deeper than race, a sense of humanity that has made us *sensitive to the sufferings of all mankind*, that has made us increasingly human in a world that is rapidly losing its claim to humanity."[50] This yearning for solidarity with all human beings is at odds with Wright's proclaimed detachment from human bonds, the Cynic position; rather, springing from a specific heritage to embrace the universal, it fits precisely the definition for Stoic cosmopolitanism cited above.

It should not come as a surprise then, when Michel Fabre claims that Wright remained all of his life "very much a humanist."[51] Like Sartre, Wright believed in the importance of political commitment, which was expressed in their joint engagement in the Rassemblement Démocratique Révolutionnaire (RDR), a radical left group that rejected both American capitalism and Soviet communism, and that was committed to finding a third (transnational) political way.[52] According to Fabre, while in France Wright developed three major preoccupations, which led, among other things, to his involvement in the RDR: "how to inject a personal philosophy into Marxist theory; how to restore morality to political action; and how to save mankind from . . . destruction through the reactivation of humanistic values."[53] Indeed, all of his nonfiction books of the 1950s turn away from race relations in the United States, and show concern instead about the future of the world in general and the situation of decolonization movements in particular. While his horizon widens to include now a transnational and transracial group of people whose members live all over the world, his sense of loyalty remains partial—it is with those who are the victims of oppression.

Stoic cosmopolitanism allows for such particular concerns, for "special loyalties to more specific communities" within the framework of world citizenship[54] while also advocating universal allegiance to humanity. In spite of his repeated declarations to the contrary, Wright clearly always had such "special loyalties." The concrete object of his loyalty, however, shifted over time. While his earlier loyalty was to African Americans, the primary allegiance of his later years was to the global community of the oppressed. This shift was as much predicated on his specific historical situatedness as an African American as it was a result of his frequent and diverse encounters with the cultural "Other." In neither case, however, did these primary allegiances efface a deeper identification with an abstract idea of America, an idea inextricably tied to Enlightenment principles.

If one's historical situatedness is simply an accident of birth, as Martha Nussbaum claims, it is certainly a decisive one, and Wright dedicated much of his literary career to a minute examination of the injuries that result from the specific historical accident of being born black in twentieth-century America. "The Negro American," he writes in *White Man Listen!* "is the only American in America who says, 'I want to be an American.' More or less all the other Americans are born Americans and take their Americanism for granted."[55] As a result of this paradoxical existence, Wright claims, the

African American cannot help but become "a kind of negative American."[56] To be American in the United States, he said in a 1947 interview, "means to be white, Protestant, and very rich. This excludes almost entirely black people and anyone else who can be easily identified."[57] Apparently, Wright understood that despite such exclusion he never would—indeed, never could—entirely stop being American.

AMERICANISM VERSUS COSMOPOLITANISM?

Fabre claims that the question of Wright's "Americanness" is best addressed in an unpublished piece that he presumably wrote for a French audience, giving not one but eighty-six answers to the question "Am I an American?" Every single answer starts with "I am an American but,"[58] and Fabre suggests that the "but" is the most important point of these answers. However, given his speculation that the text was written in the late 1950s—which would mean either after or concurrently with both *Pagan Spain* and *White Man Listen!* it is quite remarkable that Wright identified himself as an American at all, much less eighty-six times in a row. The American he presented himself as being, though, was an American with a twist:

> I am an American but tomorrow I could surrender my citizenship and still be an American. . . .
> I am an American but not of today's America. . . .
> I am an American but I can live without America and still be an American, which ought to—I feel—prove what an American is or ought to be.[59]

It would not be going too far to say that, when writing this speech, Wright seems still to have felt attached to "America." The idea or ideal that connected him emotionally to America was one he had grown up with and could not help but embrace, but it was also an idea that conflicted so brutally with his experiences that he had to leave the country to keep it alive. Only in a non-American framework could he experience freedom, equality, justice, and the rest. To be American, for Wright, was thus not to pledge allegiance to the American flag or to own an American passport (although he would learn painfully the significance of the latter); to be American meant to be thoroughly cosmopolitan. "I am *that* sort of American," he writes, "an amalgam of many races and many continents and cultures, [and] I feel that the real end and aim of being an American is to be able to live as a man anywhere," respecting "the sacredness that I feel resides in human personality."[60] His assertion should not be confused with the oft-heard argument that America's melting-pot policy equals a micro-cosmopolitanism.[61] Wright does not claim that U.S. society is even remotely cosmopolitan, nor does he imply that the

United States is in any position to "educate," "police," or otherwise colonize other countries. He is an American, he declares, but unlike many of his countrymen, he need "not use the ideals of my country as an excuse to ask you to give me access to the minerals or the strategic positions of your country."[62]

Acutely aware of U.S. realities, Wright does not, perhaps cannot, disconnect his cosmopolitan ideals from their perceived Americanness, not even in the late 1950s, after a decade of expatriation. "American" ideals, most of which he can only experience in a non-American framework, do not, for all that, stop being American for him. This is the tricky nature of historical situatedness: it cannot be fully renounced or left behind, because it shapes the way we see and think, and even the way we imagine a different way of seeing or thinking. This difference is why, as James T. Campbell has noted, "innumerable African American travelers in Africa have experienced . . . moments of disillusionment, moments bringing them face-to-face with Africa's unfamiliarity and their own painful Americanness."[63]

INTERCULTURAL HERMENEUTICS FROM THE PERSPECTIVE OF COLONIALITY

In his 1960 *Wahrheit und Methode* (*Truth and Method*), Hans-Georg Gadamer is concerned with the structures of (intercultural) understanding. Gadamer's rehabilitation of prejudice in *Truth and Method* springs from a recognition of the inevitable historical situatedness of every human being—the historically conditioned character of understanding—coupled with the hermeneutic imperative that one must engage with this limitation. For Gadamer, the only way out of the prison of one's historically conditioned understanding lies in interaction with an Other. Only the fruitful interaction between the contexts of the Self and the Other, according to Gadamer, can produce new human understanding. To analyze the process of such understanding, Gadamer examines the etymology and half-hidden second meaning of "pre-judice"—in German, *Vor-urteil*—which he understands as a *vorläufiges Urteil*, a pre-judgment. He argues that, rather than closing us off, our prejudices (or "pre-judgments') govern our ability to open up to "what is to be understood," in this case the cultural Other (or any Other that we try to understand, for that matter, including a historical text). Gadamer takes the Heideggerian notion of a prior hermeneutical situatedness and frames it in terms of the "fore-structures" of understanding. A prejudice (or pre-judgment), he explains, is an anticipatory structure that allows the Other to be grasped in a preliminary fashion. Not only are pre-judgments deriving from our own cultural-historical situatedness unavoidable, they are absolutely essential, in their roles as anticipatory structures, to our processes of understanding. Understanding, according to Gadamer, always involves an "anticipation of completeness": a continuously revisable presupposition of what is yet to be understood.

If prejudices are as vital to understanding as they are inevitable, the capacity to avoid getting stuck with a prejudice, but instead to treat it as a "continuously revisable" pre-judgment, is wholly dependent on what Gadamer calls "openness" or "goodwill." "Openness to the Other," he writes, "involves recognizing that I myself must accept some things that are against me, even though no one else forces me to."[64] Without goodwill, there is no readiness to open up and revise previous pre-judgments into new pre-judgments. However, this disposition is how we function as understanding beings—by having our assumptions constantly challenged by other, new and differing information, without ever arriving at a fixed or final judgment.

Gadamer's reliance on goodwill for successful mediation and understanding is mirrored in an important passage in *White Man Listen!*: "If good will is lacking," Wright asserts, "everything is lost and a dialogue between men becomes not only useless, but dangerous, and sometimes even incriminating."[65] Wright not only shares with Gadamer an insistence on the importance of goodwill, but also joins him in the conviction of the utter impossibility of an objective, eternally true standpoint: "Obviously no striving for an objectivity of attitude is ever complete. Tomorrow, or the day after, someone will discover some fact, some element, or a nuance that I've forgotten to take into account, and, accordingly, my attitude will have to be revised, discarded, or extended, as the case may be."[66] Our attitudes, or our preliminary judgments, to invoke Gadamer's terminology, must be constantly revised, Wright claims, because as human beings we are inevitably "the slaves of our assumptions, of time and circumstance; we are the victims of our passions and illusions; and the most that our critics can ask of us is this: Have you taken your passions, your illusions, your time, and your circumstances into account? That is what I am attempting to do. More than that no reasonable man of good will can demand."[67]

Wright's and Gadamer's trust in the power of open-minded interaction to help individuals take their own circumstances into account, however, was and is by no means shared by everyone. After the initial publication of *Truth and Method*, Gadamer was widely criticized for his "naïve" reliance on goodwill and the possibility of (interpersonal as well as intercultural) understanding, most famously by Jacques Derrida.[68] Conversely, throughout all his public debate with Derrida, Gadamer never lost confidence in the beneficial effects of interactions with the Other. Against Derrida's insistence on the totality of otherness, Gadamer maintained that interaction with the Other, even if it remains incomprehensible to some degree, is central to human understanding: "To allow the Other to be valid against oneself . . . is not only to recognize in principle the limitation of one's own framework, but is also to allow one to go beyond one's own possibilities, precisely in a dialogical, communicative, hermeneutic process."[69] Trying to understand the Other, Gadamer suggests, is not only important for intercultural or interpersonal understanding. It is crucial for *self-understanding* as well. Real self-understanding, he maintains, even requires the "strengthening of the Other against me"[70]

If taken seriously, such a definition of understanding has rather serious implications for the cosmopolitan endeavor. Gadamer argues effectively for not only accepting or tolerating the Other, but for giving the benefit of the doubt, assuming from the start of a conversation that indeed the Other could well be right. Without the challenges offered us by our Others, he claims, we cannot see as constructed what we have learned to see as natural. Only the Other can save us from eternal confinement in the narrow little box that we believe to be the world.[71] In one of *Black Power*'s most revealing passages, Wright shows how this important process works:

> And suddenly I was self-conscious; I began to question myself, my assumptions. I was assuming that these people had to be pulled out of this life, out of these conditions of poverty, had to become literate and eventually industrialized. But why? Was not the desire for that mostly on my part rather than theirs? I was literate, Western, disinherited, and industrialized and I felt each day the pain and anxiety of it. Why then must I advocate the dragging of these people into my trap?[72]

Wright's moment of doubt reveals the important flipside of an honest and goodwill-driven engagement with new contexts and cultural realms: the interrogation and renegotiation of where one comes from.

This is why African cultural theorist Manthia Diawara calls *Black Power* a "magnificent book." In spite of all the problems that the travelogue manifests, Diawara is deeply impressed by Wright's vulnerable self-exposure of his conflicting emotions of "identification and estrangement, love and hate"[73] toward Africans as well as toward his own background.[74] Wright himself exposes these conflicting emotions again, in another passage in *Black Power*:

> The American Negro's passionate identification with America stem[s] from two considerations: first, it was a natural part of his assimilation of Americanism; second, so long had Africa been described as something shameful, barbaric, a land in which one went about naked, a land in which his ancestors had sold their kith and kin as slaves—so long had he heard all this that he wanted to disassociate himself in his mind from all such realities.[75]

Wright was not able to transcend these Western prejudices about Africa, but he was aware that his biases were culturally conditioned. The constant interrogation of currently held prejudices, through (often painful) self-awareness, offers the cosmopolitan the chance not only to better understand the cultural Other, but also to question and resist the societal forces that form him or her. As Paul Gilroy puts it in *Against Race* (2000), the uses of cosmopolitanism seem to lie in seeing "how an understanding of one's own particularity or identity might be transformed as a result of a principled exposure to the claims of otherness."[76] Thus, Mignolo and other contemporary theorists have emphasized the importance of the Other's voice in one's conceiving of a cosmopolitanism that can go beyond Western benevolence within the framework of coloniality.

FROM "CRITICAL" COSMOPOLITANISM TO COSMOPOLITANISM IN PROCESS

Wright's and Gadamer's shared emphasis on the importance of good-willed conversation and critical self-examination does indeed resonate with Mignolo's demands for a critical and dialogical cosmopolitanism. "Critical and dialogic cosmopolitanism as a regulative principle," Mignolo writes, "demands yielding generously ('convivially' said Vitoria; 'friendly' said Kant) to diversity as a universal and cosmopolitan project in which everyone participates instead of 'being participated.'"[77] To the happy list of "generously," "convivially," and "friendly," one could easily add Gadamer's and Wright's "good-willed." All of these statements, from Wright to Mignolo, sound in turn remarkably like that of the Stoic Marcus Aurelius, who wrote in his *Meditations*: "Accustom yourself not to be inattentive to what another person says, and as far as possible enter into that person's mind . . . Generally, one must first learn many things before one can judge another's action with understanding."[78] What should make Wright more interesting for Mignolo's project than Marcus Aurelius is that, as an African American, he is indeed writing from the perspective of *coloniality*.[79] Only this viewpoint, Mignolo has claimed, can develop a cosmopolitanism that will not get caught—willingly or unwillingly—in the trap of perpetual Eurocentricity.

Wright himself would certainly have agreed. After all, he writes of himself as "ahead of the West," as a result of the fact that, while being a Westerner himself, his stance "conflicts at several vital points with the present, dominant outlook of the West."[80] Consequently, his rejection in *Black Power* of a "racial explanation" for his being in Africa need not lead, as Appiah has insisted, to a "paranoid hermeneutics." One could argue instead with S. Shankar that Wright introduces a *third* position into the discussion. Instead of wholly identifying with either "(black) race" or "(Western) culture," "Wright prefers to act in the arena of transnational and transracial politics."[81] Such a move is made possible only *because* of Wright's anti-essentialist stance on race. Among African Americans, as Paul Gilroy has noted, Wright was among those thinkers "prepared to renounce the claims of African American exceptionalism in favor of a global, coalitional politics in which anti-imperialism and anti-racism might be seen to interact if not to fuse."[82] If the primary concern of Wright's later works was with those who have been the victims of *coloniality*, to use Mignolo's term, his first allegiance was with those who thought like him, those with whom he could form ties built on *insight*. Rather than seeking his allies and attachments in racial or national realms, Wright chooses political grounds for this solidarity. One of the main things that initially attracted him to the Pan-Africanist movement, Virginia Whatley Smith reminds us, was their decidedly socialist world-view.[83] Wright's prolonged engagement with transnational Pan-Africanism has been thoroughly discussed elsewhere, but it is important to note for our context that transnationalism is not the same as cosmopolitanism.[84] While transnationalism denotes primarily the material fact of transcending national borders, cosmopolitanism has always some ethical or moral premise to it. Wright, while sharing many interests and goals with Kwame Nkrumah, George Padmore, Léopold Senghor and other Pan-Africanists, did not, ultimately, want to stop at a community of the transnational African diaspora. Instead, he hoped for a system of living that would respect "the sacredness that I feel resides in human personality."[85] This is why he bonded with Sartre and other French intellectuals, with whom he also shared a Marxist—and internationalist—vision. When it served the right political cause he was clearly willing to "cross the color line" in his choice of allegiance. While not personally victimized in the way people of color were, these intellectuals sided with the oppressed and therefore shared a political vision with Wright, regardless of their racial and ethnic background. And such were the kind of political alliances he was looking for.

What is unambiguous, however, is that at the end of his life, Wright was, in Hazel Rowley's words, "a lonely outsider"[86] —despite his many calls for human connectedness. After all, his similarities with all the groups and individuals he was affiliated with politically—the Pan-African intellectuals as well as the French existentialists—only went so far: practically none of them were African American, and those who were did not share his cosmopolitan and transracial vision. In a letter to James Holness in 1959, he wrote not without bitterness that, as an "American Negro," he was completely "alone. I belong to no gang or clique or party or organization. If I'm attacked there is nobody to come to my aid or defense."[87] However, in the very same letter, he also writes of his "right to fight for the Africans," thus clearly declaring his cosmopolitan solidarity with other human beings, and even with particular groups.[88] This is again the same ambivalence that we find in *The Outsider*, and in many of his nonfiction texts. The detached vision of the Cynic and the multiply attached vision of the Stoic both stayed with Wright as ideals until the very end of his life, and the enormous tension between the two—finding expression in many of his writings—seems at times to almost have torn him apart. But while this particular combination of allegiances on the one hand and radical outsiderness on the other eventually estranged Wright from most of his compatriots, it also makes him fascinating. The mixed success and failure of Wright's shifting system of allegiances indicates that he lived out a "critical" cosmopolitanism that always remained in process.[89]

The fact that Wright never succeeded in becoming an *ideal* cosmopolitan could, together with the pronounced unhappiness of his final days, be understood to support the claims of those conservative critics who insist that we cannot get by without a firm grounding in family and nation. However, one of the values in studying Wright's life and work is exactly that it helps us see how patriotic attachments are not nearly so straight-forwardly available to those who, like Wright, embody Mignolo's notion of border thinking. Wright's insider-outsiderness to American society sparked not only his critical stance toward American realities, but also, in the long run, his cosmopolitan process. The fact that this process involved and included a life-long struggle with American ideas and ideals illustrates how difficult it is to transcend one's historical situatedness and the ideological interpellations that come along with it, the best of intentions notwithstanding. This is the inevitable dilemma of the "in-process" cosmopolitan. What matters most, though, are Wright's efforts to fulfill a cosmopolitan ideal. As he said once to a young woman who asked him if his ideas and ideals would be suited to make people happy, "My dear, I do not deal in happiness; I deal in meaning."[90]

NOTES

1. Richard Wright, *White Man Listen!* (New York: Harper Perennial, 1957), xxix.
2. Richard Wright, *White Man Listen!*, xxix.
3. Richard Wright, *White Man Listen!*, xxix.
4. Martha C. Nussbaum, *For Love of Country: Debating the Limits of Patriotism*, ed. Joshua Cohen (Boston: Beacon Press, 1996), 6–7.
5. Richard Wright, *White Man Listen!*, xxix.
6. For the "in-process" terminology I use to denote cosmopolitanism I advocate here, I am indebted to Dean and Mohanty, who both develop the notion of an "in-process understanding" of solidarity.
7. Kwame Anthony Appiah, *Cosmopolitanism: Ethics in a World of Strangers* (New York: Norton, 2006), xv.
8. "Practice" is not understood here in the Marxist sense of revolutionary change, but as the alternative to the teleological. My use of the term roughly parallels that of Posnock and Mignolo.

9. Walter Mignolo, "The Many Faces of Cosmo-polis: Border Thinking and Critical Cosmopolitanism," *Public Culture* 12, no. 3 (2000): 736.

10. Kleingeld and Brown explain: "By identifying himself not as a citizen of Sinope but as a citizen of the world, Diogenes was refusing to agree that he owed special service to Sinope and the Sinopeans. So understood, 'I am a citizen of the cosmos' is a negative claim, and we might wonder if there is any positive content to the Cynic's world-citizenship." Pauline Klein-geld and Eric Brown. "Cosmopolitanism" in *Stanford Encyclopedia of Philosophy*, htt://plato.stanford.edu/entries/cosmopolitanism.

11. The current work of Robbins, Cheah, Mignolo, Posnock, Calhoun, Appiah, Gilroy, and Held, among others, explores such perspectives, and these theorists offer a range of convincing explanations of why we should concern ourselves with redefinitions of cosmopolitanism in a world characterized by the geopolitical shift of globalization or global capitalism. Unsurprisingly, such redefinitions come with a myriad of modifiers, such as realistic cosmopolitanism/ cosmopolitan realism (Beck), critical cosmopolitanism/dialogical cosmopolitanism (Mignolo), rooted cosmopolitanism/cosmopolitan patriotism/partial cosmopolitanism (Appiah), actually existing cosmopolitanism (Robbins), radical cosmopolitanism/cosmopolitics (Cheah), and post-identity cosmopolitanism (Posnock).

12. Bruce Robbins, "Actually Existing Cosmopolitanism" in *Cosmopolitics: Feeling and Thinking beyond the Nation*, ed. Pheng Cheah and Bruce Robbins (Minneapolis: University of Minnesota Press, 1998), 2.

13. Mignolo frames his essay with the claim that coloniality "is the hidden face of modernity and its very condition of possibility." For this reason, he examines cosmopolitanism "within the scope of the modern/colonial world—that is, located chronologically in the 1500s and spatially in the northwest Mediterranean and the North Atlantic." That this "hidden dark face of modernity" that is coloniality "remains difficult to understand as the darker side of modernity," Mignolo argues, "is due to the fact that most stories of modernity have been told from the perspective of modernity itself, including, of course, those told by its internal critics." In consequence, Mignolo sees a need for a re-conception of "cosmopolitanism from the perspective of coloniality" (722).

14. Walter Mignolo, "The Many Faces of Cosmo-polis: Border Thinking and Critical Cosmopolitanism," 744. Mignolo reads the term "global designs" as global narratives with a "managerial" orientation: "Narratives of cosmopolitan orientation could be either managerial (what I call global designs—as in Christianity, nineteenth-century imperialism, or late-twentieth-century neoliberal globalization) or emancipatory (what I call cosmopolitanism—as in Vitoria, Kant, or Karl Marx, leaving aside the differences in each of these projects), even if they are oblivious to the saying of the people that are supposed to be emancipated. The need for a critical cosmopolitanism arises from the shortcomings of both" (722).

15. Wright's estrangement from the U.S. public in general and from African American communities in particular has recently been read anew; see Rowley, "The 'Exile' Years?" Rowley maintains: "It was one thing to hail Wright as a talented black son in his own house, but Americans did not expect this black man to stride out through the front door. The black community tended to regard Wright as a deserter" (15). Stovall similarly asserts that "in criticizing America from Paris, Wright had crossed the Rubicon" (221).

16. Michel Fabre, *The World of Richard Wright* (Jackson: University Press of Mississippi, 1985), 306.

17. Baldwin's term, taken from the title of an article he wrote for *Esquire* in July 1961 (215).

18. Brent Hayes Edwards, *The Practice of Diaspora: Literature, Translation, and the Rise of Black Internationalism* (Cambridge, MA: Harvard University Press, 2003), 4.

19. Kevin Gaines, "Revisiting Richard Wright in Ghana: Black Radicalism and the Dialectics of Diaspora," *Social Text* 19, no. 2 (2001): 76.

20. James Baldwin, "Alas, Poor Richard," in *Nobody Knows My Name: More Notes of a Native Son* (New York: Dial Press, 1961), 203.

21. James Baldwin, "Alas, Poor Richard," in *Nobody Knows My Name: More Notes of a Native Son*, 184.

22. James Baldwin, "Alas, Poor Richard," in *Nobody Knows My Name: More Notes of a Native Son*, 203. As James Campbell, Rowley, and others have shown, another problem was that in the increasingly paranoid atmosphere of the McCarthy years, Wright, like many other black intellectuals in the Paris expatriate community (among them William Gardner Smith and Richard Gibson) was suspected of spying for the U.S. government. James Campbell cites a letter that Kay Boyle wrote to Wright in 1956, warning him "that you are known to be working with the State Department, or the FBI . . . and that you give information about other Americans in order to keep your passport and be able to travel" (James Campbell 197). This accusation seems to have been not quite as outrageously wrong as one might assume at first: Campbell quotes from U.S. embassy memos that show clearly that Wright, while almost certainly never on a government payroll, did indeed give somewhat denunciatory information to the American consul in Paris, Agnes Schneider, to secure his passport (Campbell 102, 191–92).

23. Kwame Anthony Appiah, "A Long Way From Home: Wright in the Gold Coast," in *Richard Wright*, ed. Harold Bloom (New York: Chelsea House, 1987), 188.

24. Paul Gilroy, *The Black Atlantic: Modernity and Double Consciousness* (Cambridge, MA: Harvard University Press, 1993), 173.

25. Kevin Gaines, "Revisiting Richard Wright in Ghana: Black Radicalism and the Dialectics of Diaspora," 77.

26. Kevin Gaines, "Revisiting Richard Wright in Ghana: Black Radicalism and the Dialectics of Diaspora," 76.

27. I am grateful to Edwards for clarifying his understanding of diaspora in a private e-mail conversation on October 2, 2006.

28. Ross Posnock, "The Dream of Deracination: The Uses of Cosmopolitanism," *American Literary History* 12, no. 4 (2002): 808.

29. Richard Wright, *Pagan Spain* (New York: Harper Perennial, 1995), 21.

30. Critical distinctions between the first two books and the existentialist third date back to Edward Margolies (113–14).

31. Richard Wright, *Black Power: A Record of Reactions in a Land of Pathos* (New York: Harper Perennial, 1995), 42.

32. Richard Wright, *Black Power: A Record of Reactions in a Land of Pathos*, 43.

33. Richard Wright, *Black Power: A Record of Reactions in a Land of Pathos*, 42.

34. Richard Wright, *Black Power: A Record of Reactions in a Land of Pathos*, 42.

35. Kwame Anthony Appiah, "A Long Way from Home: Wright in the Gold Coast," 178.

36. James T. Campbell, *Middle Passages: African American Journeys to Africa, 1787–2005* (New York: Penguin, 2006), 296.

37. James T. Campbell, *Middle Passages: African American Journeys to Africa, 1787–2005*, 300.

38. James T. Campbell, *Middle Passages: African American Journeys to Africa, 1787–2005*, 309.

39. See Chiwengo and also Shankar. Moreover, Fabre wrote on the relationship between the two books much earlier in *The World of Richard Wright*. Fabre's bibliographical "Wright's First Hundred Books," in *The World of Richard Wright*, cites Wright's familiarity with Conrad's books and his ownership of them (20).

40. Passages in both *Heart of Darkness* and *Black Power* depict Africans in exotic and dehumanizing terms; Conrad draws Africans as bestial and savage, and, in a more mid-twentieth-century idiom, Wright describes African men as robot-like and only half-human. For both authors, "the Africans" are submissive and indifferent; they go about their difficult labor without resistance and pay no or almost no attention to the (non-African) observer. Interestingly, the respective narrators of *Heart of Darkness* and *Black Power* express a certain shuddering compassion mixed with disapproval for the African men they observe.

41. Richard Wright, *Black Power: A Record of Reactions in a Land of Pathos*, 139.

42. Richard Wright, *Black Power: A Record of Reactions in a Land of Pathos*, 140.

43. Chinua Achebe, "An Image of Africa: Racism in Conrad's *Heart of Darkness*," in *Heart of Darkness: An Authoritative Text, Backgrounds and Sources, Criticism*, ed. Robert Kimbrough (New York: Norton, 1988), 252.

44. S. Shankar, "Richard Wright's *Black Power*: Colonial Politics and the Travel Narrative," in *Richard Wright's Travel Writings: New Reflections*, ed. Virginia Whatley Smith (Jackson: University Press of Mississippi, 2001), 18.

45. James T. Campbell, *Middle Passages: African American Journeys to Africa, 1787–2005*, 384.

46. Richard Wright, *The Outsider* (New York: Harper Perennial, 2003), 585.

47. Jean-Paul Sartre, *Existentialism and Humanism* (New York: Philosophical Library, 1947), 52.

48. Michel Fabre, *The World of Richard Wright*, 172.

49. Paul Gilroy, *The Black Atlantic*, 154.

50. Richard Wright, *Black Power: A Record of Reactions in a Land of Pathos*, 84; emphasis added.

51. Michel Fabre, *The World of Richard Wright*, 159.

52. Sartre in turn made Wright one of the prime examples of a politically committed writer in his *What Is Literature?* (1948).

53. Michel Fabre, *The World of Richard Wright*, 159.

54. Martha Nussbaum, *For Love of Country: Debating the Limits of Patriotism*, 7.

55. Richard Wright, *Black Power: A Record of Reactions in a Land of Pathos*, 17.

56. Richard Wright, *Black Power: A Record of Reactions in a Land of Pathos*, 17.

57. Richard Wright, "I Feel More at Home in France than Where I Was Born" in *Conversations with Richard Wright*, ed. Keneth Kinnamon and Michel Fabre, trans. Michel Fabre. (Jackson: University Press of Mississippi, 1993), 126–27.

58. Richard Wright, "I Feel More at Home in France than Where I Was Born," 188.

59. Michel Fabre, *The World of Richard Wright*, 188–89.

60. Michel Fabre, *The World of Richard Wright*, 188; emphasis added.

61. This argument can be found, for example, in Barber and also in McConnell.

62. Michel Fabre, *The World of Richard Wright*, 190.

63. James T. Campbell, *Middle Passages: African American Journeys to Africa, 1787–2005*, 211.

64. Hans-Georg Gadamer, *Truth and Method*, trans. Joel Weinsheimer (New York: Continuum, 2004), 361.

65. Richard Wright, *White Man, Listen!* 47.

66. Richard Wright, *White Man, Listen!* 48.

67. Richard Wright, *White Man, Listen!* 48.

68. Derrida not only doubted the effectiveness of Gadamer's goodwill; he rejected the possibility of intersubjective understanding wholesale. In "Three Questions to Hans-Georg Gadamer" (1981), he follows Nietzsche in insisting that the Other is absolutely and incomprehensibly alien, and that interpretation of this Otherness is never an understanding mediation, but "the translation of what is alien into one's self" (53), and therefore appropriation, a "saming" of the Other. Derrida conceptualizes understanding as a necessarily subsuming, colonizing, and imperial project easily linked to the Eurocentric cosmopolitan tradition that Mignolo sees epitomized in the writings of Francisco de Vitoria, Bartolomé de Las Casas, and Immanuel Kant (Mignolo 727).

69. Hans-Georg Gadamer, "Subjectivity and Intersubjectivity: Subject and Person," *Continental Philosophy Review* 33, no. 3 (2000): 284.

70. Hans-Georg Gadamer, "Subjectivity and Intersubjectivity: Subject and Person," 285.

71. While Gadamer's philosophical hermeneutics does provide valuable tools for the practice of cosmopolitanism, he has been reasonably excluded from virtually all current debates on the topic. Even if we reject Derrida's sweeping critique, we need to come to terms with the problems posed by Gadamer's Eurocentric outlook as well as by the prominence of tradition in his work and his almost complete silence about women and other Others. Looking with Gadamer at Gadamer, his own perspective must be seen as an inevitably limited and historically situated one, one that can be only improved and widened by a conversation that allows engagement with a different perspective. The rare feminist and intercultural criticisms of Gadamer's work demonstrate effective use of Gadamer's concepts without accepting his conservative philosophical outlook wholesale. In her provocatively titled "Why Feminists Do Not Read

Gadamer"—the introduction to a collection of sixteen essays of feminists who do read Gadamer—Lorraine Code compares appropriations of Gadamerian thought in feminist theory to those of Nietzsche's work. "Gadamerian hermeneutics," she claims, "in which knowing is engaged, situated, dialogic, and historically conscious—has so much to offer to feminists and other theorists of subjectivity, agency, history, and knowledge who are disillusioned with an empiricist-positivist legacy that manifests itself in epistemologies of domination" (*Feminist Interpretations of Hans-Georg Gadamer* [University Park: Pennsylvania State University Press, 2003], 4). Gadamer's hermeneutic interpretive conversation, Code suggests, is valuable because it "enables recognition of the other and cognizance of the situatedness of human life and knowledge," making us aware of the conflict that emerges "between hermeneutic requirements for openness and the limitations imposed by situatedness" (21). Code's view is shared by other feminists, including Linda Alcoff, who goes as far as to claim that some of Gadamer's central positions "are nascently feminist," regardless of his own beliefs (232).

72. Richard Wright, *Black Power: A Record of Reactions in a Land of Pathos*, 163.

73. Manthia Diawara, *In Search of Africa* (Cambridge, MA: Harvard University Press, 1998), 72.

74. Diawara, a Malian expatriate in the United States, executed in many ways the inverse of Wright's journey, and has expressed cogently the dilemma of the would-be cosmopolitan. "I wonder if I have become the cosmopolitan individual of my dreams, or if I am still trapped in a racial or ethnic group," he writes in *We Won't Budge : An African Exile in the World* (New York: Basic Civitas Books, 2003).

75. Manthia Diawara, *In Search of Africa*, 73.

76. Paul Gilroy, *Against Race: Imagining Political Culture beyond the Color Line* (Cambridge, MA: Harvard University Press, 2001), 115.

77. Walter Mignolo, "The Many Faces of Cosmo-polis: Border Thinking and Critical Cosmopolitanism." 747.

78. Martha Nussbaum, *For Love of Country: Debating the Limits of Patriotism*, 10.

79. Coloniality, for Mignolo, is a product of the colonial project and "the exteriority of modernity," meaning not "something lying untouched beyond capitalism and modernity, but the outside that is needed by the inside" (724). As an African American, Wright looks back to a long and very specific colonial history which continues to affect Wright's present. Continuously "Othered" by American society, he necessarily writes from the perspective of coloniality, the perspective of "the outside that is needed by the inside," even as he is not a colonial subject. For an interesting investigation into the "confluences" between postcolonial and African American cultural criticism see John Cullen Gruesser's *Confluences: Postcolonialism, African American Literary Studies, and the Black Atlantic* (London: University of Georgia Press, 2005).

80. Richard Wright, *White Man, Listen!* 55.

81. S. Shankar, "Richard Wright's *Black Power*: Colonial Politics and the Travel Narrative," 15.

82. Paul Gilroy, *Against Race*, 225.

83. Virginia Whatley Smith, ed. *Richard Wright's Travel Writings: New Reflections* (Jackson: University Press of Mississippi, 2001), 176.

84. For example, Michel Fabre, *The World of Richard Wright*; Hazel Rowley, *Richard Wright: The Life and Times* (New York: Holt, 2001); Virginia Whatley Smith, ed., *Richard Wright's Travel Writings : New Reflections*; and Kevin Gaines, *American Africans in Ghana: Black Expatriates and the Civil Rights Era* (Chapel Hill: University of North Carolina Press, 2006).

85. Michel Fabre, *The World of Richard Wright*, 189.

86. Hazel Rowley, *Richard Wright: The Life and Times*, 477.

87. Wright to James Holness, July 7, 1959, quoted in Hazel Rowley, *Richard Wright: The Life and Times*, 475.

88. Wright to James Holness, July 7, 1959, quoted in Hazel Rowley, *Richard Wright: The Life and Times*, 475.

89. Ross Posnock, interestingly, also called Wright a "critical cosmopolitan," even before the appearance of Mignolo's article. "Wright's critical cosmopolitanism," he writes in *Color and Culture : Black Writers and the Making of the Modern Intellectual* (Cambridge, MA: Harvard University Press, 2000), "and its interrogation of race belong to what has been called an 'eclipsed tradition in black intellectual culture'" (10). Like Paul Gilroy, Posnock sees Wright's "transracial utopia" as one of the pillars of his emerging cosmopolitanism.

90. Richard Wright, *White Man, Listen!* xxix.

Chapter Seven

On Richard Wright and Our Contemporary Situation

Jerry W. Ward, Jr., Dillard University

"Are you still interested in Richard Wright?" Someone asked my young colleague Howard Rambsy II this question, and I was momentarily irritated. Imagine substituting another writer's name. "Are you still interested in William Faulkner?" The person who asked that question might be considered a career-oriented academic or a bamboozled scholar, a person with minimal interest in the obligations of American intellectual or literary history. It is difficult, at least from the perspective of intellectual history, to find a justifiable reason for losing interest in Wright's challenging works of fiction or in his provocative nonfiction. Indeed, our *contemporary situation*, which is constituted by a welter of immediate and long-term crises, unfolding anxieties, acts of courage, and denials, invites me and others to have a more profound investment in the study of Wright and in how the body of his published and unpublished works might assist us in dealing with the chaos of the twenty-first century. Our contemporary situation invites us to meditate on writers ancient and modern, especially those who raise disturbing questions about the designs human beings have upon other human beings. A person is entitled, of course, not to be interested in a writer, because interest is both a professional and personal choice. The choice of being interested, for me, is at once pragmatic and existential, devoid of trembling in the face of contradictions. In the case of Richard Wright, I choose to think about refractions of human absurdity through the prisms of his works.

WRIGHT ORIENTS US TO POINTS OF REFERENCE

Recognition that Wright was born at a time when race permeated life and thought most visibly helps us to appreciate aspects of creative pragmatism in his works, and we might say that his choices as an engaged writer were paradoxically free and bound. Wright was free not to create the icon Bigger Thomas in *Native Son* (1940), for example, because the horrors of race and ethnography would have begot a Bigger eventually. Yet, Wright chose not to wait for a delayed birth and made a historically angled response to *his* contemporary situation. Having chosen to create Bigger, however, Wright was bound by logic to pursue his inquiry in creating varieties of Bigger in Cross Damon (*The Outsider*) and Erskine Fowler (*Savage Holiday*) and lesser protagonists in his fiction.[1] As we ponder the vast uncertainties of our contemporary situation, Wright's fictions caution us about the dangers in post-racial card games just as his nonfiction writings alert us to certain traps present in failure to scrutinize globalization.

It is not a single work by Richard Wright that assists us in dealing with the lack of metaphysical absolutes to secure our sense that life has meaning; it is the whole body of his work that serves as a question-generating machine and enables us to grasp that Wright was an accidental philosopher in the traditions of blues people.[2]

The short fiction in *Uncle Tom's Children* forces us to deal with the idea of regional differences in the United States, with historical dimensions of social and labor relations, with the permanence of race, racialism, and racism in America, and with the fact that domestic terrorism threatened certain Americans at least a century prior to their being threatened by the international terrorism of 9/11. *Native Son* forces us to think seriously about the dynamics of man-made institutions which sponsor possession or absence of free will among our fellow citizens, to think about the nature of our vernacular political economy, and to view with dread the dramas enacted in urban environments. Consider that Bigger Thomas has been "rescued" from the electric chair, displaced from Chicago to New Orleans, and refashioned as a dedicated looter rather than as an environmentally determined adolescent. The alienation and nihilism of the adolescent in 2010 is more clearly addressed in *Rite of Passage* (c. 1945; published 1994). *12 Million Black Voices*, which Wright proclaimed in 1941 was a folk history, exposes the unstable grounds upon which human histories are constructed and revised. Moreover, given that some photographs used in the book came from the Farm Security Administration, our interest in the uses of visual evidence to broadcast state propaganda is quickened.[3] *Black Boy*, Wright's "autobiography," urges us to think afresh about an inscription of the self within multiple, gendered, and racialized traditions as these might be related to black identity politics and life-history theory. Wright's 1953 novel *The Outsider* obligates us to consider that philosophical meditations and commonsense thinking about life can result in our own abject alienation. *Eight Men* bids us to examine how banal are the stereotypes in our lives, and *Savage Holiday* provides a glimpse of non-black pathologies and a reminder that adequate discussion of pathology is deliberately repressed in white ethnic discourses. *The Long Dream* and *A Father's Law* beget questions about fathers and sons, moral riddles, economics and amoral corruption, and social death.[4] The posthumously published *Lawd Today!* takes us into the realms of African American folklore, ethnographic description, and generic imitation of James Joyce's *Ulysses*; Wright's 817 haiku (*Haiku: This Other World*) lead to questions about American uses of Asian aesthetics. Wright's travel writing— *Pagan Spain, Black Power, The Color Curtain*, and *White Man, Listen!*— provides yet another framework for posing unanswerable questions about world order and disorder; about human responses to natural disasters and recovery; about imperialism and its relationship with terrorism.[5] The full range of Wright's works allows us to make practical use of philosophy by exercising transactional reading without violating his integrity as a literary artist.[6]

WRIGHT PROMOTES DEEPER INQUIRY ABOUT THE AFTERMATH OF RECENT DISASTERS

Richard Wright's works became for me in the days following August 29, 2005, in a rather new sense, instruments or catalysts for thinking about the aftermath of September 11, 2001, and the national tragedy of unpreparedness and disinformation in the wake of Hurricanes Katrina and Rita and the global implications of April 20, 2010, and British Petroleum's Deepwater Horizon oil rig. Wright hinted in his writing at the end of his life that the history of Western imperialism might be usefully examined as surreal, irrational, and effective immoral acts in the service of power. One of the key phrases in our current situation is "homeland security," a phrase that served as a warrant for the passage of the USA Patriot Act, a legal entity that authorizes suspension of constitutional guarantees. This act has done much to create a climate for "legitimate" transgression of human rights. To the extent that American citizens can be persuaded to be patriotic without question and to survive on a diet of misinformation, the immense power unleashed by the act can oil that path that leads from American democracy as we knew it to the American fascism that we imagined would never come into existence on our soil. What has slouched into our contemporary situation is horror that not even Wright's most prophetic vision could prepare us to deal with.

Wright's fictive treatment of the Mississippi River flood of 1927 in the short stories "Silt" (later retitled "The Man Who Saw the Flood") and "Down by the Riverside" does prepare us partially for the national tragedy that is unfolding as the national gaze on the plight of New Orleans segues into macrodiscourses about government preparedness for responding to natural disasters, about poverty (which is being treated as an amazing new discovery); about the long-term effects of various toxins on ecosystems and on public health in the southeastern United States; about race as an inevitable American dilemma; about probable government appropriation of private property in New Orleans by using a fairly obscure concept—usufruct—as one recovery strategy.

Wright's story "Down by the Riverside" makes us aware that natural disaster and its subsequent traumas do not necessarily lead to any transcending of racial differentiation and skin privilege. That can be seen in the way our mass media used various kinds of print and visual narratives to report on New Orleans, a regressive process of demonizing one portion of the city's population and of erasing the existence of other portions. The classic binary of black and white was showcased with a vengeance. It is now very easy to believe that no Latinas/Latinos, no Haitians, no Vietnamese, no Japanese, no Chinese, no people of Asian descent inhabited the city. They are a significant absence in the ongoing discourse. Such is the implacable power of imperialism, power, and avarice.

So, what is the fallout that might be anticipated? Listen to this small excerpt from the screenplay of *Hotel Rwanda*.

> Paul [Rusesabagina]: I am glad that you have shot this footage—and that the world will see it. It is the only way we have a chance that people might intervene.
>   Jack glances down.
>   Jack: Yeah, and if no one intervenes, is it still a good thing to show?
>   Paul: How can they not intervene—when they witness such atrocities?
>   Jack: (sighs) I think if people see this footage they'll say, "Oh my God, that's horrible," and then go on eating their dinners. [7]

A more dismal forecast comes from Slavoj Zizek, a Slovenian philosopher and senior researcher at the Institute for Advanced Study in the Humanities in Essen, Germany. He concludes his article "The Subject Supposed to Loot and Rape: Reality and Fantasy in New Orleans" with a chilling paragraph:

> New Orleans is one of those cities within the United States most heavily marked by the internal wall that separates the affluent from ghettoized blacks. And it is about those on the other side of the wall that we fantasize: More and more, they live in another world, in a blank zone that offers itself as a screen for the projection of our fears, anxieties and secret desires. The "subject supposed to loot and rape" is on the other side of the Wall—this is the subject

about whom [William] Bennett can afford to make his slips of the tongue and
confess in a censored mode his murderous dreams. More than anything else,
the rumors and fake reports from the aftermath of Katrina bear witness to the
deep class division of American society. [8]

The best that Richard Wright's works can do to alleviate our pessimism and
despair is to remind us that human beings do survive enormous tragedies. I
grant that may be very true, but I still ask if in the absence of ruthless
philosophical conversations about what it means to be an American, it is
possible for Americans to survive one another. It is quite conceivable that
benign, highly selective genocide can occur here under the guise of homeland security or whatever the buzzword of choice might be. Wright's example of engaging dangerous issues by way of his actively "reading" contemporary situations and writing about them is one we might wish to emulate.

When I sum up my investment in Richard Wright and our contemporary
situation, my attitudes are expressed concisely in the third stanza of my poem
"After the Hurricanes."

> Hope is not devoid of its deceit,
> Nor immune to misleading into swamps.
> Careful. Don't move left. Quicksand be there.
> Don't move right. Gators will kiss you.
> Learn from the fugitive enslaved.
> Befriend moccasins.
> Capture and coffle the cruel,
> The arrogant, the mammon cold.
> Send them on middle passages into the blues.

Permit me to leave you with an unarticulated but certainly intended warning
in the imperative of the final line "Send them on middle passages into the
blues." Remember, of course, that you will be on the same awe-filled journey. Richard Wright and I are very unlike Ralph Ellison's invisible narrator
who *spoke for* you perhaps at the lower frequencies. Our current situation
demands that we speak *to you* of anguished efforts to uncover a truth, of
transactional gestures to discover a grain of consolation in philosophy.

NOTES

1. Influenced perhaps by his interests in sociology and psychology and his work for the
WPA Illinois Writers' Project in the 1930s, Wright's first novel *Lawd Today!* (c. 1934–1935)
focuses on debasement. This novel stands in sharp contrast to *Uncle Tom's Children* (1938)
and subsequent fictions where Wright exploits themes of defying debasement in a racist society.

2. My claim that Wright is an "accidental" philosopher is predicated on his having derived
philosophical insights in the process of concentric enlargement of perspectives: from the rural
South to the urban North in the United States prior to World War II, and from France to the

international arenas of Africa and the so-called Third World during the Cold War period. Even in acknowledging Wright's indebtedness to Marxist philosophy, we ought to be aware of his penchant for innovation based on his extensive reading and his avoidance of the "enslavements" professional philosophers endure. We would profit from re-examining Wright under the spotlight of LeRoi Jones's *Blues People* (New York: William Morrow, 1963).

3. One can be greatly enlightened about *12 Million Black Voices* by reading Virginia Whatley Smith, "Image, Text and Voice: Oppositions of Meanings in the Wright-Rosskam Photographic Text," *Obsidian* 8, no. 2 (1993): 1–27.

4. Abdul R. JanMohamed's brilliant *The Death-Bound-Subject: Richard Wright's Archaeology of Death* (Durham, NC: Duke University Press, 2005) provides a methodology for delving into Wright's oeuvre.

5. See Virginia Whatley Smith, ed. *Richard Wright's Travel Writings: New Reflections* (Jackson: University Press of Mississippi, 2001).

6. See Louise M. Rosenblatt, *The Reader, the Text, the Poem: The Transactional Theory of the Literary Work* (Carbondale: Southern Illinois University Press, 1978); and Edward W. Said, *Culture and Imperialism* (New York: Alfred A. Knopf, 1993).

7. Terry George, ed. *Hotel Rwanda* (New York: Newmarket Press, 2005), 170.

8. Slavoj Zizek, "The Subject Supposed to Loot and Rape," In These Times, October 20, 2005, www.inthesetimes.com/site/main/article/2361.

Selected Bibliography

Kwame Anthony Appiah, "A Long Way from Home: Wright in the Gold Coast" in *Debating Cosmopolitics*, ed. Daniele Archibugi (London: Verso, 2003).

Arturo Arias, "Rigoberta Menchú's History" in *The Rigoberta Menchú Controversy*, ed. Arturo Arias (Minneapolis: University of Minnesota Press, 2001).

J. L. Austin, *How To Do Things with Words* (Oxford: Oxford University Press, 1975).

William Barrett, *Irrational Man: A Study in Existential Philosophy* (New York: Random House, 1962).

Simone de Beauvoir, *Force of Circumstance: The Autobiography of Simone de Beauvoir*, trans. R. Howard (New York: Paragon House, 1992).

Harold Bloom, ed., *Richard Wright* (New York: Chelsea House, 1987).

Robert Bone, *Richard Wright* (Minneapolis: University of Minnesota Press, 1969).

James Campbell, *Exiled in Paris: Richard Wright, James Baldwin, Samuel Beckett and Others on the Left Bank* (New York: Scribner, 1995).

James T. Campbell, *Middle Passages: African American Journeys to Africa, 1787–2005* (New York: Penguin, 2006).

Ernst Cassirer, *The Question of Jean-Jacques Rousseau*, trans. Peter Gay (Bloomington: Indiana University Press, 1963).

Pheng Cheah and Bruce Robbins, eds., *Cosmopolitics: Feeling and Thinking beyond the Nation* (Minneapolis: University of Minnesota Press, 1998).

Charles Chestnutt, *The Marrow of Tradition* (Ann Arbor: University of Michigan Press, 1969).

Eldridge Cleaver, *Soul on Ice* (New York: Delta, [1968] 1991).

Lorraine Code, ed., *Feminist Interpretations of Hans-Georg Gadamer* (University Park: Pennsylvania State University Press, 2003).

Martin Cohen, *Philosophical Tales: Being an Alternative History Revealing the Characters, the Plots, and the Hidden Scenes That Make Up the True Story of Philosophy* (Malden, MA: Wiley-Blackwell, 2008).

Anna Julia Cooper, *The Voice of Anna Julia Cooper, including "A Voice from the South" and Other Important Essays, Papers and Letters*, ed. Charles Lemert and Esme Bhan (Lanham, MD: Rowman & Littlefield, 1998).

Andrew Cross, *Kierkegaard* (New York: Routledge, 2004).

Jodi Dean, *Solidarity of Strangers: Feminism after Identity Politics* (Berkeley: University of California Press, 1996).

Daniel Dennett, *Consciousness Explained* (Boston: Little, Brown and Company, 1991).

Manthia Diawara, *In Search of Africa* (Cambridge, MA: Harvard University Press, 1998).

————. *We Won't Budge: An African Exile in the World* (New York: BasicCivitas Books, 2003).

Fyodor Dostoevsky, *The Idiot* (New York: Vintage, 2003).

————. *Notes from Underground* (New York: Penguin Classics, 2009).

Frederick Douglass, *Narrative of the Life of Frederick Douglass, an American Slave, Written by Himself* (New York: New American Library, 1968).

W. E. B. DuBois, *The Conservation of the Races* (Washington, DC: Negro Academy, 1898).

————. *The Souls of Black Folk: Essays and Sketches* (Chicago: A.C. McClurg, 1903).

————. *The Autobiography of W. E. B. Du Bois: A Soliloquy on Viewing My Life from the Last Decade of Its First Century* (New York: International Publishers, 1968).

Brent Hayes Edwards, *The Practice of Diaspora: Literature, Translation, and the Rise of Black Internationalism* (Cambridge, MA: Harvard University Press, 2003).

Michel Fabre, *The World of Richard Wright* (Jackson: University Press of Mississippi, 1985).

Franz Fanon, *The Wretched of the Earth*, trans. Constance Farrington (New York: Grove Press, 1963).

————. *Black Skin, White Masks*, trans. Charles Lamm Markman (New York: Grove Press, 1967).

Richard K. Fenn, *The Secularization of Sin: An Investigation of the Daedalus Complex* (Louisville, KY: Westminster/John Knox, 1991).

Hans-Georg Gadamer, *Truth and Method*, trans. Joel Weinsheimer (New York: Continuum, [1960] 2004).

Kevin K. Gaines, *American Africans in Ghana: Black Expatriates and the Civil Rights Era* (Chapel Hill: University of North Carolina Press, 2006).

Henry Louis Gates and K. A. Appiah, eds., *Richard Wright: Critical Perspectives Past and Present* (New York: Amistad Press, 1993).

Paul Gilroy, *The Black Atlantic: Modernity and Double Consciousness* (Cambridge, MA: Harvard University Press, 1993).

————. *Against Race: Imagining Political Culture beyond the Color Line* (Cambridge, MA: Harvard University Press, 2001).

Jane Anna Gordon and Lewis R. Gordon, *Of Divine Warning: Reading Disaster in the Modern Age* (Boulder, CO: Paradigm Publishers, 2009).

Lewis R. Gordon, *Bad Faith and Antiblack Racism* (Atlantic Highlands, NJ: Humanities International Press, 1995).

————, ed., *Existence in Black: An Anthology of Black Existential Philosophy* (New York: Routledge, 1997).

————. *An Introduction to Africana Philosophy* (Cambridge: Cambridge University Press, 2008).

Antonio Gramsci, *The Prison Notebooks*, ed. and trans. Quintine Hoare and Geoffrey Nowell Smith (London: Lawrence and Wishart, 1971).

Yoshinobu Hakutani, *Richard Wright and Racial Discourse* (Columbia: University of Missouri Press, 1996).

Leonard Harris, ed., *Philosophy Born of Struggle: Anthology of Afro-American Philosophy from 1917* (Dubuque, IA: Kendall/Hunt, 1983).

Ronald Hayman, *Sartre: A Biography* (New York: Carroll & Graf, 1987).

G. W. F. Hegel, *Phenomenology of Spirit* (Oxford: Oxford University Press, 1977).

David Held, *Democracy and Global Order: From the Nation-State to Cosmopolitanism Governance* (Cambridge: Polity, 1995).

Essex Hemphill, ed., *Brother to Brother: New Writings by Black Gay Men.* (Boston: Alyson, 1991).

Lawrence Jackson, *Ralph Ellison: Emergence of Genius* (New York: Wiley & Sons, 2002).

Abdul R. JanMohamed, *The Death-Bound-Subject: Richard Wright's Archaeology of Death* (Durham, NC: Duke University Press, 2005).

Abdul JanMohamed and David Lloyd, eds., *The Nature and Context of Minority Discourse* (New York: Oxford University Press, 1990).

E. Patrick Johnson and G. Mae Henderson, eds., *Black Queer Studies: A Critical Anthology* (Durham, NC: Duke University Press, 2005).

LeRoi Jones, *Blues People* (New York: William Morrow, 1963).

Immanuel Kant, *Perpetual Peace: A Philosophical Essay*, trans. M. Campbell (New York: Garland, [1795] 1972).

Walter Kaufmann, *Existentialism from Dostoevsky to Sartre* (New York: Meridian Books, 1959).

Søren Kierkegaard, *Fear and Trembling* (New York: Penguin Classics, 1985).

Robert Kimbrough, ed., *Heart of Darkness: An Authoritative Text, Backgrounds and Sources, Criticism* (New York: Norton, 1988).

Audrey Lorde, *Sister Outsider* (Berkeley, CA: Crossing Press, [1984] 2007).

Edward Margolies, *The Art of Richard Wright* (Carbondale: Southern Illinois University Press, 1969).

Maurice Merleau-Ponty, *The Visible and the Invisible* (Evanston, IL: Northwestern University Press, [1964] 1968).

Diane Michelfelder and Richard Palmer, eds., *Dialogue and Deconstruction: The Gadamer-Derrida Encounter* (Albany: State University of New York Press, 1989).

Chandra Talpade Mohanty, *Feminism without Borders: Decolonizing Theory, Practicing Solidarity* (Durham, NC: Duke University Press, 2003).

Friedrich Nietzsche, *Beyond Good and Evil: Prelude to a Philosophy of the Future*, trans. Walter Kaufmann (New York: Vintage, 1966).

Martha Nussbaum, *For Love of Country: Debating the Limits of Patriotism*, ed. Joshua Cohen (Boston: Beacon Press, 1996).

Ross Posnock, *Color and Culture: Black Writers and the Making of the Modern Intellectual* (Cambridge, MA: Harvard University Press, 2000).

Arnold Rampersad, ed., *Richard Wright: A Collection of Critical Essays* (Englewood Cliffs, NJ: Prentice Hall, 1995).

Robert Reid-Pharr, *Black Gay Man: Essays* (New York: New York University Press, 2001).

Louise M. Rosenblatt, *The Reader, the Text, the Poem: The Transactional Theory of the Literary Work* (Carbondale: Southern Illinois University Press, 1978).

Edward W. Said, *Culture and Imperialism* (New York: Alfred A. Knopf, 1993).

Virginia Whatley Smith, ed., *Richard Wright's Travel Writings: New Reflections* (Jackson: University Press of Mississippi, 2001).

Tyler Stovall, *Paris Noir: African Americans in the City of Light* (Boston: Houghton Mifflin, 1996).

Margaret Walker, *Richard Wright: Demonic Genius* (New York: Warner Books, 1988).

Constance Webb, *Richard Wright: A Biography* (New York: G. P. Putnam's Sons, 1968).

Richard Wright, "The Voodoo of Hell's Half Acre," *Southern Register* (1924).

———. *Native Son* (New York: Milestone Editions, 1940).

———. *Uncle Tom's Children* (New York: Harper & Brothers, 1940).

———. *12 Million Black Voices* (New York: Thunder Mouth Press, 1941).

———. *Black Boy* (New York: HarperCollins Publishers, [1944, 1945] 2005).

———. *Black Power: A Record of Reactions in a Land of Pathos* (New York: Harper Perennial, [1954] 1995).

———. *The Color Curtain: A Report on the Bandung Conference* (Jackson: University Press of Mississippi, [1956] 1995).

———. *Pagan Spain* (New York: Harper Perennial, [1957] 1995).

———. *White Man Listen!* (New York: Harper Perennial, [1957] 1995).

———. *American Hunger* (New York: Harper & Row, 1977).

———. *The Outsider*, with an introduction by Maryemma Graham (New York: Harper Perennial, 1993).

George Yancy, *Black Bodies, White Gazes* (Lanham, MD: Rowman & Littlefield, 2008).

Index

Achebe, Chinua, 106, 107, 119n43
African American literature and
  philosophy, xiii, xiv, xxviiin19,
  xxviiin20, xxviiin21, 4; ethics, xiv;
  figurative writing, 83; figurative writing
  versus theory, 83, 84; figurative writing
  versus theory (constative), 84, 86, 95;
  figurative writing versus theory
  (illocutionary), 84, 86, 87, 95; function
  of art (literature), 84. *See also* race and
  narrative form; self-narration
African American philosophy, xxvin11, 4
Appiah, Kwame Anthony, 100, 103, 106,
  107, 115
Aurelius, Marcus, 115

black existential philosopher versus black
  existential critic, 4

Camus, Albert, xi, xxivn3, 47n49, 51
Cooper, Anna Julia, 3, 18n5
Conrad, Joseph, 106; *The Heart of
  Darkness*, 106, 119n40, 107
constituting identity versus constituted
  identity, 88, 90; Lacan, Jacques, 88, 91
cosmopolitanism, xxiii, 100, 101, 118n11,
  103, 104, 111, 120n72, 121n74, 116;
  rootless cosmopolitan, xxiii, 99

Derrida, Jacques, 113, 120n69

dialectic, 8, 19n24, 14, 70, 92; dialectic
  typography, 7, 9, 89; Douglass,
  Frederick, 95
Du Bois, W. E. B., xviii, 3, 18n3, 5, 19n12,
  19n13, 6, 24, 100. *See also* race and
  double consciousness

existentialism, xx, 51, 103, 105, 108, 123;
  American, xxivn4; black, xxivn3, 18n1,
  4, 16, 17; existential phenomenology,
  xxi, xxiii; the human condition, 51;
  intersubjective communication, xx, 3,
  11; irony, 4, 44n28; lived-experience, 5,
  52, 54, 59, 61, 100. *See also*
  phenomenology, phenomenological
  return

Fanon, Frantz, 3, 18n2, 8, 19n26, 28;
  "secretion" of blackness, 19n15
freedom, 7, 9, 19n28; being-at-home, 7
forces/vectors, 24, 42n13, 31, 38

Gilroy, Paul, 103, 109, 115; Diaspora, 103,
  104; *The Black Atlantic*, 103
Gramsci, Antonio, 85, 96n6, 90

intercultural hermeneutics, 100; Gadamer,
  Hans-Georg, 100, 112, 113, 114,
  120n72; good-will, 113; prejudice, 112,
  113; *Truth and Method*, 112

133

Lightning Source UK Ltd.
Milton Keynes UK
UKOW041417170912

199152UK00002B/1/P